THE ARCHIVAL POLITICS
OF INTERNATIONAL COURTS

The archives produced by international courts have received little empirical, theoretical or methodological attention within international criminal justice (ICJ) or international relations (IR) studies. Yet, as this book argues, these archives both contain a significant record of past violence, and also help to constitute the international community as a particular reality. As such, this book first offers an interdisciplinary reading of archives, integrating new insights from IR, archival science and post-colonial anthropology to establish the link between archives and community formation. It then focuses on the International Criminal Tribunal for Rwanda's archive, to offer a critical reading of how knowledge is produced in international courts, provide an account of the type of international community that is imagined within these archives, and establish the importance of the materiality of archives for understanding how knowledge is produced and contested within the international domain.

HENRY REDWOOD is Lecturer in International Relations at London South Bank University. He is co-editor of *Reconciliation* (2021), co-author of *Impact and International Affairs* (2021), and has published with *Review of International Studies* (2019), *Millennium* (2020) and *Critical Studies on Security* (2021).

T0384514

CAMBRIDGE STUDIES IN LAW AND SOCIETY

Founded in 1997, Cambridge Studies in Law and Society is a hub for leading scholarship in socio-legal studies. Located at the intersection of law, the humanities, and the social sciences, it publishes empirically innovative and theoretically sophisticated work on law's manifestations in everyday life: from discourses to practices, and from institutions to cultures. The series editors have longstanding expertise in the interdisciplinary study of law, and welcome contributions that place legal phenomena in national, comparative, or international perspective. Series authors come from a range of disciplines, including anthropology, history, law, literature, political science, and sociology.

Series Editors

Mark Fathi Massoud, *University of California, Santa Cruz*

Jens Meierhenrich, *London School of Economics and Political Science*

Rachel E. Stern, *University of California, Berkeley*

THE ARCHIVAL POLITICS OF INTERNATIONAL COURTS

Henry Alexander Redwood

London South Bank University

CAMBRIDGE
UNIVERSITY PRESS

CAMBRIDGE
UNIVERSITY PRESS

Shaftesbury Road, Cambridge CB2 8EA, United Kingdom

One Liberty Plaza, 20th Floor, New York, NY 10006, USA

477 Williamstown Road, Port Melbourne, VIC 3207, Australia

314–321, 3rd Floor, Plot 3, Splendor Forum, Jasola District Centre, New Delhi – 110025, India

103 Penang Road, #05–06/07, Visioncrest Commercial, Singapore 238467

Cambridge University Press is part of Cambridge University Press & Assessment, a department of the University of Cambridge.

We share the University's mission to contribute to society through the pursuit of education, learning and research at the highest international levels of excellence.

www.cambridge.org
Information on this title: www.cambridge.org/9781108948838

DOI: 10.1017/9781108953498

First published 2021
First paperback edition 2023

A catalogue record for this publication is available from the British Library

Library of Congress Cataloging-in-Publication data
Names: Redwood, Henry, 1988– author.
Title: The archival politics of international courts / Henry Alexander Redwood, London South Bank University, London.
Description: Cambridge, United Kingdom ; New York, NY : Cambridge University Press, 2021. | Series: Cambridge studies in law and society | Based on author's thesis (doctoral - King's College London, 2018) issued under title: Accounting for violence : the production, power and ownership of the International Criminal Tribunal for Rwanda's archive. | Includes bibliographical references and index.
Identifiers: LCCN 2021027176 (print) | LCCN 2021027177 (ebook) | ISBN 9781108844741 (hardback) | ISBN 9781108953498 (ebook)
Subjects: LCSH: International Criminal Tribunal for Rwanda – Archives. | Court records – Tanzania – Arusha. | International criminal courts – Archival resources.
Classification: LCC KZ1201.A12 R43 2021 (print) | LCC KZ1201.A12 (ebook) | DDC 345/.0123–dc23
LC record available at https://lccn.loc.gov/2021027176
LC ebook record available at https://lccn.loc.gov/2021027177

ISBN   978-1-108-84474-1   Hardback
ISBN   978-1-108-94883-8   Paperback

CONTENTS

ACKNOWLEDGEMENTS

This book has been a long time in the making. The ideas that underpin this began to emerge ten years ago during a third-year module I took at the University of Bristol, 'History, Law and Memory', under the inspirational tuition of Tim Cole. This started a fascination with the accounts of violence that courts produce, and how these help, or often hinder, communities' transition from war to peace. Much has changed, however, en route to writing this book, and the influence of peers, mentors, colleagues, family and friends has defined the course that this research has taken.

The majority of this research was completed whilst I was an Economic and Social Research Council (ESRC) funded PhD student in the Department of War Studies at King's College London, under the supervision of James Gow and Rachel Kerr. Their patience, support and intellectual stimulation throughout the PhD were invaluable to me and helped to shape me and my research in profound ways. They also opened my eyes to a whole new approach to research through their incredible Arts and Humanity Research Council (AHRC) project *Art and Reconciliation*, which I was fortunate enough to work on after my PhD. I am similarly indebted to Claudia Aradau for her mentorship during an ESRC post-doc, where her academic insights and guidance helped me to navigate the difficult waters of being an early-career researcher. This book has also been fundamentally inspired by the environment of the Department of War Studies as a whole. The emphasis on interdisciplinarity and the diversity of approaches to the study of war has really made this book what it is. Especially under the leadership of Michael Goodman, the department has been an incredibly supportive and rewarding place to be an early-career researcher. The department is, of course, made what it is by those who work there, and I am grateful to the support and encouragement of colleagues and friends, including Leonie Ansems de Vries, Peter Busch, Amanda Chisholm, Rebekka Friedman, Lola Frost, Vivienne Jabri, Hannah Ketola, Emma McCluskey, Milena Michalski, Pablo de Orellana and

Jayne Peake. I left the department for a permanent position at London South Bank University (LSBU) in the middle of COVID-19, and it was odd not to say goodbye properly after eight years, so this is also a goodbye and heartfelt thanks to War Studies. I would also like to thank the School of Law and Social Science at LSBU for such a warm welcome in such strange times, and I very much look forward to working with my inspiring new colleagues in the coming years.

This book has also relied on the great generosity of a number of other institutions. First amongst them is the research councils whose continued support of PhD and ECR research allowed me to conduct the work underpinning this book. I would also like to thank the International Criminal Tribunal for Rwanda (ICTR), those who gave up their time to be interviewed for this project, and in particular the Office of the Prosecutor (OTP) and the archive sections of the tribunal. With the former, I was lucky enough to spend some time as part of my PhD working in the OTP and through this I met so many inspiring people who have dedicated their lives to the pursuit of justice. And for the archivists, particularly Tom Adami, Martha Hunt and Romain Ledauphin, a huge thanks for the support in accessing records but also for what is an unrivalled passion for maintaining the archives as a core aspect of the ICTR's legacy, often in difficult conditions. Whilst this book at times offers a critical reading of the ICTR, this is not to specifically criticise the work of individuals at the tribunal, many of whom I know worked tirelessly to make a positive contribution to the international community. The critique of the systems of power that produced the archive is much broader than the actions of any individual, and indeed many of the individuals I have met personally worked hard to contest some of the problematic aspects of the tribunal's practice discussed in the book.

As a result of my engagement with the ICTR, I have been extremely fortunate to spend time in Rwanda, where I have met so many inspirational individuals, each of whom in some way has contributed to this book, and more generally to how I think about research and the wider world. This includes Celse Ngaruye from Indiba Arts, Nicolette Nsabimana from Centre Marembo, Vivienne Mugunga at rYico and Assumpta Mugiraneza from IRIBA. Whilst from a different aspect of my research, I am also incredibly grateful for the time and insights offered to me from those I have met as a result of my research in the Western Balkans, and particularly those who contributed to IZAZOV! and *Art and Reconciliation*. Through my exchanges with these wonderful and dedicated artists, activists and community organisers, I have rethought how I approach the questions associated with rebuilding communities after war. Through these projects, moreover, I was lucky enough to meet Vladimir Miladinović, whose artwork has helped me to re-conceptualise the archive; he was kind enough to produce a new piece of work for the front cover of this book.

A big thank you goes to the team at Cambridge University Press for being so encouraging and patient throughout this process, and in particular to Jens Meierhenrich and Finola O'Sullivan for being supportive of the original idea and including it in the Cambridge Studies in Law and Society series. It is a huge privilege to be included in this series amongst so many august scholars, and the series has been incredibly important in informing the ideas of the book. And thanks go to Marianne Field for her assistance in pulling the final book together. I also wish to thank everyone who has offered feedback and comments either on specific drafts or sections of this book, or on the ideas that underpin this. It would be impossible to name everyone here, but I particularly thank Nigel Eltringham, Kirsten Campbell, Claudia Aradau, James Gow, Rachel Kerr, Hannah Partis-Jennings, Andreas Papamichail, Scarlet Brown, Barrie Sander Alister Wedderburn and the three anonymous reviewers.

Hannah Goozee offered some really valuable research assistance later on in this project, and I am very grateful to her for all the outstanding work she did helping this get over the line. Her astute research also provided some additional supporting evidence used in Chapter 5.

I have also been fortunate to have met many inspirational academics along this path who have also become the best of friends and offered both academic inspiration and, more importantly, a sense of solidarity and support, along with a whole lot of joy, as we try to figure out what it means to be academics. Whilst more could be named, my inexpressible thanks go to Scarlet Brown, Clara Eroukhmanoff, Tiffany Fairey, Ciaran Gillespie, Lucas Donna Hedlund, Mark Griffiths, Andreas Papamichail, Hannah Partis-Jennings, Ivor Sokolic and Alister Wedderburn.

And finally, and most importantly, I thank my family for their unwavering support, and Ella for being there every step of the way, and offering intellectual and emotional guidance and companionship. We have just welcomed our first child into what is a pretty mad world, but they, and I, are incredibly lucky to have you by our sides. This book is for you.

ABBREVIATIONS

APA	Arusha Peace Accords
CDR	*Coalition pour la Défense de la République*
ESC	United Nations Economics and Social Council
FAR	Rwandan Armed Forces
ICC	International Criminal Court
ICTR	International Criminal Tribunal for Rwanda
ICTY	International Criminal Tribunal for the Former Yugoslavia
IHL	International Humanitarian Law
JCE	Joint Criminal Enterprise
MDR	*Mouvement Démocratique Républicain*
MICT	International Residual Mechanism for Criminal Tribunals
MRND	*Mouvement Républicain National pour la Démocratie et le Développmenent*
OIOS	United Nations Office of Internal Oversight Services
OTP	Office of the Prosecutor
RPE	Rules of Procedure and Evidence
RPF	Rwanda Patriotic Front
RTLM	*Radio Télévision Libre des Mille Collines*
SCLC	Special Court of Sierra Leone
UN	United Nations
UNAMIR	United Nations Assistance Mission for Rwanda
UNGA	United Nations General Assembly
UNSC	United Nations Security Council
UNSG	United Nations Secretary General

CHAPTER ONE

THE POLITICS OF ARCHIVAL KNOWLEDGE IN INTERNATIONAL COURTS

We should admit that power produces knowledge (and not simply by encouraging it because it serves power, or by applying it because it is useful); that power and knowledge directly imply one another; that there is no power relation without the correlative constitution of a field of knowledge, nor any knowledge that does not presuppose and constitute at the same time power relations.[1]

INTRODUCTION

International criminal trials produce an overwhelming volume of information. The International Criminal Tribunal for Rwanda's (ICTR) judicial archive, based in Arusha, Tanzania, alone contains thousands of linear metres of documents.[2] Sitting at the heart of the ICTR's archive is the testimony of the witnesses, which formed the main evidence base at the ICTR. This totals approximately 26,000 hours of testimony, produced by 3,200 witnesses across 6,000 trial days.[3] In addition, thousands of exhibits have been entered into the archive, along with the countless motions, decisions and other records of the tribunal's day-to-day activities. The archive is not, then, only

---

[1] Michel Foucault, *Discipline and Punish: The Birth of the Prison* (New York: Vintage, 1977), 27.
[2] Tom Adami, 'Judicial Record Management/Archiving', *ICTR Legacy Symposium – 20 Years of Challenging Impunity*, 6 November 2014.
[3] United Nations Security Council (hereafter UNSC), S/PV.6678, *6678th Meeting*, 7 December 2011, 8; UNSC, S/2015/884, *Letter Dated 17 November 2015 From the President of The International Criminal Tribunal for Rwanda Addressed to The President of The Security Council: Report on The Completion of The Mandate of The International Criminal Tribunal for Rwanda as at 15 November 2015*, 17 November 2015, 5.

a considerable record of the violence that engulfed Rwanda in 1994, when in just 100 days nearly one million people – the majority of whom were Tutsi – were killed. It is also a record of the tribunal as an institution created by the United Nations Security Council (UNSC) on 8 November 1994 to bring peace and security to the Great Lakes region, and the international community more widely.[4] UNSC delegates at the tribunal's conception further suggested that the ICTR was an expression of the 'conscience of mankind' – a trope that continued to reappear throughout the tribunal's existence.[5] As such, the archive is also a record of, or perhaps monument to, that conscience, contributing towards the constitution of an 'international community'.[6]

However, archives are not neutral repositories of information where the past is preserved *as it was*.[7] They are, as the quote from Michel Foucault mentioned earlier suggests, sites intertwined with power. This much is already suggested in the logic that underpinned the creation of the tribunal, where it was thought that constructing *an* account of the violence in Rwanda could play a political role and bring peace to Rwanda and help to (re)constitute the international community. Taking the archive as the focus of analysis, this book, as such, determines: what account of violence was constructed within the archive as a result of the prosecutions at the ICTR? What systems of power account for this? What understanding of the international community and how it should be governed was constituted as a result? This is, then, a question of the interrelationship between law, knowledge and governance in international courts and archives.

As the following section demonstrates, the archive is a site where these themes of law, knowledge and governance coalesce to give an archive, as well as its corresponding community, a particular form. Having made this case, by drawing on the work of post-colonial scholars, anthropologists and archival scientists, the chapter then examines how the relationship between law, knowledge and governance has been assessed by disciplines more typically associated with the

[4] UNSC, S/RES/955, 8 November 1994. See Richard Goldstone, 'Justice as a Tool for Peace-Making: Truth Commissions and International Criminal Tribunals', *Journal of International Law and Politics* 28 (1995): 485–504.
[5] UNSC, S/PV.3453, 3453rd Meeting, 8 November 1994, 3–15; United Nations General Assembly (hereafter UNGA), A/51/PV.78, 51st Session, 78th Plenary Meeting, 10 December 1996, 18.
[6] S/PV.6678, 8.
[7] Carolyn Steedman, 'Something She Called a Fever: Michelet, Derrida, and Dust', *The American History Review* 106:4 (2001): 1170–72.

work of international courts, such as international law, history and transitional justice. The chapter then returns to the concept of the archive, as I outline the methodological approach which underpins my reading of the ICTR's archive and its constitution of the international community, the focus of the remainder of the book.[8]

ARCHIVAL POLITICS: LAW, KNOWLEDGE AND GOVERNANCE

The link between law, knowledge and governance was anchored within the idea of the archive from its very conception.[9] The word 'archive' first emerged in ancient Greece in relation to the work of the *archons* (the magistrates) and the archon's house, which was known as the *arkeion* (the archive). The archive was the place where the community's records were kept, separated and secured from the rest of society. The magistrates' authority rested with their ability to protect and interpret the records and, as such, create law.[10] This placed at a very early point a clear link between archives, law, knowledge and governance as the archive, as Jacques Derrida notes, functioned as a site of commencement, as an ontology and history were created as real, and as a site of commandment, as the law was created and then declared so.[11]

Turning to the institutional history of archives demonstrates this link further as, especially from the nineteenth century onwards, archives played a crucial role in the governing of populations and producing identities and norms of the individual, collective and nation.[12] One of the problems for the modern European state throughout this time was how to control an ever-growing population in an increasingly connected yet secular society – where a sovereign's divinity no longer meant automatic loyalty to the state. Nationalism played an important role in this respect, and archives in turn helped to construct a shared identity through the collection and consignation of objects that

---

[8] This analytical framework is discussed in greater depth in Henry Redwood, 'Archiving (In)Justice: Building Archives and Imagining Community', *Millennium: Online First* (October 2020).

[9] Joan Schwartz and Terry Cook, 'Archives, Records, and Power: The Making of Modern Memory', *Archival Science* 2:1 (2002): 9–11.

[10] Jacques Derrida, 'Archive Fever: A Freudian Impression', *Diacritics* 25:2 (1995): 9–10.

[11] Irving Velody, 'The Archive and the Human Sciences: Notes towards a Theory of the Archive', *History of the Human Sciences* 11:4 (1998): 1–2.

[12] Steedman, 'Something She Called a Fever', 1159–63.

produced a sense of the nation's past – its identity.[13] Nineteenth-century historians, such as Jules Michelet in France, played a vital role here as they used these records to write nationalist histories, constructing a shared (monolithic) past.[14]

The archival drive is very much predicated on this attempt at a totalising (and exclusionary), pure and truthful depiction of the past.[15] The synergy, then, between the archive and nationalism – as a technique of governance – goes beyond its practical utility in managing populations. Rather, the archival drive (the process of producing, ordering, fixing, excluding records for the archive and reifying the existence of particular subjects and objects) mirrors the very logics of nationalism. Underneath the clamours of this 'total history' lies a need to categorise, to name, but therefore also to exclude and to render unknowable. At its extreme, these logics – an obsessiveness for categorising, ordering and excluding – also unpin acts of violence such as genocide. It is for this reason that Derrida sees that there is a sort of sickness within the heart of the archive.[16]

The relationship between law, knowledge and governance within the archive continued during, and was crucial to, colonial expansion, as archives helped to produce the colonial state as a particular reality,[17] and render indigenous populations as knowable and governable subjects.[18] Benedict Anderson has shown how, through meticulous record-keeping, colonisers invented subsections of colonial societies with specific 'objectively' identifiable identities. Within these records it was apparent that, whereas the colonisers' sentimentalities and lived experiences shaped these identity categories, the local populations' lived experiences and ways of knowing were ignored. For instance, whereas the Philippines' census records fixated on class (e.g. noblemen), which the Spanish conquistadors mobilised wherever they landed, in the Indonesian archipelago the Dutch colonisers' Asian

---

[13] Richard Brown and Beth Davis-Brown, 'The Making of Memory: The Politics of the Archive, Libraries and Museums in the Construction of National Consciousness', *History of Human Sciences* 11:4 (1998): 18–20; Derrida, 'Archive Fever', 10; Pierre Nora, 'Between Memory and History: Les Lieux de Mémoire', *Representations* 26 (1989): 12–14.

[14] Steedman, 'Something She Called a Fever', 1171–72; Carolyn Steedman, 'After the Archive', *Comparative Critical Studies* 8:2–3 (2011): 333–37.

[15] Steedman, 'Something She Called a Fever', 1162–63.

[16] Derrida, 'Archive Fever'.

[17] Ann Stoler, *Along the Archival Grain: Epistemic Anxiety and Colonial Common Sense* (Princeton: Princeton University Press, 2010), 28–29.

[18] *Ibid.*, 97–98; Thomas Osborne, 'The Ordinariness of the Archives', *History of Human Sciences* 12:2 (1999): 51–64; Jeanette Bastian, 'Reading Colonial Records Through an Archival Lens: The Provenance of Place, Space and Creation', *Archival Science* 6 (2007): 267–84.

trading networks led to more regionally specific, yet highly racialised, categories, such as 'Chinees'.[19] With time, funnelling different subjects through different institutions based on these imagined identities, and giving them different opportunities and standings, 'gave real social life to the state's earlier fantasies'.[20] As such, Ann Stoler argues that these archives reveal

> the force of writing and the feel of documents, about lettered governance and written traces of colonial lives. It is about the commitment to paper, and the political and personal work that such inscriptions perform. Not least about the colonial archive as sites of the expectant and conjured – about dreams of comforting futures and foreboding future failures.[21]

The archive is a space of imagination and creation.[22] As Stoler suggests, however, the archive's rules are not fixed but represent the archivist's anxiety as they attempt to bring order to the archive and community, and archive (and produce) new objects.[23] Yet, as the reference to failure suggests, the archivist's command over the archive's objects is never complete; there is always an *excess* of meaning within the archives as records push back against the archival drive to rationalise, organise, categorise and exclude. This also means that the archive can never capture the complete vision of a community it desires. Indeed, as Michel-Rolph Trouillot has argued, archives are always filled with silences produced by the limits of the archivist's epistemology and imagination.[24]

Rwanda offers a good, if not extreme, example of the potential consequence of this form of archiving, and evidences Derrida's link between genocide and the archive. In Rwanda, prior to colonisation, Hutus, Tutsis and Twas (the three main groups in Rwanda) reflected relative socio-economic standing, and so remained fluid identity categories. However, the German and then Belgian colonisers viewed the Hutus, Tutsis and Twas as racially distinct groups.[25] Drawing on the

---

[19] Benedict Anderson, *Imagined Communities: Reflections on the Origin and Spread of Nationalism* (London: Verso, 2006), 168–70.
[20] *Ibid.*, 169.
[21] Stoler, *Along the Archival Grain* 1 and 97.
[22] See also Michel-Rolph Trouillot, *Power and the Production of History* (Boston: Beacon Press, 1995), 72–73.
[23] *Ibid.*, 2–3, 32–33, and 41–43.
[24] Trouillot, *Power* 72–82; Derrida, 'Archive Fever', 51–53; Anjali Arondekar, 'Without a Trace: Sexuality and the Colonial Archive', *Journal of the History of Sexuality* 14:1–2 (2005): 27.
[25] Nigel Eltringham, '"Invaders Who Have Stolen the Country": The Hamitic Hypothesis, Race and the Rwandan Genocide', *Social Identities* 12:4 (2006): 425–46.

Hamitic myth, the colonisers determined that the Tutsis – the minority socio-economic group that wielded considerable power – originated from Ethiopia and were, as such, racially closer to white Europeans than Rwanda's 'natives', the Hutus (the majority group) and Twas (the smallest group).[26] Mirroring Anderson's findings, these artificial demarcations became lived realities through the production of records, such as ID cards, and determining which pathways through life would be available for the different groups. This became particularly important in the Second Republic under President Juvénal Habyarimana when a quota system was implemented under the guise of ensuring a fair representation of the three groups in all sections of society. In reality, however, the system helped to systematically discriminate against Tutsis, establishing them as second-class (or perhaps even non-) citizens.

The arbitrary determination that these categories constituted distinct races became key during the genocide. For example, the genocidal discourse urged perpetrators to send the Tutsis back to Ethiopia via the Nyabarongo river (a code that Tutsis should be killed and thrown in the water), and victims were killed at roadblocks for 'looking like a Tutsis'. As was stated at the 1936 Congress of German Archivists:

> There is no practice of racial politics without the mobilisation of source documents informing us on the origin and development of race and people ... . There is no racial politics without archives, without archivists.[27]

The production of records, as such, can carry severe, and sometimes violent, consequences within the communities that they help to constitute.

Archives need not *necessarily* align, however, with 'hegemonic power' – and so reproduce restricted notions of community and nation. Post-colonial International Relations (IR) scholars have, for example, demonstrated that whilst the ability to rescue the subaltern's voice from colonial archives might be in question (discussed more subsequently), it is possible to find 'anti-colonial' archives which challenge colonialism's (and the archival drive's) orderings of society.[28] Importantly,

---

[26] Alison Des Forges, *Leave None to Tell the Story: Genocide in Rwanda* (New York: Human Rights Watch, 1999), 34–35.
[27] Velody, 'Archive', 5.
[28] Shiera el-Malik and Isaac Kamola (eds.), *Politics of African Anticolonial Archive* (London: Rowman & Littlefield International, 2017).

however, doing so requires reconceptualising the archive away from the bounded material site of state and colonial administrative centres and towards a more amorphous and dynamic notion of the archive.[29] Whilst these anti-colonial archives are important for understanding how communities – including the international community – might be reimagined, it is equally important to understand how what might be termed 'hegemonic archives' constitute and govern the international community in particular ways and with particular effects. I argue that, as important liberal international institutions that seek to regulate norms and actions within the international community, the archives of international courts represent exactly this type of hegemonic archive, and it is for this reason that the book takes these archives as its central concern.

This section has shown that there has been a clear and consistent link between archives, law, knowledge and governance as archives help to constitute, as well as govern, community. As the work of postcolonial scholars, in particular, shows, archives were key to the development of states and nationalist ideologies in both Europe and the colonies. Archives are, then, an important, yet I would argue underutilised, site that can help us to understand how communities are imagined and constituted as reality.

Whilst scholarship on international courts has to date, for the most part, overlooked the role of archives as empirical sites of interest in and of themselves, the composite themes of knowledge production and governance have received some attention. The following section briefly discusses this work before outlining the methodological approach that underpins the rest of the book.

KNOWLEDGE-MAKING IN INTERNATIONAL COURTS

The relationship between international courts and the production of knowledge has been examined by both historians and political scientists. Whilst for historians, a fascination with the accounts produced by war crimes courts was prompted by the prosecutions of those

---

[29] Shiera el-Malik and Isaac Kamola, 'Introduction: Politics of African Anticolonial Archive', in *Politics of African Anticolonial Archive*, eds. Shiera el-Malik and Isaac Kamola (London: Rowman & Littlefield International, 2017), 3–4. See also Michelle Caswell, 'Defining Human Rights Archives: Introduction to the Special Double Issue on Archives and Human Rights', *Archival Science* 14 (2014): 207–13; Verne Harris, 'Antonyms of Our Remembering', *Archival Science* 14:3–4 (2014): 215–29; Stewart Motha and Honni van Rijswijk (eds.), *Law, Memory and Violence: Uncovering the Counter Archive* (London: Routledge, 2016).

responsible for the Holocaust in the aftermath of World War II (the 'Holocaust trials'), for political scientists it was the creation of truth commissions and ad hoc international courts in the 1990s, and the emergence of a sub-discipline of transitional justice, which led to an engagement with these issues.[30]

Despite the relative (and surprising) lack of cross-referencing between these bodies of work, uniting these enquiries is a sense that courts struggle to produce historically accurate, or 'truthful', accounts of past violence. There is something about the legal nature of courts that seems to place them squarely at odds with truth-telling and the correlative benefits this has for a transitioning society.[31] Donald Bloxham, for instance, demonstrates that at the Nuremberg trial (1945–46), the London Charter (the court's statute) meant that crimes against humanity (the charge arguably best suited to capturing the Holocaust) had to be linked to a charge relating to crimes of aggression, meaning that the Holocaust became subsumed in a narrative of aggressive war, rather than treated as a distinct atrocity.[32] Similarly, the drive to secure a verdict, rather than provide a comprehensive account, meant that the prosecution presented a stunted historical narrative that conflated similar acts of violence together. For instance, all Nazi camps were treated as being identical, and other aspects of the planning and execution of the Holocaust were ignored when deemed superfluous to the court's legal purpose (such as 'Operation Reinhardt' – a key moment in the evolution of the Holocaust).[33] For the French historian Henry Rousso, the incommensurability of law and history was so stark that he refused to participate as an expert witness in the 1994 trial of

---

[30] Pierre Hazan, *Judging War, Judging History: Behind Truth and Reconciliation* (Stanford: Stanford University Press, 2010), 12.

[31] Arguably, one of the first scholars to point to the incongruity of the relationship between law and history was Hannah Arendt. Arendt, for instance, addresses law's inability to deal with the banality of Adolf Eichmann during his trial in Jerusalem (1961), as the bureaucratic and essentially modern nature of the Holocaust 'explode[d] the limits of law'. Nancy Wood, 'Memory on Trial in Contemporary France: The Case of Maurice Papon', *History and Memory* 11:1 (1999): 41; Hannah Arendt, *Eichmann in Jerusalem: A Report on the Banality of Evil* (London: Penguin Books, 2006).

[32] Donald Bloxham, *Genocide on Trial: War Crimes Trials and the Formation of Holocaust History and Memory* (Oxford: Oxford University Press, 2001); Laurence Douglas, *The Memory of Judgment: Making Law and History in the Trials of the Holocaust* (New Haven: Yale University Press, 2001), 48–49.

[33] Bloxham, *Genocide on Trial* 101, 114–15, 123 and 127. For similar argument regarding the Frankfurt Auschwitz trials (1963–65), see: Devin Pendas, *The Frankfurt Auschwitz Trial, 1963–1965: Genocide, History and the Limits of the Law* (Cambridge: Cambridge University Press, 2006); Rebecca Wittmann, *Beyond Justice: The Auschwitz Trial* (Cambridge: Harvard University Press, 2005); Ian Buruma, *Wages of Guilt* (London: Atlantic, 2009), 153.

Maurice Papon (a Vichy bureaucrat) in Paris, believing that the trial would not only produce an inadequate history, but that it would *damage* the decades of rigorous historical work that had tried to understand Vichy France.[34]

In a similar vein, transitional justice scholars argue that courts' legal priorities and drive for a verdict mean that they cannot perform the truth-seeking function that remains central to transitional justice discourse and practice. This is particularly because of how courts treat witnesses, as the perpetrator-centric nature of their procedures and the pursuit of a legal verdict mean that witnesses, often the victims of the crimes, are prevented from telling *their* story in full.[35] Especially in the wake of the claimed successes of the South African Truth and Reconciliation Commission, trials were seen as more likely to 'silence' victims than offer them a space for cathartic truth-telling.[36] Nicola Henry and Katherine Franke argue that in re-silencing the victims the power relations at the core of the original act of violence are reproduced, which potentially re-traumatises the witness.[37] As

---

[34] Henry Rousso, *The Haunting Past: History, Memory and Justice in Contemporary France* (Pennsylvania: University of Pennsylvania Press, 2002), 73.

[35] Jonathan Tepperman, 'Truth and Consequences', *Foreign Affairs* 81:2 (2002): 130; Audrey Chapman and Patrick Ball, 'The Truth of Truth Commissions: Comparative Lessons from Haiti, South Africa, and Guatemala', *Human Rights Quarterly* 23:1 (2001): 3.

[36] Marie-Bénédicte Dembour and Emily Haslam, 'Silencing Hearings? Victim-Witnesses at War Crime Trials', *European Journal of International Law* 15:1 (2004): 163–65; Kieran McEvoy and Kirsten McConnachie, 'Victims and Transitional Justice: Voice, Agency and Blame', *Social and Legal Studies* 22:4 (2013): 492–95; Nicola Henry, 'The Impossibility of Bearing Witness: Wartime Rape and the Promise of Justice', *Violence against Women* 16:10 (2010): 1107–10; Rosalind Dixon, 'Rape as a Crime in International Humanitarian Law: Where to from Here?', *European Journal of International Law* 13:3 (2002): 705; Claire Garbett, 'The Truth and the Trial: Victim Participation, Restorative Justice, and the International Criminal Court', *Contemporary Justice Review* 16:2 (2013): 194–95; Martha Minow, 'The Hope for Healing: What Can Truth Commissions Do?', in *Truth V. Justice: The Morality of Truth Commissions*, ed. Robert Rotberg and Dennis Thompson (Princeton: Princeton University Press, 2000), 236–98; Martha Minow, 'Making History or Making Peace: When Prosecutions Should Give Way to Truth Commissions and Peace Negotiations', *Journal of Human Rights* 7:2 (2008): 177. There is now, more generally, a skepticism about the idea that speaking out is *necessarily* cathartic. Erin Daly, 'Truth Scepticism: An Inquiry into the Value of Truth in Times of Transition', *International Journal of Transitional Justice* 2:1 (2008): 30–32.

[37] Henry, 'The Impossibility of Bearing Witness', 1100–1 and 1109; Katherine Franke, 'Gendered Subjects of Transitional Justice', *Journal of Gender and Law* 15:3 (2006): 818–20. This closely mirrors Walter Benjamin's concern that history so often subsumes and co-opts victims' voices, neutralising their disruptive potential. In the face of the co-option of the victim's voice by both *history and language*, Benjamin argues that sometimes the only real response to trauma is silence. Shoshana Felman, *The Juridical Unconscious: Trials and Traumas in the Twentieth Century* (London: Harvard University Press, 2002), 34–37.

such, courts are often seen as sites *devoid* of truth, producing what might be considered a 'knowledge deficit'.[38]

As the first section demonstrated, paying attention to what is excluded from (legal) archives is important when understanding the archive's politics. However, much is concealed by focusing on what is absent from courts' accounts of violence. First, this elides the generative and constituting nature of these records – even in spite of these absences. As Lawrence Douglas argues, despite producing a somewhat problematic and limited account of the Holocaust, the Holocaust trials captured the public's imagination *exactly because* they were trials, and the spectacle and dramatic nature of these events enabled the creation of a shared historical consciousness concerning the Holocaust.[39] At *Nuremberg*, the screening of the Nazi Concentration Camp film 'imprinted on the western consciousness the images which came to characterise the Final Solution' and the figure of six million dead became an accepted truth.[40] The trial of Adolf Eichmann in Jerusalem (1961) embedded the Holocaust as a pivotal moment in Israel's, and arguably the world's, collective history.[41] As Mark Osiel argues, trials help to generate a collective memory for a community;[42] this memory fundamentally shapes what it means to be part of that community, and what type of future it will realise.

Second, and related, the criticisms of courts as spaces devoid of historical truth artificially draw a line around what 'history' is. There is vested interest in attempting to neatly demarcate particular fields of enquiry and expertise – as is true of all disciplinary boundary making – which needs to be questioned.[43] Yet, the boundaries between law and

---

[38] This argument should not be confused with the one put forward by Nancy Combs. Combs would likely be supportive of the idea of a 'knowledge deficit' but for Combs this is because witnesses frequently lied whilst testifying. This argument is questionable in a number of respects (not least Combs's attribution of 'culture' as being a primary factor behind witnesses' wilful perjury). However, I am not interested here in determining whether the accounts produced were 'correct', but rather in determining why it is that they exist as they do. Nancy Combs, *Fact-Finding without Facts: The Uncertain Evidentiary Foundations of International Criminal Law* (Cambridge: Cambridge University Press, 2010), 4–10.

[39] Douglas, *Memory of Judgment*, 66 and 71; Michael Marrus, 'The Holocaust at Nuremberg', *Yad Vashem Studies* 26 (1998): 1–32.

[40] Douglas, *Memory of Judgment* 62 and 70.

[41] *Ibid.*, 103 and 156–57; Shoshana Felman, 'Theatres of Justice: Arendt in Jerusalem, the Eichmann Trial, and the Redefinition of Legal Meaning in the Wake of the Holocaust', *Theoretical Inquiries in Law* 1:2 (2000): 465–508.

[42] Mark Osiel, *Mass Atrocity, Collective Memory, and the Law* (New Jersey: Transaction Publishers, 2000), 1–6.

[43] Christine Bell, 'Transitional Justice, Interdisciplinarity and the State of the "Field" or "Non-Field"', *International Journal of Transitional Justice* 3 (2009): 5–27. A keen advocate of this line between history and law is Richard Evans, also author of *In Defence of History* (2000).

history are blurred. Advocates of international courts continue to claim that one of these courts' functions is the determination of an accurate record of 'what happened'.[44] Richard Wilson has shown that the use of historical and social science expert knowledge in international trials means that far from being in opposition to law, history has become *legally relevant* in international trials.[45] Nigel Eltringham suggests that international courts' archives should be considered as 'oral history archives'; both law and history entice testimony from witnesses, shape these around particular interests and adopt a particular understanding of how it is that the agents of history act.[46] Similarly, Charles Maier argues that both judges and historians turn the complex social world into a comprehensible story with a false sense of cohesion, finality and impartiality.[47] As the opening quote suggests, knowledge is *always already* imbued with power, which renders the search of an Archimedean point a fruitless activity. Acknowledging this shifts the question from whether or not courts produce 'good' or 'bad' histories to consider what history, why and to what effect? This question leads to the core focus of this book, which interrogates the archives of international courts to understand which accounts of violence courts produce, why and how this results in particular imaginings of the international community.

---

[44] Barrie Sander problematises this idea by considering the pluralist nature of courts accounts, but also shows how this notion of the sociopolitical value of the court is contested by those adhering to a more strictly adjudicative view of the function of trials. Barrie Sander, 'Unveiling the Historical Function of International Criminal Courts: Between Adjudicative and Sociopolitical Justice', *International Journal of Transitional Justice* 12:2 (2018): 334–55; Barrie Sander, 'History on Trial: Historical Narrative Pluralism within and beyond International Criminal Courts', *International & Comparative Law Quarterly* 67:3 (2018): 547–76.

[45] Richard Wilson, *Writing History in International Criminal Trials* (Cambridge: Cambridge University Press, 2011), 12–20, 69–86, 112–13 and 121–28; Ruti Teitel, *Transitional Justice* (Oxford: Oxford University Press, 2000), 69–75; Gerry Simpson, *War and Crime: War Crimes Trials and the Reinvention of International Law* (Cambridge: Polity Press, 2007), 79–80; Nigel Eltringham, 'Illuminating the Broader Context: Anthropological and Historical Knowledge at the International Criminal Tribunal for Rwanda', *Journal of the Royal Anthropological Institute* 19:2 (2013): 342.

[46] Nigel Eltringham, '"We Are Not a Truth Commission": Fragmented Narratives and the Historical Record at the International Criminal Tribunal for Rwanda', *Journal of Genocide Research* 11:1 (2009): 55–65. See also Austin Sarat and Thomas Kearns, 'Writing History and Registering Memory in Legal Decisions and Legal Practices: An Introduction', in *History, Memory, and the Law*, ed. Austin Sarat and Thomas R Kearns (Michigan: University of Michigan Press, 1999), 1–24.

[47] Charles Maier, '"Doing History, Doing Justice": The Narrative of the Historian and of the Truth Commission', in *Truth V. Justice: The Morality of Truth Commissions*, ed. Robert Rotberg and Dennis Thompson (Princeton: Princeton University Press), 270–71.

INTERNATIONAL CRIMINAL JUSTICE AS GOVERNANCE

The role of international courts in the governance of international affairs has long garnered scholarly interest. The first (at least partially) international courts at Nuremberg and Tokyo in the aftermath of World War II were, in this respect, embroiled in claims of 'victor's justice', as the powerful victors of the war punished the vanquished, and ignored their own – not inconsequential – crimes. At the Tokyo trial, Judge Pal forced home this point in his dissenting opinion, which argued that the Allies' execution of selective justice rendered the whole process illegitimate.

The new era of international justice that emerged at the end of the Cold War promised to address many of these concerns. With the establishment of both the ICTR and ICTY, and then the International Criminal Court (ICC), international justice could claim to be, unlike Nuremberg or Tokyo, truly international in terms of personnel, jurisdiction and state support. The universal reach of international criminal justice is such that the ICC's jurisdiction covers even those states that refuse to recognise the court's legitimacy.

Yet, despite this claim to universalism, these courts have also failed to carve out an independent sphere of action and remained embroiled in the power dynamics of international politics. This is, as Kenneth Rodman shows, in part because international courts remain at the whims of nation states due to their dependence on national governments for enforcement, staff assistance and finance.[48] This is not to say that politics necessarily *obstructs* these courts' work.[49] Rachel Kerr, for instance, has shown that international politics is *essential* to what these courts do: At the ICTY, politics brought the court to life – through UNSC RES 827, under Chapter VII of the UN Charter – and gave it power to function, through state diplomacy; and its ultimate goal of achieving peace was very much political.[50] As such, these courts function as important sites through which international politics is practised, and the international community regulated.

---

[48] Kenneth Rodman, 'Justice as a Dialogue between Law and Politics', *Journal of International Criminal Justice* 12:3 (2014): 437–69.

[49] Rachel Kerr, *The International Criminal Tribunal for the Former Yugoslavia: An Exercise in Law, Politics, and Diplomacy* (Oxford: Oxford University Press, 2004), 212. See also Michael Humphrey, 'International Intervention, Justice and National Reconciliation: The Role of the ICTY and ICTR in Bosnia and Rwanda', *Journal of Human Rights* 2:4 (2003): 495–505.

[50] Kerr, ICTY, 2; Rodman, 'Justice as a Dialogue', 437–69; James Gow, 'The ICTY, War Crimes Enforcement and Dayton: The Ghost in the Machine', *Ethnopolitics* 5:1 (2006): 49–65.

This has not stopped, however, these courts from being accused of delivering uneven, and even a form of 'victor's', justice. Two points are particularly important in this respect when thinking about courts as practices of governance: the 'distanced' nature of these courts and the selective application of the law.

Distanced Justice

The accusations that international courts, along with other transitional justice mechanisms, represent a distanced form of justice centre on both the physical distance between these courts and communities where the crimes occurred, and the epistemological distance between law's ways of knowing and how those affected by the violence understand these crimes.[51] Tim Kelsall found in relation to the Special Court for Sierra Leone that even the hybrid nature of that court (which supposedly integrated a 'local' element into the procedure) could not overcome the gap between the practice of international law and local Sierra Leonean culture.[52] This was particularly the case when it came to the court's less than adequate understanding of forced marriages, child soldiers and magic.[53] Joseph Fink has argued that the deontological nature of international criminal law means that it is inevitably incapable of understanding the specificity and cultural contexts within which violence occurs, as it generalises and abstracts episodes of violence.[54] As such, law here is seen as enforcing a particular understanding of the social world – according to Fink, to the point of deontological abstraction – which inhibits its ability to truly *know* the crimes it processes.

[51] Phil Clark, *Distant Justice: The Impact of the International Criminal Court on African Politics* (Cambridge: Cambridge University Press), 34–46 and 309–12; Gready, 'Reconceptualising Transitional Justice', 11–3; Peter Uvin and Charles Mironko, 'Western and Local Approaches to Justice in Rwanda', *Global Governance* 9 (2003), 220; and Drumbl, 'Punishment, Postgenocide', 1314–26. Miriam Aukerman, 'Extraordinary Evil, Ordinary Crime: A Framework for Understanding Transitional Justice', *Harvard Human Rights Journal* 15 (2002): 47.

[52] As Eltringham rightly critiques, this is not to essentialise culture as the obstacle here – as discussed more in Chapter 6.

[53] Tim Kelsall, *Culture under Cross-Examination: International Justice and the Special Court for Sierra Leone* (Cambridge: Cambridge University Press, 2010), 8–16. See Alison Des Forges and Timothy Longman, 'Legal Response to Genocide in Rwanda', in *My Neighbour, My Enemy*, ed. Harvey Weinstein and Eric Stover (Cambridge: Cambridge University Press, 2004), 56.

[54] Joseph Fink, 'Deontological Retributivism and the Legal Practice of International Jurisprudence: The Case of the International Criminal Tribunal for Rwanda', *Journal of African Law* 49:2 (2005): 115–23. Payam Akhavan has similarly noted his concern with what happens when the legal idiom attempts to generalise between different types of traumatic experience. Payam Akhavan, *Reducing Genocide to Law: Definition, Meaning, and the Ultimate Crime* (Cambridge: Cambridge University Press, 2012), 1–78 and 141–44.

Whilst over-emphasising the passivity of the communities that are subjected to international law,[55] and returning, somewhat unhelpfully, to the 'truth vs justice debate' of the 1990s (as international law is treated simply as being *incapable* of understanding violence), this at least points to the fact that law is not, and cannot be, interpreted simply as the application of rules, but is a reflection, and enforcement, of a particular perspective. It is worth quoting Catherine MacKinnon at length in this respect:

> In reality begins principle. The loftiest abstractions, however, strenuously empty of social specificity on the surface are born of social life: amid the intercourse of particular groups, in the presumptive ease of the deciding classes, through the trauma of specific atrocities, at the expense of the silent and excluded, as a victory (usually compromised often pyrrhic) for the powerless. Law does not grow by syllogistic compulsion; it is pushed by the social logic of domination and challenge to domination, forged in the interaction of change and resistance to change. It is not only in the common law that life of the law is experience, not logic. Behind all law is someone's story; someone whose blood, if you read closely, leaks thought he lines. Text does not beget text; life does. The question – a question of politics and history and therefore law – is whose experience grounds what law.[56]

Law does not neatly reflect the social world, then, but plays a role in actively shaping it from a *particular perspective*.[57] These ideas are echoed

---

[55] Clarke, *Distant Justice* 18; Kamari Clarke, Abel S. Knottnerus and Eefje De Volder (eds.), *Africa and the ICC: Perceptions of Justice* (Cambridge: Cambridge University Press, 2016). Roger Mac Ginty, 'Hybrid Peace: The Interaction between Top-Down and Bottom-Up Peace', *Security Dialogue* 41:4 (2010): 391–412. Moreover, as post-colonial scholarship has shown, as a result of colonial encounters, actors from the Global South and the Global North co-constituted each other, fundamentally altering each other's existence and that these encounters had a significant impact on the nature of international system and international law. This, then, further complicates the notion of 'distant justice' or the ability to neatly disentangle different 'stakeholders' in international criminal justice. Antony Anghie, *Imperialism, Sovereignty and the Making of International Law* (Cambridge: Cambridge University Press, 2005), 1–12 and 250–53; Diane Otto, 'Subalternity and International Law: The Problem of Global Community and the Incommensurability of Difference', *Social and Legal Studies* 5:3 (1996), 339–54; Makau Mutua, 'Savages, Victims, and Saviors: The Metaphor of Human Rights', *Harvard International Law* Journal 42:1 (2001), 212–14; Sundhya Pahuja, 'The Postcoloniality of International Law', *Harvard International Law Journal* 46:2 (2005), 460–68; and Frédéric Mégret, 'From "Savages" to 'Unlawful Combatants': A Postcolonial Look at International Humanitarian Law's Other', in *International Law and Its Others*, ed. Ann Orford (Cambridge: Cambridge University Press, 2006), 265–318.

[56] Catherine MacKinnon, 'Crimes of War, Crimes of Peace', *UCLA Women's Law Journal* 4 (1993): 59.

[57] This mirrors James White's argument that courts *translate* the social world into law, and as with all translations this contains both exuberance (as meaning is added) and deficiency (as meaning is lost). James White, *Justice as Translation: An Essay in Cultural and Legal Criticism*

in Michael Shapiro's analysis of war crimes, as he argues that scholars need to move beyond seeing justice as a static concept and to focus on 'when, where, how, from whose perspective(s), and under whose control it is activated as an issue and implemented through justice related apparatuses'.[58]

Critical legal studies offers further evidence of the politically charged nature of law and adds greater insight, and nuance, to thinking about how criminal law's epistemology reproduces particular societal dynamics and power relations. For instance, numerous studies have now shown how gender and race influence how a trial unfolds, and as such, reinforce particular racial and gendered assumptions about society. John O'Barr and William Conley's examination of the treatment of sexual violence testimony in municipal courts shows that the presence of patriarchal discourses means that this type of testimony is less likely to be believed.[59] Martha Minow similarly shows how race affects trial outcomes in the United States and in particular that the race of a defendant and their alleged victim plays a significant role in determining the severity of sentence.[60] These non-legal discourses, then, help create the conditions where legal decisions of guilt can be rendered. Law is shaped through a particular world view and how law is practised has consequences for (re)creating this world view. As Chris Reus-Smit argues, law is both constituting and constitutive of politics.[61]

(Chicago: Chicago University Press, 1992), 2239–69; Clark Cunningham, 'The Lawyer as Translator, Representation as Text: Towards an Ethnography of Legal Discourse', *Cornell Law Review* 77:6 (1992): 1298–387.

[58] Michael Shapiro, *War Crimes, Atrocity and Justice* (Cambridge: Polity Press, 2015), 11–12.

[59] A 'double bind' is placed over a rape victim's testimony that sees the chances of it being accepted by the courtroom diminish. This is the case, O'Barr and Conley argue, because the victim either adopts a powerful speech style and is deemed unreliable for either failing to play out their gender 'properly' or because it indicates that the witness is 'too together' to have experienced a traumatic experience like rape, or they adopt powerless speech style, conform to the gendered stereotype, and are seen as irrational and unreliable; John Conley and William O'Barr, *Just Words: Law, Language, and Power*, 2nd ed. (Chicago: University of Chicago Press, 2005), 32–39. William O'Barr, *et al.*, 'Speech Style and Impression Formation in a Court Setting: The Effects of "Powerful" and "Powerless" Speech', *Journal of Experimental Social Psychology* 14:3 (1978), 266–79.

[60] Martha Minow, *Making All the Difference: Inclusion, Exclusion, and American Law* (London: Cornell University Press, 1990), 66–67; Martha Minow 'Foreword: Justice Engendered', *Harvard Law Review* 101:10 (1987): 14; Kimberley Crenshaw, 'Mapping the Margins: Intersectionality, Identity Politics, and Violence against Women of Color', *Stanford Law Review* 43:6 (1991): 1241–99.

[61] Chris Reus-Smit, 'The Politics of International Law', in *The Politics of International Law*, ed. Chris Reus-Smit (Cambridge: Cambridge University Press, 2004), 14.

Rather than simply treating international criminal justice as being necessarily incapable of understanding a particular act of violence, this work from critical legal studies shows there is a need to more closely understand how international law functions from an epistemological perspective and with what consequences. Doing so brings to the fore, once more, the question of how law reproduces *particular* accounts of violence and community.

Justice and Community

The second relevant critique of international courts relates to Rosemary Nagy's suggestion that to understand the politics of transitional justice as discourse and practice, scholars need to ask who, when and what these interventions focus on.[62] For international courts, the answer here is relatively explicit: These courts have almost entirely focused on communities in the Global South and, in particular, those from the African continent.[63] The sole exception to date is the prosecution of a Belgian national, George Ruggiu, who was tried at the ICTR for his role as radio host on the notorious RTLM radio station. As such, even in this instance, the gaze of the international justice remained on the Global South.

The imbalance of these courts', and in particular the ICC's, focus in part led to the African Union's threat of mass withdrawal in 2017. Whilst the threat was never fully realised – with only Burundi withdrawing, followed in 2018 by the Philippines – this has done little to dampen critics' claims that the ICC's near-exclusive focus on the Global South renders it a site of neo-colonial governance. The two defences that could be made against this allegation are, first, that the majority of international criminal cases are initiated by actors from the Global South, and, second, that investigations are ongoing into a number of Western states' actions, including the United Kingdom in relation to the Iraq War. With the latter, along with the incredibly slow pace of these proceedings against Western powers, the fact remains that with three of the five permanent members of the UNSC yet to ratify the Rome Statute, some of the most powerful actors in global politics remain

---

[62] Rosemary Nagy, 'Transitional Justice as Global Project: Critical Reflections', *Third World Quarterly* 29:2 (2008): 275–89.

[63] The exceptions here would be the International Criminal Tribunal for the Former Yugoslavia, the Extraordinary Chambers in the Courts of Cambodia, Special Panels of the Dili District Court, and the Special Tribunal for Lebanon.

immune from the court's justice as non-signatories are only able to be referred through the UNSC.[64]

The role of African state leaders in initiating proceedings offers a stronger challenge to these neo-colonial claims.[65] Yet it is also the case that colonial power has always relied on the colonised to execute much of its work.[66] Overall, the design and practice of international criminal justice today appear to mirror the power dynamics embedded in international law at its conception; directed at securing the role and legitimacy of 'civilised' states to intervene in, and discipline, uncivilised, barbaric and backward states in need of 'saving'.[67] Whilst the success of modern-day 'civilising missions', in the form of humanitarian interventions and international prosecutions, is more than questionable,[68] what is of equal importance here is that these interventions instil a particular set of power relations within the international domain which presents the Global South as failing victim, and the Global North as benevolent saviour, ensuring that inequality is reproduced within the international domain.[69] Moreover, whilst who initiates these proceedings is one thing, who controls them once they are underway, and in whose interests they serve, is a different matter. When thinking about courts as sites of governance, it is, therefore, important to think about how power is exercised *within* these courts, what role the post-colonial subject – so often the focus of international courts – plays in this process, and how particular accounts of violence and community are produced as a result. Such is the focus of the analysis offered in this book.

---

[64] Jessica Whyte, "Always on Top"? The "Responsibility to Protect" and the Persistence of Colonialism', in *The Postcolonial World*, eds. Jyotsna Singh and David Kim (London: Routledge, 2016): 316–17.

[65] Clark, *Distant Justice* 18.

[66] Dianne, Otto, 'Subalternity and International Law: The Problems of Global Community and the Incommensurability of Difference', *Social & Legal Studies*, 5:3(1996): 337–64; Gayatri Spivak, 'Can the Subaltern Speak?', in *Colonial Discourse and Post-Colonial Theory: A Reader*, eds. Patrick Williams and Laura Chrisman (New York: Colombia University Press, 1994), 90–110.

[67] Vivienne Jabri, 'Peacebuilding, the Local and the International: A Colonial or a Postcolonial Rationality?', *Peacebuilding* 1:1 (2013): 6–7 and 14; Kamari Clarke, 'Affective Justice: The Racialized Imaginaries of International Justice', *PoLAR* 42:2 (2019): 244–57.

[68] Phil Clark has clearly shown how the ICC's interventions, despite the court's failure to acknowledge its own embeddedness in the contexts in which it functions, has led to disastrous effects for those communities subjected to it's jurisdiction, *Distant Justice* 18–19.

[69] Whyte, 'Always on Top'; Mahmood Mamdani, 'Responsibility to Protect or Right to Punish?', *Journal of Intervention and Statebuilding* 4:1 (2010): 53–67; Clarke, 'Affective Justice'; Muppidi Himadeep, 'Colonial and Postcolonial Global Governance', in *Power in Global Governance*, eds. Michael Barnett, and Raymond Duvall (Cambridge and New York: Cambridge University Press, 2005): 273–93.

Moreover, whilst these interventions are often made on behalf of the 'international community' this should not disguise the ambiguity and transience of this community. Following Vivienne Jabri, the international community should be considered 'a distinct juridical-political space' where the constitution of, and relations between, different subjects is defined and regulated by an ever-changing, and unevenly applied, set of rules and norms. This means the international community is not ontologically stable but is constantly reformulated as it encounters new problems and subjects.[70] As Michael Dillion and Julian Reid have suggested, interventions on behalf of the international community become important for articulating a sense of, and making real, the 'international community',[71] contributing to 'the normative construction of the international' itself.[72]

In this respect, throughout the ICTR's history, beyond helping Rwanda, the tribunal's advocates also stressed what these trials would do for the 'international community' – whether as an expression of its conscience, a means to solidify the rules and norms of the community or to achieve 'international peace and security'. The ICTR, then, offers a chance to examine what particular idea of the international community emerged through the tribunal's operations and, by interrogating the inner operations of the court and the ways in which the archive is produced, *who* controls this process and, returning to the above, *whose* perspective is enforced and *whose* vision of justice realised.

As this chapter has argued, turning to the archive, as a site where these strands of law, knowledge and governance coalesce, offers the opportunity to get the heart of these questions of why a particular account of violence was produced and how this led to certain conceptions of community. The archive is, however, not only the empirical site through which imaginings of community can be excavated. The archive is also, as the following section argues, a methodological approach that is used to examine how archives produce and restrict knowledge in particular ways and so produce particular imaginings of community.

---

[70] Jabri, 'Peacebuilding', 3–4; Colin Koopman, 'Foucault's Historiographical Expansion: Adding Genealogy to Archaeology', *Journal of the Philosophy of History* 2:3(2008): 359.

[71] Michael Dillon and Julian Reid, 'Global Governance, Liberal Peace, and Complex Emergency', *Alternatives* 25:1 (2000): 117–43.

[72] Jabri, 'Peacebuilding', 6–7 and 14. See also Clarke, 'Affective Justice', 244–57.

ARCHIVES AS METHODOLOGY

In the 1980s and 1990s, the question of how to analyse colonial archives was an important point of debate in post-colonial studies. Some scholars argued that there was a need to read archives *against the grain* to recover the subaltern's voice in the face of the archive's exclusionary logics.[73] However, Gayatri Spivak questioned the validity of this approach, arguing that the archival force was such that attempting to find agency in those lives recorded in the archive was futile.[74] Stoler, supporting this approach, consequently argued that colonial archives (and arguably any archive) should be read *along the grain* and analysed from an ethnographic perspective to examine how 'credible' knowledge is produced and the effects that this has within particular societies.[75] This resonates with Foucault's description of the archive as part of his archaeological methodology,[76] which Colin Gordon describes as follows:

> [T]he study of forms of knowledge and rationality at the level of their *material manifestation* as bodies of discourse composed of finite sets of oral or written utterances. The aim is to render these discourses accessible to description and analysis as constituting a specific order of historical reality. (emphasis added)[77]

In order to understand the politics of the archive, then, it is important to ascertain what rules underpin the production of knowledge – Foucault calls these the rules of formation.[78] Foucault's archaeological methodology offers a way to determine these rules, by analysing the regularity with which statements and records are made for (and excluded from) the archive and how they relate to each other, structuring, ordering, restricting and *enabling* discourse.[79]

---

[73] See also Bastian, 'Colonial Records', 273. For a similar account of the ability, and need, to reclaim 'lost voices', see Arlette Farge, *The Allure of the Archive*, trans. Thomas Scott-Railton (London: Yale University Press, 2013).

[74] Gayatri Spivak, 'The Rani of Sirmur: An Essay in Reading the Archives', *History and Theory* 24:3 (1985): 271; Dianne Otto, 'Subalternity and International Law: The Problems of Global Community and the Incommensurability of Difference', *Social & Legal Studies* 5:3 (1996): 354–55.

[75] Ann Stoler, 'Colonial Archives and the Arts of Governance', *Archival Science* 2:1 (2002): 87–109.

[76] Michel Foucault, *The Archaeology of Knowledge and the Discourse on Language*, trans. Alan Sheridan (New York: Pantheon Books, 1972).

[77] Colin Gordon, 'Afterword', in *Power/Knowledge: Selected Interviews and Other Writings 1972–1977*, ed. Colin Gordon (New York: Pantheon Books, 1980), 243–44.

[78] Foucault, *Archaeology of Knowledge* 127; Gilles Deleuze, *Foucault*, trans. Seán Hand (London: University of Minnesota Press, 1988), 3–8.

[79] Foucault, *Archaeology of Knowledge* 45.

Statements – grouped into four categories, or levels of analysis: objects, enunciative modalities, concepts and strategies – are not understood as regularly conceived of, as explicable through grammatical units such as sentences. Rather they are utterances that are intelligible only as components of the larger whole – a discourse or *archive*.[80] The way in which Foucault describes these different types of statement offers an insight into how Foucault conceives of the archive and how the regularity *and specificity* of particular statements can be exposed.

Objects are not found external to discourse but take on a particular appearance as a result of the way that a discourse refracts light, as Gilles Deleuze puts it, in a particular manner to make these visible.[81] In rendering these objects visible *in a particular way*, the discourse itself is rejuvenated. This co-constituting nature is the case for each of these categories of statement, each of which is made possible by, and makes possible, a particular discourse.[82] In relation to the ICTR's archive, this might, then, consider how 'victims' and 'perpetrators' are produced as objects of enquiry.

Enunciative modalities are the possible subject positions that can be taken up by different actors and the rules that determine how these actors participate in the construction of the discourse. This further highlights the need to look at actors' positions within particular institutions and the position of the institutions themselves within wider society and hence draws attention to the relationship between the discursive and non-discursive.[83] When analysing international criminal justice this might, for instance, look at the interactions between prosecutors and witnesses in the production of the archive. This also draws attention to the question of voice and resonates with the post-colonial concern with *who* has the right to speak and produce records for the archive. Moreover, following Jens Meierhenrich and Eltringham, this pushes back against any notion that these tribunals are homogenous and disembodied spaces. Rather, as will be made clear throughout the book, international courts are brought to life by different subjects who bring with them their own vision of justice and community.[84]

---

[80] *Ibid.*, 27, 32–38 and 79–99.
[81] *Ibid.*, 40–49; Gilles Deleuze, 'What Is Dispositif?', in *Michel Foucault: Philosopher*, ed. Timothy Armstrong (Hempstead: Harvester Wheatsheaf, 1992), 160.
[82] Lene Hansen, *Security as Practice: Discourse Analysis and the Bosnian War* (London: Routledge, 2013), 9.
[83] Foucault, *Archaeology of Knowledge* 50–55 and 106.
[84] Nigel Eltringham, *Genocide Never Sleeps: Living Law at the International Criminal Tribunal for Rwanda* (Cambridge: Cambridge University Press, 2019): 6–8; Jens Meierhenrich, 'The

What is important when understanding the concepts that underpin the archive is the manner in which these relate to each other, which orders the discourse and provides a grid of intelligibility.[85] For example, in international criminal justice, the concept of genocide exists only in relation to other crimes, such as crimes against humanity.[86] For each of these categories, the interrelation *within* and *between* categories is crucial when articulating the rules of formation.[87] Finally, strategies are the overriding principles that direct the discourse and help settle conflicts, or hold conflicting possibilities in productive relation to each other.[88] For international courts, one of the most important strategies underlying its function is to deliver 'justice'. What this, as with all of these categories, means in practice, however, is a product of the archive's rules of formation and so something that needs determining through careful analysis of the archive's records.

The archaeological approach also encourages analysis to move beyond a focus on the discursive. As the quote from Gordon suggests, there is a materiality to the archive. First, the archive is a site where the materiality of a discourse manifests; the archive produces material artefacts and records in a particular way due to the rules that determine the contours of legitimate knowledge. As Stoler argues, archives should be seen 'as monuments of states as well as sites of state ethnography'.[89] As such, reading the materiality of the archive can provide a way to understand the discourse(s) that underpin it. Second, the archive also materially effects the social world. Whether this is how particular people should be classified or what constitutes the 'reality' of a nation's past, the archive produces particular conditions and logics that resonate beyond the archive, producing particular lived experiences. But, as the first section of this chapter argued, the archive's attempts to tame are always bound to, at least partially, fail. What this means is that there is the possibility that certain material fragments are located within the archive which sit in tension with the archive's rules and offer a disruptive potential. This also, and following Arlette Farage, means that Spivak's claims that the force of the archive is such

---

Practice of International Law: A Theoretical Analysis', *Law and Contemporary Problems* 76:3–4 (2013): 1–83.

[85] Foucault, *Archaeology of Knowledge* 56–63.

[86] Claire Moon, 'Narrating Political Reconciliation: Truth and Reconciliation in South Africa', *Social Legal Studies* 15:2 (2006): 261–66.

[87] Foucault, *Archaeology of Knowledge* 45.

[88] Ibid., 64–70 and 72.

[89] Stoler, *Along the Archival Grain* 90.

that it *erases* the subaltern's voice completely should be treated with caution.[90]

The analysis conducted throughout this book draws on this analytical and methodological approach to explore how knowledge is produced within the ICTR's archive and how this links to the production of certain ideas of community. Following the approach set out earlier, it asks: What account of violence was produced within the archive? What rules and power relations underpin the archive? And how do these records constitute, as such, a particular imagining of community?

Adopting this approach to the analysis of the ICTR's archive offers a step change in how international law is analysed. Empirically, few scholars that have considered the archives of international courts as important research sites in and of themselves, and even those that have, on the whole, tended to skirt over the explicit question of the politics of archival knowledge. As such, they treat the archive in more traditional terms as a repository of a neutral account of the past, which is seen as contributing towards peace and reconciliation.[91] The exception here is the work of Kirsten Campbell, whose analysis of the ICTY's archive comes closest to exploring this link between law, knowledge and governance. Campbell highlights several frameworks surrounding the ICTY that shaped the archive, including the tribunal's mandate to determine a legal judgment, its role in representing the international community's norms, and its contribution to the Western Balkans' transition to peace. As such, Campbell shows how the archive's records, and hence the memory of the violence, are *constructed* rather than found and are therefore politically charged.[92]

This book builds on Campbell's analysis in a number of ways. First, whereas Campbell begins analysis with the structures surrounding the ICTY, suggesting, in turn, that these inevitably produced particular types of records, the book begins its analysis with the records themselves, and meticulously traces how the records were produced and in the process reproduced particular world views, and draws inspiration

[90] Farage, *Allure of the Archive.*
[91] Adami, 'Judicial Record Management/Archiving'; Tom Adami and Martha Hunt, 'Genocidal Archives: The African Context', *Journal of the Society of Archivists* 26: 1 (2005): 177; and Tom Adami, '"Who Will Be Left to Tell the Tale?" Recordkeeping and International Criminal Jurisprudence', *Archival Science* 7 (2007): 213–21; Eric Ketlaar, 'Truths, Memories and Histories in the Archives of the International Criminal Tribunal for the Former Yugoslavia', *Genocide Convention: The Legacy of 60 Years*, eds. Hugo Van der Wilt et al. (Leiden: Brill, 2012), 220–21.
[92] Kirsten Campbell, 'The Laws of Memory: The ICTY, Archive, and Transitional Justice', *Social and Legal Studies* 22:2 (2013): 251–53.

from the post-colonial concern with *who* has the right to construct the archive.[93] This also looks to emphasise the ways that the archival process is contested. As such, the book is concerned not only with how the archive contributes to what Jef Huysmans and Joao Pontes Nogueira refer to as 'boundary making', but also how certain practices in the production of the archive might *fracture* or disrupt those boundaries.[94] Second, whilst Campbell points to the archive as a site of norm projection, by ascertaining the archive's rules the book offers an understanding of what exactly these norms are and how these relate to particular notions of community. This analysis is also, then, important for IR scholars interested in how the international community is demarcated and constituted as a particular reality, and specifically this association between legal archives and the international community is a new and important contribution of this book.[95] Finally, the granular approach to determining how the archives records are produced leads to a deeper exploration of the very contents of the archive and determines which material traces of the tribunal's existence and the genocide have been deemed worthy of protection and preservation for future use and what this tells us about the politics of the archive.

When taken together, moreover, these developments offer a theoretical advance in the analysis of international courts by bringing some of the ideas and concepts from critical legal scholarship and IR into the study of international courts. These perspectives, although growing in prominence, still remain marginalised in the study of international criminal law.[96] This is, then, about moving analysis beyond the black letter of the law and instead understanding how law is brought to life and with what consequence.[97] In doing so the book demonstrates that international courts should be seen as performative sites where law, knowledge and imaginings of community are produced in highly contested and dynamic ways.

Analysing the ICTR Archive

Whilst the book considers the ICTR's archive as a whole, the source base of this research focused in more narrowly on three trials. This was

---

[93] Stoler, *Along the Archival Grain* 1.

[94] Jef Huysmans and João Pontes Nogueira, 'Ten Years of IPS: Fracturing IR', *International Political Sociology* 10:4 (2016): 303–4.

[95] *Ibid.*

[96] Eltringham, *Genocide Never Sleeps*; Meierhenrich, 'The Practice of International Law'; Clarke, *Affective Justice.*

[97] Eltringham, *Genocide Never Sleeps* 6–8.

to get an in-depth understanding of the processes and conditions through which records were produced for the archive. This, for instance, allowed for a close analysis of the way that the records of witnesses' testimony were constructed – which remain, arguably, the most important record within the archive. The three trials selected were spread over the lifespan of the tribunal: Jean-Paul Akayesu (1998); Emanuel Bagambiki, Samuel Imanishimwe and André Ntagerura, otherwise known as *Cyangugu* (2004); and Jean-Baptiste Gatete (2011).[98] Throughout the book, the analysis is more concerned with the rules that allow particular statements to be made within the archive, rather than a detailed account of each trial. As such, an overview of these trials can be found at the end of Chapter 2.

These trials were chosen for several reasons. From a methodological perspective, these were selected because they dealt with prosecutions spread over the tribunal's history, relatively similar subject matter (making it possible to identify the (dis)similarities with which these subjects were treated), and instances of prosecutorial success (*Akayesu* and *Gatete*) and failure (*Cyangugu*). Whilst being not representative of all ICTR trials, these offer a way to systematically analyse how records were constructed for the archive and how differing contexts (e.g. the temporality of the trial) affected this process.

The analysis drew on three main types of sources. The first, and main, set was each trial's case files, which contain pre-trial statements (only rarely available), indictments, trial transcripts (of both the trial and appeals hearings), trial exhibits, correspondence, motions, decisions and judgments (of both the trial and appeals hearings). These amounted to a considerable volume of source material; *Cyangugu* alone contains in the region of 100,000 pages of records. Each of these case files was examined to determine the rules and regularities with which the different actors in the courtroom constructed accounts of violence. In addition to this, I drew on documents from other ICTR trials (particularly judgments) to supplement my analysis where required.

Here, I acknowledge Eltringham's observation about how much is lost from the courtroom process by only looking at trial transcripts, which do not capture the embodied and deeply social nature of the trial process. This is, certainly, a limitation of this study. However, in many respects, the book is, like Eltringham, concerned with moving beyond

---

[98] These dates represent the year of the trial judgments.

a 'black letter' approach to the study of law and to understand the conditions and rules, often unspoken, which animate law and bring it to life in particular ways and with particular effects. Whilst perhaps the affective register is lost for the most part in these transcripts, it is nonetheless possible to meticulously trace and build up an image of the rules that underpin which records can be made for the archive and which cannot. Indeed, because my source base is largely written documentation I have been able to analyse a much larger volume of data than would have been possible with a purely ethnographic approach. However, to compensate for some of this loss, I have both observed ICTR trials in person and conducted a series of interviews with tribunal personnel, discussed later.[99]

Second, to see how the political landscape that surrounded the court affected the archive, I also drew on administrative documents held largely in the UN's online archive,[100] including external reports (such as by the UN's Fifth Committee), internal reports (particularly ICTR biannual reports to the UNSC and UN General Assembly [UNGA]), strategy documents (such as those by the Office for Internal Oversight Services), and UNGA and UNSC discussions of the ICTR. I attempted to place these UN discussions within broader context of UN activity throughout this period and so additionally analysed policy briefings and reports that were produced by the UNSC and Secretary General (UNSG) on similar topics (such as peacebuilding and transitional justice).

Finally, as mentioned, I conducted twenty-two semi-structured interviews with actors from each of the tribunal's organs (prosecution, chambers and registry) and the defence to elucidate how the trials' participants approached the trials at the tribunal and how changes both inside and outside the tribunal affected this. These included a number of senior officials, including two former presidents of the tribunal and a prosecutor, registrar, head of appeals, and head of the archives section. This allowed for a potential dissonance to come to the fore as individual actors had the chance to express their motivations and experiences of the tribunal in a manner that might challenge how I understood these processes to have unfolded.[101] These interviews were supplemented by

---

[99] Eltringham, *Genocide Never Sleeps* 4 and 8.

[100] UN, 'Documents: Online Archive', found: www.un.org/en/documents/index.html (last accessed 30 August 2019).

[101] Nigel Eltringham, '"When We Walk out, What Was It All About?": Views on New Beginnings from within the International Criminal Tribunal for Rwanda', *Development and Change* 45:3 (2014): 545.

other publicly accessible interviews with tribunal employees, such as the 'Voice from the Rwanda Tribunal' project.[102]

In conducting the analysis, I made use of the qualitative analysis software NVIVO.[103] This offers a number of tools to identify and record various patterns found in these sources. In particular, it allows the user to create 'nodes' which facilitate the manual 'coding' of files against different themes. At the outset, then, I identified a number of themes linked with Foucault's four categories of statements – objects, enunciative modalities, concepts and strategies – which became the nodes which then structured my reading of the files. For example, whilst the following is indicative, rather than exhaustive, for objects, I created nodes for 'victims', 'perpetrators', etc.; for enunciative modalities, 'prosecution', 'witnesses', etc.; for concepts, 'genocide', 'crimes against humanity', etc.; and for strategies, the initial node was, more broadly, 'strategic function', which recorded when and where the function of the court was discussed. Whilst the initial nodes were those more or less obviously associated with the practice of international criminal justice, as analysis continued, more nodes and sub-nodes were added to offer a fine-grained analysis. For instance, under the perpetrator node I created sub-nodes about the different narrative tropes that were created about the defendants. One such example, discussed in Chapter 3, was, that the defendants 'did what they could.' Having 'coded' the documents according to these nodes, it was then possible to return to the file extracts associated with the nodes to further analyse the patterns of how these different objects, enunciative modalities, concepts and strategies emerged and changed over time. Piecing together the results from this in-depth qualitative research produced the analysis that follows.

Chapter 2, 'The ICTR and It's Archive', sets out the archive's strategies at the tribunal's outset, by tracing the UN's involvement in Rwanda from the build-up to the genocide to the creation of the tribunal and the archive. In particular, it looks at why, having been willing to stand by during the genocide, the UN came to see an international court as a potential solution to the violence in Rwanda and what this reveals about the politics and purpose of the archive. Here I argue that the introduction of the legal terminology of 'genocide' during the violence marked a key turning point in the UN's

---

[102] Batya Friedman *et al.*, 'Voices from the Rwandan Tribunal', found: http://tribunalvoices.org/voices/ (last accessed 22 August 2020).
[103] See www.qsrinternational.com/nvivo/what-is-nvivo (last accessed 20 December 2017).

intervention, as the violence then became something that targeted the international community as a whole. The chapter also offers a brief overview of the ICTR and the archive and here shows that, at the start of the tribunal, a very broad set of strategies underpinned the archive orientated around the principles of truth, justice and reconciliation. This emphasised the tribunal's role in determining individual responsibility, establishing the truth, providing a space for victims to testify and reconcile with their pasts, and contributing to the development of international criminal law. This broad function had significant consequences for how knowledge was produced for the archive, and the rules that were to underpin it at the outset.

Chapter 3, 'The Force of Law', focuses on the archive's concepts and objects. The chapter first examines how the tribunal's legal rules shaped the archive, setting out how the court's statute and ever-evolving jurisprudence created the framework through which the archive's records were produced. Beginning to get to the political nature of this account, the chapter also demonstrates how certain interpretations of the law ended up preventing records from being produced – such as about the international nature of the genocide – and cemented the use of trials as a key governance tool within the international community. The second part zeros in on arguably the two most important objects for the archive: victims and perpetrators. Exploring how these were constituted in particular ways points to how this produced distinctive visions of community and also how this resulted in a number of conflicts between the archives strategies.

Chapters 4 and 5 explore how various subject positions (or what Foucault describes as enunciative modalities) influenced how knowledge was produced within the archive, from which perspective records were constructed, and, ultimately, what was to be archived. In Chapter 4, 'Contesting the Archive', I focus on the witnesses, who played a far more significant role in constructing the archive than scholars normally credit. Whilst this shows how legal actors constrained what witnesses could record within the archive, it also demonstrates how witnesses were able to contest these parameters both in terms of which crimes would be recorded, but also how the law was to account for violence. This contestation also destabilised many of the objects and subjects that the legal discourse tried to produce, such as what constituted a victim or perpetrator.

Chapter 5, 'Reconstituting Justice', looks at how other actors involved in the production of knowledge at the ICTR tried to influence the way in which the archive was constructed. It begins by returning to the themes set out at the end of Chapter 2 and explores how the legal actors of the court, in the tribunal's formative years, pursued an expansive approach to the trials in search of truth, justice and reconciliation. This shows how this influenced what was recorded within the archive and that initially the archive was underpinned by a broader understanding of justice, which can be seen as a weak form of restorative justice. However, this approach to prosecutions changed over time as the tribunal began to focus simply on getting as many verdicts as possible, as quickly as possible. As such, the conception of justice underpinning the archive became far more restricted and more closely resembled a more traditional form of retributive justice. This, then, shows the fragmenting of the tribunal's initial purpose. This chapter identifies three main factors behind this shift: the solidification of the legal rules that underpinned the trials; the relationship between the tribunal and other UN organs – and particularly the Security Council's decision in early 2000 that the tribunal had to close down as quickly as possible; and the ICTR's acquiescence to the RPF's demands that the tribunal halt investigations into RPF crimes during the genocide.

Chapter 6, 'Imagining Community', brings together, and builds on, the findings made throughout the book about the nature of the international community imagined within the archive. This shows that whilst the tribunal functioned as a site of liberal international governance, underneath this liberal vision sat a distinctly illiberal understanding of community. In particular this shows that the archive divided the international community into the international, as a site of peace and order, and the local, as a site of barbarity; protected a space wherein violence was a legitimate aspect of international relations; and projected a patriarchal and colonial vision of community as the voices of the subaltern was denied.

Chapter 7, 'The Residual Mechanism and the Archive', turns to the Residual Mechanism for the International Criminal Tribunals (MICT), the institution that took over the remaining functions of the ICTR after it closed down. This looks at the extent to which the logics that underpinned the ICTR's archive were replicated at the MICT, specifically through a reading of the materiality of the archive, which sits at the heart of the new MICT complex in Arusha. In doing so, this demonstrates that whilst the rhetoric that surrounded the MICT revived the broad idea of justice that underpinned the ICTR at its inception, the reality was that an even narrower vision of justice came to underpin the archive. This also draws on Pierre Nora's understanding of *lieux de memoire* to examine the dynamic between remembering and forgetting that is at the heart of the archive.[104]

The conclusion, 'The ICTR's Archive', brings these findings together and considers what this tells us about the role of the archive in international criminal justice and international politics. This reveals a complex picture whereby the principles and strategies that under-pinned knowledge production at the tribunal shifted considerably as the tribunal progressed, from a form of restorative justice to a more strictly retributive model. This also meant a shift from more far-reaching records of violence produced under the witnesses' influence to a more legalistic record of violence. Over time, the archive, then, less closely reflected the needs and priorities of those affected by the genocide and arguably also produced a more conservative, and concerning, vision of the international community. The chapter also examines the extent to which these dynamics are an inevitable part of the international criminal justice project, in part by examining ICC trial practice. This argues that, whilst there is little to suggest international criminal justice must necessarily act with such a reductionist view of its mandate, regrettably, the rules underpinning the ICTR/MICT archive continue to frame how justice is imagined and practised at the ICC.

---

[104] Pierre Nora, 'Between Memory and History: *Les Lieux de Mémoire*', *Representations* 2 (1989): 7–24.

CHAPTER TWO

THE INTERNATIONAL CRIMINAL TRIBUNAL FOR RWANDA AND ITS ARCHIVE

An archive's strategies, Foucault reminds us, give it a sense of purpose and coherence, as conflicts between different statements are settled or held together in productive tension. Yet, as with all of the types of statements outlined in Foucault's archaeological methodology, what these strategies are should not be taken at face value. Rather, as with the objects, concepts and enunciative modalities, strategies are constituted in particular ways within the archive and so have rules that need to be excavated. As will become clear throughout the book, strategies are also subject to change over time as they interact with, and are defined in relation to, the other categories of statements. This chapter is concerned with outlining what strategies underpinned the archive at the tribunal's outset, as it came to be seen as a tool of international governance that could introduce international peace and security, and bring reconciliation to Rwanda.

Whilst the use of international trials in the present is a relatively established (if not still highly contested) aspect of how the international community is governed, this should not lead to a warped teleological sense that such an outcome was inevitable.[1] There was, prior to the 1990s, very little prospect of this.[2] The emergence of two

[1] Michel Foucault, 'Nietzsche, Genealogy, History', in *Foucault Reader*, ed. Paul Rainbow (London: Random House, 1984), 76–101; Colin Koopman, 'Foucault's Historiographical Expansion: Adding Genealogy to Archaeology', *Journal of the Philosophy of History* 2:3 (2008): 338–55.

[2] Mark Drumbl, 'Pluralising International Criminal Justice: From Nuremberg to the Hague: The Future of International Criminal Justice by Philippe Sands', *Michigan Law Review* 103:6 (2005): 1300–301.

international courts in quick succession in the early 1990s – one for the former Yugoslavia (ICTY) and then Rwanda (ICTR) – needs to be understood within the historical moment they emerged in, allowing for the conditionality of their emergence to come to the fore. This will, as outlined throughout this chapter, offer an insight into what exactly it was hoped the ICTR could achieve as a response to the Rwandan genocide and, through this, what strategies emerged within the archive as a result.

The following section traces the UN's entanglement with Rwanda from the eve of the genocide to the formation of tribunal and archive. Towards the end of the chapter, I also provide an overview of the trials that underpin the subsequent analysis of the book, both to introduce these trials to those readers unfamiliar with ICTR cases and as a means to briefly survey some of the ways that the tribunal and the archive strategies changed over time.

RWANDA AND THE UN

War and the Arusha Peace Accords

On 1 October 1990 an intense conflict broke out in Rwanda, as the Rwandan Patriotic Front (RPF) invaded from its base in Uganda. The RPF was a force largely made up of exiled Tutsis that had fled Rwanda during the purges of the 1960s, after the establishment of the First Republic under President Kayibanda, and settled in Uganda – many, including future President Paul Kagame, serving with the Ugandan army. Having failed to return to Rwanda by peaceful means, the RPF invaded in 1990 to claim its right to return. This started the period of instability that ultimately would lead to the genocide, as the political landscape in Rwanda became dominated with anti-Tutsi rhetoric.[3] During this initial conflict, the early signs of genocide could already be seen. Léon Mugesera's notorious 1992 speech outlined the core elements of the génocidaires' Hutu power ideology, and the Bugesera massacre in 1992 can be interpreted as a prototype of the systematic targeting and killing of Tutsis that was to spread across the country in

---

[3] Here, it is important to note that drawing this link between Tutsis inside the country and the RPF was an explicit part of the propaganda campaign in the run-up to the genocide. Moreover, there is a long history in Rwanda of Hutu power advocates using (and sometimes inventing) the threat of a 'Tutsi invasion' in order to persecute and kill Tutsis in Rwanda as a means of securing political capital. Alison Des Forges, *Leave None to Tell the Story* (New York: Human Rights Watch, 1999), 61–65.

1994.[4] The media outlets that became instrumental in the killing were also established at this time. *Kangura* magazine was launched in 1990, with issue 6 (December 1990) publishing the 'Hutu 10 Commandments' – encapsulating the Hutu power call to fear, oppose and destroy the Tutsis. The radio station *Radio Télévision Libre des Mille Collines* (RTLM) was established in 1993, quickly becoming the mouthpiece of the génocidaires.

In February 1993, after three years of conflict, the two sides agreed to a ceasefire that resulted in the signing of the Arusha Peace Accords (APA). With the assistance of the French government, who convinced Rwanda's president, Juvénal Habyarimana, of the merits of the agreement, both the RPF and the Rwandan government lobbied the UN to send in a UN peacekeeping force as part of the APA to ensure the maintenance of the ceasefire and to aid both parties to implement the agreement.[5] After some initial reluctance – due, in part, to the UN's wariness caused by its ill-fated intervention in Somalia that led to deaths of a number of US and Pakistani peacekeepers – the UNSC increasingly came around to the idea of intervening in the resolution of the conflict.[6] Given the apparent support from both parties, the task was interpreted as a simple handholding exercise. Demonstrating a deep ignorance to the political climate in, and history of, Rwanda, the UN came to see Rwanda as an 'easy win' – a chance to re-establish the UN's roles as guardians, as well as enforcers, of international peace and security after its failure in Somalia.[7]

The APA were finally signed on 4 August 1993. As Michael Barnett has argued, however, despite the UN provisionally agreeing to its presence in Rwanda prior to this, the UN's slow-moving bureaucratic cogs led to a delayed introduction of the UN force in Rwanda.[8] It took until October 1993 for the UN to finally approve the United Nations Assistance Mission for Rwanda (UNAMIR), which was only deployed in Rwanda in November 1993.[9] Even then, the strength of the force

[4] Samantha Power, *A Problem from Hell: America and the Age of Genocide* (London: Flamingo, 2003), 338; UNSC, S/1999/1257, *Report of the Independent Inquiry into the Actions of the United Nations during the Rwandan Genocide*, 16 December 1999, 6; UNSC, S/PV.7155, *7155th Meeting*, 16 April 2014, 4.
[5] Michael Barnett, *Eyewitness to Genocide: The United Nations and Rwanda* (London: Cornell University Press, 2002), 60–61.
[6] S/1999/1257, 41.
[7] Barnett, *Eyewitness to Genocide*, 13 and 65; Linda Melvern, *A People Betrayed: The Role of the West in Rwanda's Genocide* (London: Zed Books: 2nd edition, 2009), 94.
[8] Barnett, *Eyewitness to Genocide*, 62–63.
[9] S/1999/1257, 8.

and the scope of its mandate were far less than what was initially anticipated, and even when 'fully formed' UNAMIR lacked basic equipment.[10] This meant that the reduced force with its reduced mandate never reached full capacity and by late February 1994 UNAMIR was so weak that it had to stop foot patrols.[11] From the very outset, both a lack of political will and certain bureaucratic practices influenced how the UN responded to the violence in Rwanda, something that was also seen in the failure to pass on to UNAMIR the Special Rapporteur for Rwanda's 1993 report, which suggested genocide had already occurred during the initial civil war.[12]

Any hopes that Rwanda was going to be a quick win for the UN were quickly revised. The deteriorating conditions inside the country, the Rwandan government's obstruction over the installation of a broad-based transitional government – one of the key pillars of the APA – and a spike in politically motivated assassinations made it apparent that something more was going on than just the mere stalling of the peace process. If any doubt existed over the potential seriousness of the situation, then this should have been finally set straight by General Dallaire's (the head of UNAMIR forces on the ground) famous 11 January 1994 cable, now known as the 'genocide fax'. This cable passed on key information to the UN Secretariat that Dallaire had received convincing evidence from an informant that extremist Hutu elements had begun to systematically prepare for a campaign against the Tutsis by compiling lists of potential victims, stockpiling weapons and converting the civil defence forces into armed militia.[13] The cable – sent from Dallaire to Kofi Annan – was never passed on to the UNSC for consideration, and when Dallaire requested permission to intervene and seize the stockpiled weapons, he was told that those actions would exceed his mandate and that he should stand down.[14]

This response is often presented as the watershed moment in the UN's involvement in Rwanda. Adam LeBor goes as far as to suggest that raiding the caches could have stopped the genocide.[15] Showing at

---

[10] This was due to both the United Kingdom's and the United States' successful attempts to water down the mandate to make it less costly and some genuine concern for the capabilities of an overstretched UN peacekeeping office. Melvern, *People Betrayed*, 94; S/1999/1257, 30–32; Barnett, *Eyewitness to Genocide*, 70–71.

[11] S/1999/1257, 40; Melvern, *People Betrayed*, 116.

[12] S/1999/1257, 31.

[13] *Ibid.*, 10.

[14] Adam LeBor, '*Complicity with Evil*': *The United Nations in the Age of Modern Genocide* (London: Yale University Press, 2006), 168; Melvern, *People Betrayed*, 107–9.

[15] LeBor, '*Complicity with Evil*', 168–70; Melvern, *People Betrayed*, 107–9.

best negligence, and at worst calculated indifference, this (in)action set a trend for what came next, when the UN stood idly by whilst the massacres of up to one million Tutsis and 'moderate Hutus' occurred.

The Genocide

Whilst, then, there is a much longer history to the genocide, the killing began in earnest when Habyarimana's plane was shot down close to Kigali Airport in the early hours of 6 April 1994. This triggered the resumption of violence between the RPF and the Rwandan government and military, and the start of a highly coordinated campaign that saw close to a million victims murdered in just a hundred days. Almost immediately after the plane crash, 'Hutu extremists' within the major political parties formed a coalition that became known as the 'interim government', which coordinated the violence throughout Rwanda. Whilst, as will be discussed in Chapter 3, the violence was more complicated than simply being ethnically rooted, largely the perpetrators of the violence were Hutus aligned to the ruling coalition of Hutu power advocates, and Tutsis made up the vast majority of the victims. However, it should be noted that the first to be killed in the early hours of the genocide were those Hutus opposed to the 'Hutu power' ideology (such as Prime Minister Uwilingiyimana), and throughout the genocide Hutus played roles as victims, protectors and saviours, as well as genocidaires.

Whilst the campaign was nationally orchestrated, violence was interwoven within local power structures, and the genocide took place at different moments, with varying intensity, in different locations across Rwanda.[16] Crucial to the execution of the genocide was the *Interahamwe* (the youth militia affiliated with the main political party, the *Mouvement Républicain National pour la Démocratie et le Développmenent* – MRND), who roamed between areas setting up roadblocks – one of the main sites of killing – and igniting violence within localities that resisted the call to genocide. Equally as important was RTLM, which was used as a means to communicate with genocidaires (and even directed them to where Tutsis could be found) and also encouraged others to participate in the killing.[17] For example, on

---

[16] For histories of the genocide, see Des Forges, *Leave None to Tell the Story*; Lee Fujii, *Killing Neighbours: Webs of Violence in Rwanda* (London: Cornell University Press, 2009); Scott Straus, *The Order of Genocide: Race, Power and War in Rwanda* (London: Cornell University Press, 2006).

[17] For the role of the media in the genocide, see Allan Thompson (ed.), *The Media and the Rwandan Genocide* (London: Pluto Press, 2007).

2 June 1994, Hasan Ngeze – a major shareholder of RTLM, leader of the *Coalition pour la Défense de la République* (CDR), and founder and editor of *Kangura* – appeared on RTLM to ensure that the *Interahamwe* at the roadblocks were carrying out their work correctly:

> [Y]ou find these last few days that there are roadblocks where you arrive, you are thin, you have a small nose, you were born that way, and they say you are a Tutsi, even if you have an identity card showing that you are Hutu. Or they say that you are an accomplice. Then if you are a Hutu born thin with a small nose, he shows you his identity card that he is Hutu, he tells you his commune and you refuse saying: 'it is not possible, there is no Hutu like you.' You take him and kill him. [18]

Large amounts of the violence took place in locations where people had sought refuge, such as hospitals, schools, churches and local centres of government. Sometimes these acted as strongholds of resistance where the refugees fought off wave after wave of attacks.[19] In other instances, persons who were tasked with protecting these sites, and those who had sought refuge within them, helped the attackers to kill those congregated.[20]

The RPF ultimately declared victory on 17 June 1994, bringing an end to the genocide. After a short period under a coalition government, the RPF came to dominate Rwanda's post-genocide political landscape. Paul Kagame, who spearheaded the RPF invasion, subsequently took power and, at the time of writing, has retained control of the country for twenty years. Whilst not of comparable scale or intensity to the genocide, as the RPF swept through the country they committed numerous and serious violations of international law, largely committed against the Hutu population.[21]

---

[18] *Prosecutor v. Ferdinand Nahimana, Jean-Bosco Barayagwiza and Hassan Ngeze*, Judgment (ICTR-99-52-T), 3 December 2003, 253–54.

[19] For examples from witness testimony at the ICTR, see *Prosecutor v. André Ntagerura, Emmanuel Bagambiki and Samuel Imanishimwe*, Case No. ICTR–99–46 (hereafter ICTR–99–46), TRA001796/1, *[Cyangugu] – Ntagerura et al – Redacted Transcript of 23/10/2002*, 23 October 2002, 9–11; ICTR–99–46, TRA000122/01, *[Cyangugu] – Ntagerura et al – Redacted Transcript of 09/10/2000*, 09 October 2000, 13–34; *Prosecutor v. Jean Baptiste Gatete*, Case No. ICTR–00–61 (hereafter ICTR–00–61), TRA005458, *Gatete – Redacted Transcript of 22/10/2009*, 22 October 2009, 46–48.

[20] ICTR–00–61, ICTR–00–61–0240/1, *Gatete – Judgement and Sentence*, 31 March 2011, 4, 9 and 90; *Prosecutor v. Grégoire Ndahimana*, Case No. ICTR–01–68, *Trial Judgement*, 30 December 2001), 143–53.

[21] *Ibid.*, 57–58.

The UN and the Genocide

As has been well documented, despite the presence of the UNAMIR force, the UN – and the international community more generally – largely stood by whilst the genocide took hold of the country.[22] Whilst it is often stated that just 5,000 troops could have brought the genocide to an end, the UN actually *reduced* the number of UNAMIR troops in the first weeks of the genocide, convinced that it was no longer possible to neutrally keep the peace when there was none to be kept.[23] This is widely seen as giving the genocidaires a green light to step up the intensity of the killing in the knowledge that the international community would not intervene.[24] A number of other incidents further tarnished the UN's reputation, including the evacuation of all foreign personnel from Rwanda in April, leaving domestic staff to their own fate and marking the only moment where a stronger mandate was given to the UNAMIR force.[25]

Numerous reasons have been offered for why the UN was willing to stand by and let the genocide spread, including: the shadow of the Somalia crisis, a lack of political interest in Rwanda by leading global powers and the misconstrual (or deliberate misrepresentation) of the violence as 'tribal' rather than genocide.[26] This latter issue meant that as an (almost inevitable) outpouring of violence based on 'ancient hatreds' there was nothing that could be done to stop the violence in Rwanda (more on which in Chapter 6). This description of the violence predominated the media's representation of the violence too. Within the Western media, in particular, the portrayal of bloodlust and an innate will to violence, when coupled with the 'distant' nature of the violence, meant that there was no obligation for the international community to intervene.[27]

---

[22] Melvern, 'A People Betrayed'; Barnett, Eyewitness to Genocide; Adam LeBor, 'Complicity with Evil'; Power, A Problem from Hell.

[23] Melvern, 'People Betrayed', 134–70.

[24] LeBor, 'Complicity with Evil', 177; Helen Hintjens, 'Explaining the 1994 Genocide in Rwanda', The Journal of Modern African Studies 37:2 (1999): 274; Victor Peskin, International Justice in Rwanda and the Balkans: Virtual Trials and the Struggle for State Cooperation (Cambridge: Cambridge University Press, 2008), 155.

[25] Melvern, People Betrayed, 134–70.

[26] UNSC, S/PV.3377, 3377th Meeting, 16 May 1994, 8 and 11. This also resulted in the infamous statement by Madeleine Albright (US ambassador at the UN) about 'acts of genocide'. Samantha Power, 'Bystanders to Genocide: Why the United States Let the Rwandan Tragedy Happen', The Atlantic Online, September 2001, found: www1.essex.ac.uk/ARMEDCON/story_id/BystandersToGenocideRwanda.pdf (last accessed 21 September 2019).

[27] Alan Kuperman, 'How the Media Missed the Rwanda Genocide', in Media and the Rwandan Genocide, ed. Allan Thompson (London: Pluto Press, 2007), 256–60. In the UK press, even

It should be stated that this notion of the international community's inaction, as it is so often framed, conceals the deeply implicated nature of international actors in the violence in Rwanda. This, as argued by Michael Dillion and Julian Reid, allows these types of crises to be understood as being on the outskirts of the international community, rather than an important aspect, and to an extent consequence, of the community's rules and norms.[28] Beyond the effect that the UNAMIR's passivity had on the genocidaires, numerous other international actors were entangled in the violence. On the side of the RPF, the Ugandan state and military were strongly implicated, and on the side of the Rwandan government (and then the interim government), international arms companies helped to flood the country with cheap weapons, and the French government, in looking to support a Francophone ally, played a crucial role in underwriting the credit needed to purchase the weapons, training the genocidaires and then protecting them as the genocide unfolded.[29] Rather, the sleight of hand which described this violence as discrete and localised drew on and reproduced notions of the Other as a barbarous, hostile and backward place, distinguished from the peace and order of the 'civilised world'.[30]

A key shift in policy, however, began as the lexicon of law was gradually introduced to reframe the violence away from being seen as 'tribal' or mindless towards an understanding that it constituted genocide. The term 'genocide' was first implicitly used on 30 April 1994 when a UNSC statement drew on the wording of the United Nations Genocide Convention, noting: '[I]n this context the killing of members of an ethnic group with the intention of destroying such a group in whole or in part constitutes a crime which is punishable under

---

though, on the whole, the centre/left-wing press presented a more nuanced understanding of the genocide, this was peppered with a distinctive othering. See, for example, 'Blood Bath at the Bottom of the Barrel', *Guardian*, 8 April 1994; 'Rwanda PM Killed as Troops Wreak Carnage', *Guardian*, 8 April 1994; 'French Lead Flight from Rwanda', *Guardian*, 11 April 1994. For an example of the right-wing papers' discourse, see 'Britons Marooned by Massacre in the Mist', *Daily Mail*, 11 April 1994; 'Safely Home after Hell of Rwanda', *Daily Mail*, 13 April 1994; 'Massacre of Orphans', *Daily Mail*, 04 May 1994; 'Faces of Suffering Amid the Slaughter', *Daily Mail*, 16 May 1994; 'Rwanda Bloodbath Toll Hits 500,000', *Mail on Sunday*, 15 May 1994; 'Innocents in a Hospital of Hell', *Mail on Sunday*, 22 May 1994.

[28] Michael Dillon and Julian Reid, 'Global Governance, Liberal Peace, and Complex Emergency', *Alternatives* 25 (2000): 117–19.

[29] Mel McNulty, 'French Arms, War and Genocide in Rwanda', *Crime, Law and Social Change* 33:1–2 (2000), 105–29; Nelson Alusala, 'The Arming of Rwanda and the Genocide', *African Security Studies* 13:2 (2004): 137–40; Stephan Goose and Frank Smyth, 'Arming Genocide in Rwanda, the High Cost of Small Arms Transfers', *Foreign Affairs* 73:5 (1994): 86–96.

[30] Chinua Achebe, 'An Image of Africa', *Massachusetts Review* 18:4 (1977): 784.

international law.'[31] However, there continued to be reluctance within the UNSC to explicitly label the violence in Rwanda as genocide – fearing that, under the obligations of the Genocide Convention to *prevent* genocide, this would then require action [32] – and it took until 31 May 1994, nearly two months into the genocide, for the Secretary General to finally declare that 'there can be little doubt that [the killing] constituted genocide'.[33]

Whilst slow moving, this gradual introduction of the legal discourse reframed the nature of the problem being witnessed in Rwanda. It made this a violation not only of international law but also a wrong inflicted on 'humanity' as a whole.[34] As such, continued inaction by the UN was increasingly seen as damaging the integrity of the international community, as its norms and principles were violated. This also opened up a set of possible responses to that violence. First, this period saw the creation of an enlarged UNAMIR force, UNAMIR II, and a French-led 'humanitarian force' under the name *Operation Turquoise* to help to reintroduce peace (without any sensitivity to either France's colonial history or its role in assisting the genocidaires).[35] This also saw the idea emerge that as a violation of international law, a judicial response was required to reinstate peace.[36] This much was already pointed at in the reference to the genocide convention on 30 April 1994, where there

---

[31] S/PV.3377, 14. See Article II, UN General Assembly, 'Convention for the Prevention and Punishment of the Crime of Genocide' found: https://treaties.un.org/doc/publication/unts/vol ume%2078/volume-78-i-1021-english.pdf (last accessed 24 October 2019).

[32] S/PV.7155, 5; S/1999/1257, 38. The first *explicit* use of the term 'genocide' was on 16 May 1994, as the New Zealand delegate, Keating, stated, after condemning the farce that had allowed Rwanda to continue to hold a seat on the UNSC, that there needed to be an inquiry into the genocide, with the Czech delegate stating that '[i]n the view of my delegation, the proper description is genocide'. S/PV.3377, 11 and 16.

[33] S/1999/1257, 26.

[34] UNSC, S/RES/955, *Resolution 955*, 8 November 1994; UNSC, S/1995/134, *Report of the Secretary-General Pursuant to Paragraph 5 of Security Council Resolution 955 (1994)*, 13 February 1995, 4; S/1999/1257, 38.

[35] S/1999/1257, 26; UNSC, S/1994/640, *Report of the Secretary-General on the Situation in Rwanda*, 31 May 1994, 11.

[36] UNSC, S/PV.3371, *3371st Meeting*, 30 April 1994, 3; S/PV.3377, 14–15. There is also an interesting suggestion here that the turn to legal language to highlight the problem, and to law as the solution, was used as a way of 'acting without acting'. As the representative of Djibouti stated at the UNSC: 'Make no mistake; this is the crux of the matter. The killings must be stopped now. If this is so, then it is abundantly clear that we are simply deceiving ourselves in emphasizing the human rights aspect of this tragedy, however stunning it is to us. No one will deny that highlighting the criminal, genocidal and human rights violation aspects of the situation is necessary, but as an approach to the ongoing situation in Rwanda it leads us to focus on a cure after the fact, rather than dealing with the real cause and necessary prevention of the disease.' (UNSC, S/PV.3388, *3388th Meeting*, 8 June 1994, 2).

was an underlying threat that the crimes being committed were potentially 'punishable under international law'.

This started a chain reaction whereby a judicial response to genocide
became seen as a potential strategy to introduce peace in Rwanda and
the international community. A number of reports commissioned by
various UN organs in the immediate aftermath of the genocide con-
firmed that what had happened was genocide and that a court should be
established to prosecute those responsible.[37] What sealed the need for
the international court was, however, that the RPF government on
declaring victory called for the UN to follow the precedent set with the
creation of the ICTY and establish an ad hoc tribunal to bring those
most responsible for the genocide to account. This, combined with the
UN's tattered reputation for having stood by and allowed the genocide
to take place, ultimately left little choice but to create a court as, again,
the UN tried to re-establish its position as the leader of the international community. As a result, on 8 November 1994, the UNSC
under Resolution 955 created the International Criminal Tribunal for
Rwanda.[38]

What this shows is that the way the violence was framed opened up
different ways in which both the community was imagined and which
actions were seen as appropriate and necessary. At the start, the framing
of the violence as beyond the borders of the international community,
and as an act of bestial violence, made this an unfortunate incident but
not one worthy of intervention. However, the reframing of this through
a legal lens both effectively brought the violence, and so Rwanda too,
back within the borders of the international community whilst simultaneously rendering the whole community the victim of violence and
opened up a range of tools that could be used to bring peace. This also
suggests that *who* has control over these narratives matter, and here it is
clear that actors from the Global North – whether through the media or

---

[37] United Nations Economic and Social Council, E/CN.4/1995/7, *Question of the Violation of
Human Rights and Fundamental Freedoms in any Part of the World, with Particular Reference to
Colonial and Other Dependent Countries and Territories: Report on the Situation of Human Rights in
Rwanda Submitted by Mr. R. Degni-Ségui, Special Rapporteur of the Commission on Human Rights,
Under Paragraph 20 of Commission Resolution E/CN.4/S–3/1 of 25 May 1994*, 28 June 1994; S/
PV.3377, 14–5; UNSC, S/PV.3400, 3400th Meeting, 1July 1994; S/1999/1257, 28; UNSC, S/
1994/1125, *Preliminary Report of the independent Commission of Experts Established in Accordance
with Security Council Resolution 935 (1994)*, 4 October 1994, 5; UNSC, S/1994/1115, *Letter
Dated 28 September 1994 from the Permanent Representative of Rwanda to the United Nations
Addressed to the President of the Security Council: Statement Dated 28 September 1994 on the
Question of Refugees and Security in Rwanda*, 29 September 1994, 3–4; S/PV.3566, 3566th
Meeting, 16 August 1995, 8–14.
[38] S/RES/955.

diplomates in control of organs like the UNSC – were pivotal in determining how the violence was understood. Again, then, the link between law, knowledge and governance comes to the fore.

CREATING A TRIBUNAL

The UNSC gave the tribunal a mandate to prosecute those responsible for violations of international law in Rwanda and neighbouring countries from 1 January to 31 December 1994. As a UN organ created under Chapter VII of the UN Charter, this implicitly tasked the ICTR with contributing towards international peace and security. Moreover, the mandate also stated that the tribunal would 'contribute to the process of national reconciliation and to the restoration and maintenance of peace'.[39] The stipulation that the tribunal could contribute towards reconciliation had not been included in UNSC Resolution 827 that had brought the ICTY into existence in 1993 and seemingly marked a step change in what it was thought international courts could achieve. Whilst the statute and resolution remained silent as to how it was that a court could achieve these lofty goals, in an article published to advocate for the creation of the two ad hoc tribunals, the ICTY and ICTR's first prosecutor, Richard Goldstone, elucidated some of the ideas that were to underpin this claim. This, alongside statements made by other advocates of the court, points to some of the archive's initial strategies, namely achieving truth, justice, reconciliation and the reconstitution of the international community.

Goldstone presented the tribunal as a site that would uncover the truth about past violence and give a space for victims to testify and reconcile, performing a similar function to a truth commission.[40] As such, the justification for, and approach of, the tribunal was very much framed by the emerging discourse of transitional justice that was growing in strength at this time, especially after the South African Truth and Reconciliation Commission. This notion of the tribunal producing a 'historical record' was also underlined by Madeleine Albright, US Permanent Representative to the UN in 1994, who declared that the tribunal 'will establish the historical record before the guilty can

---

[39] Ibid.
[40] Payam Akhavan, 'Justice and Reconciliation in the Great Lakes Region of Africa: the Contribution of the International Criminal Tribunal for Rwanda', *Duke Journal of Comparative and International Law* 7 (1996): 340–41; Richard Goldstone, 'Justice as a Tool for Peace-Making: Truth Commissions and International Criminal Tribunals', *Journal of International Law and Politics* 28 (1995): 485–504.

reinvent the truth'.[41] Albright also presented an additional value of the court, stating:

> Our goal must be individual accountability and responsibility [. . .]. We must fix responsibility on those who have directed these acts of violence. In so doing, we can transform revenge into justice, affirm the rule of law, and hopefully bring this horrible cycle of violence to a merciful close.[42]

Justice, then, would help the victims overcome the desire for revenge and also help avoid ideas of collective guilt and responsibility, which would have seen the whole of the Hutu population charged and prosecuted for the violence.[43] Drawing strongly on the logic that also underpinned *Nuremberg*, justice here would help to identify those that were guilty so that the innocent could reintegrate into society.

This role of determining individual responsibility was seen as important in another respect too. After the genocide ended, another crisis broke as hundreds of thousands of (largely Hutu) refugees fled Rwanda to neighbouring countries. This mass exodus was seen as undermining neighbouring countries' sovereignty and further threatened international peace and security as the administrative and military structures that had been so crucial to the genocide were reformed in the camps as violence (and the genocide) continued.[44] The ICTR became part of the response to this crisis too, as it was hoped that the impartial application of the law would encourage those in the camps that they could return to Rwanda in the knowledge that they would not be subjected to arbitrary, revenge-driven acts of retribution.[45]

Beyond the Great Lakes and assisting Rwanda to reintegrate into the international community as a legitimate, fully functioning, sovereign nation, the tribunal would also, it was hoped, make important contributions to the international community itself. This was to be achieved

---

[41] 'Judgment Day', *Washington Post*, 11 October 1998.

[42] S/PV.3400, 4.

[43] Francois-Xavier Nsanzuwera, 'The ICTR Contribution to National Reconciliation', *Journal of International Criminal Justice* 3 (2005): 945–46.

[44] The refugee camps became a microcosm of Rwanda, as the camps rearranged themselves to represent the Interim Government's governing structure, and in some cases even sectors and cells were reformed. UNSC, S/1994/1157/Add.1, *Situation of Human Rights in Rwanda: Third Report on the Situation of Human Rights in Rwanda Submitted by Mr. René Degni-Ségui, Special Rapporteur of the Commission on Human Rights, Under Paragraph 20 of Resolution S–3/1 of 25 May 1994*, 14 November 1994, 15–18.

[45] 'War Crimes: Don't Let Them Get Away with It', *Washington Post*, 20 December 1994; Akhavan, 'Justice and Reconciliation', 337–38; S/PV.3453, 3453rd Meeting, 8 November 1994, 10; 'Rwanda Agrees to a U.N. War Crimes Tribunal', *New York Times*, 9 August 1994; and 'War Crimes First', *Washington Post*, 23 August 1994.

by, along with the ICTY, solidifying the principles of law that governed certain practices within the international community and by demonstrating that international criminal justice – a key mechanism in the governance of community – was a possibility.[46] As discussed more in Chapter 3, the tribunal was in many respects an experiment, as advocates of these types of courts looked to demonstrate their value to the international community. Much of the criticism lodged against the tribunal for being slow and costly (discussed in Chapter 5) fails to consider what an immense and challenging task this was.

At a more symbolic level, the tribunal marked a moment where the international community's image (and the UN's role as leader of that community) could be repaired after its reputation had been all but destroyed by the genocide. This showed that the UN was capable of bringing peace to the international community, and in this respect the tribunal reflected the 'conscience of mankind'.[47] This sentiment was echoed throughout the tribunal's history.[48]

As such, at the ICTR's creation, under the guise of achieving international peace and security, the tribunal was seen as being able to perform multiple functions for multiple actors. Not only a site of justice, it was also a site of truth and reconciliation. Not only of value for those that had been directly affected by the genocide, but also for the international community as a whole. As will become clear in the following chapters, this strategic framework had an important bearing on both how it was that the archive was constructed and in the particular way that it would ultimately constitute an understanding of the international community.

More cynically, the tribunal offered a way of making this type of statement (showing that, despite its (in)actions during the genocide, the UN was capable of bringing peace and security to the international community) but in a relatively cost-effective and risk-free manner.[49] From the very outset an 'economic' element was inserted into the tribunal's mandate, which would see it under-resourced for its duration, but particularly during its formative years. In its first budget, for instance,

---

[46] S/PV.3453, 7–8.

[47] Ibid., 3–13.

[48] In December 1996, for instance, the Malaysian delegate to the UNSC stated: '[T]he Tribunal serves as the conscience of the international community. It is the manifestation of the moral outrage of humanity over the transgressions of civilizational norms and ethics.' UNGA, A/51/PV.78, *51st Session, 78th Plenary Meeting*, 10 December 1996, 18.

[49] Frédéric Mégret, 'The Politics of International Criminal Justice', *European Journal of International Law* 13:5 (2002): 173–74.

the tribunal had a relatively meagre initial request (considering the complexity of the task at hand) of $0.5million cut by 20 per cent.[50] It is also of note here that the budget of the ICTY dwarfed that of the ICTR, as it was (as became a theme) given what can be understood as preferential treatment.[51]

For the tribunal to contribute to truth, justice, reconciliation and peace, the UN decided that an international court would be needed and that this court should be located outside of Rwanda. From a practical perspective, in addition to overcoming the difficulties of Rwanda's then destroyed infrastructure, an international court with an international jurisdiction, and backed by the UN (and most importantly the UNSC), seemed to offer the best chance of capturing and prosecuting those most responsible for the violence – the vast majority of whom had fled Rwanda.[52] It was also claimed that specifically *international* trials would ensure that an impartial and neutral justice would be delivered, thus constituting and performing a particular notion of the 'international'.[53] The RPF also acknowledged that this would be the benefit of an international court, which would help ease the refugees' concerns that Rwanda's domestic courts would become sites of revenge and 'victors' justice'.[54] Whilst plans had initially been made for the tribunal to be seated in The Hague, along with the ICTY, it was ultimately thought that an African seat was better suited to the tribunal's goals of assisting Rwanda, as this both retained the ability of the court to be independent from Rwanda, but also meant that (in theory) it would be close enough to the location of the crime to be important symbolically – justice must be *seen* to be done – and

---

[50] 'Second Class Justice', 15.

[51] UNGA, A/51/789, *Financing of the International Criminal Tribunal for the Prosecution of Persons Responsible for Genocide and Other Serious Violations of International Humanitarian Law Committed in the Territory of Rwanda and Rwandan Citizens Responsible for Genocide and Other Such Violations Committed in the Territory of Neighbouring States between 1 January and 31 December 1994: Report of the Secretary-General on the Activities of the Office of Internal Oversight Services*, 6 February 1997, 10; and UNGA, A/C.5/52/SR.68, *Fifth Committee: Summary Record of the First Part of the 68th Meeting*, 8 July 1998, 12. It also seemed like frequently the ICTY was given greater attention at UN meetings than the ICTR. See UNSC, S/PV.4229, *4229th Meeting*, 21 November 2000; UNGA, A/57/PV.36, *57th Session: 36th Plenary Meeting*, 28 October 2002, 15; and UNSC, S/2003/946, *Letter dated 3 October 2003 from the Secretary-General Addressed to the President of the Security Council: Completion Strategy of the International Criminal Tribunal for Rwanda*, 6 October 2003, 2 and 4.

[52] Interview with Member of ICTR OTP 7 (June 2015).

[53] Vivienne Jabri, 'Peacebuilding, the Local and the International: A Colonial or a Postcolonial Rationality?', *Peacebuilding* 1:1 (2013): 1–15; Clark, *Distant Justice*, 34–46 and 309–12. In this respect, the 'distant' nature of the court was held as a positive.

[54] Kingsley Moghalu, *Rwanda's Genocide: The Politics of Global Justice* (Basingstoke: Palgrave Macmillan, 2005), 29.

practically, as it would help with accessing the crime scenes and witnesses. As a result, the Arusha International Conference Centre (AICC) in Arusha, Tanzania, was selected as the place where the tribunal would sit.[55]

However, and despite initially requesting the creation of the court, ultimately as Resolution 955 came before the UNSC, Rwanda, who happened to hold one of the UNSC's temporary seats at this time, voted against it.[56] Underpinning this dispute were two competing visions of justice. Whilst the Rwandan UN delegate agreed that the UN could deliver neutral and impartial justice, they equally felt that this 'distanced justice' would not meet with Rwandan's *expectations of justice*. Geographically, Arusha was seen as too removed from Rwanda; it was thought that the narrow temporality of the statute (only covering 1994) would fail to capture the planning of the genocide and the Tutsis' historic suffering; and the lack of a death sentence meant that justice delivered internationally would not be of equal strength compared with that delivered locally.[57] Indeed, it was thought that there was something *unjust* in the fact that those that led the genocide (exactly those that the ICTR would be targeting) would receive a less severe penalty than their subordinates being prosecuted in Rwanda. The initial optimism of the ICTR being all things to all persons, then, was dented before any trial had taken place. As such, the confidence with which the tribunal was founded, and the archive's strategies established, should not conceal the tensions and contestations that were imbedded in the court from its very outset.

A TRIBUNAL IN ACTION

In spite of this tense relationship between the Rwandan government and the tribunal – which was to worsen as the tribunal went on – the ICTR was nonetheless established and, after a slow start, in 1996 the first indictments were submitted to Judge Pillay for confirmation. A makeshift court was created in the premises of AICC, where the tribunal's archive was also initially held, and in 1996, the first trial commenced against Jean-Paul Akayesu. Over the following twenty-one years, ninety-three persons were indicted with sixty-two defendants found guilty of crimes covered by the court's statute, fourteen acquitted,

---

[55] *Ibid.*, 35–38; Peskin, *International Justice*, 166–67.
[56] S/PV.3453, 14–16.
[57] *Ibid.*, and Peskin, *International Justice*, 162.

three successfully evading arrest and the rest either transferred to other jurisdictions or deceased prior to the end of their trial. As will be discussed more in Chapter 5, these indictments covered a range of different actors, from musicians to generals and politicians, and captured acts of violence committed throughout Rwanda.[58] In 2010 an agreement was reached with the Rwandan government for Rwanda to take over some of the then pending cases, and with this a total of ten case files were transferred for prosecution in Rwanda.[59] As will be discussed in Chapter 7, in 2010 the UN also created a new body, the Residual Mechanism for the International Criminal Tribunals (MICT), which would continue the tribunal's remaining work, meaning that the ICTR could begin to close down and retain only a skeleton team.[60]

As was outlined in Chapter 1, one of the motivations behind the case selection that underpins the book's analysis was to examine trials at different points in the court's history to understand how it is practice shifted over time and what conditions affected the emergence of particular accounts of violence and community. The following briefly outlines these three cases, both giving an initial sense of how the tribunal changed over the years, whilst simultaneously offering some additional information about the trials that form the heart of the book's analysis.

Akayesu

Prosecutor v. *Jean-Paul Akayesu* (ICTR-96-44) was the first defendant tried and sentenced by the court. Akayesu was a *bourgmestre* (roughly equivalent to a mayor) of the Taba commune, Gitarama Prefecture, during the genocide.[61] The initial indictment (13 February 1996) contained twelve counts ranging from genocide to war crimes and focused on Akayesu's role in leading the genocide in Taba from his position of authority as *bourgmestre*.[62] The crux of the case was that Akayesu was

---

[58] Kingsley Moghalu, *Rwanda's Genocide: The Politics of Global Justice* (Basingstoke: Palgrave Macmillan, 2005), 84; ICTR-00-61, TRA001643/1, *Gatete – Redacted Transcript of 20/10/2009*, 20 October 2009, 2.

[59] MICT, 'The ICTR in Brief', found: http://unictr.irmct.org/en/tribunal (last accessed 19 February 2019). For a discussion of the transfer of cases under Rule 11 *bis* see Nicola Palmer, 'Transfer or Transformation?: A Review of the Rule 11 bis Decisions of the International Criminal Tribunal for Rwanda', *African Journal of International and Comparative Law* 20:1 (2012): 1–21.

[60] S/PV.6041, *6041st Meeting*, 12 December 2008, 13.

[61] ICTR-96-4, ICTR-96-4-0459/1, *Akayesu – Judgement*, 2 September 1998, para 9.

[62] ICTR-96-4-0003, *Akayesu – Indictment*, 13 February 1996.

a power-hungry individual who would do anything to advance his political career. As such, he had opposed the genocide in his commune when it had politically suited him to do so. However, having attended a prefectural meeting in Gitarama on 18 April 1994, where the interim government called for all Hutus to unite against the common enemy (the Tutsi) so that the political elite could cling on to their power, Akayesu became a willing participant in the violence. Consequently, Akayesu returned to Taba where, at a meeting in Gishyeshye, he publicly incited the local population to begin killing. The killing commenced shortly after this.[63]

Specific charges were also levelled against Akayesu for the period after the violence began. Primarily this concerned the murder of eight refugees delivered from the neighbouring commune (Runda) to the bureau communal and the murder of a number of teachers and other intellectuals also at the bureau communal. Another important narrative constructed at the trial concerned Akayesu's crazed pursuit of several individuals who were seen as significant persons within the local community. These included the hunt for Emphrem Karangwa (the former Inspector of Judicial Police), which resulted in the death of his brothers in a neighbouring commune, and a similarly crazed pursuit of Alexia, wife of Pierre Ntereye (a prominent figure within the commune), which resulted in a number of victims being tortured.[64]

This story was expanded at the end of the prosecution's case, as the OTP requested leave to submit an amended indictment which would introduce three counts of sexual violence.[65] This was for Akayesu's role in overseeing the systematic rape of women at the bureau communal, which two witnesses had brought to the tribunal's attention whilst testifying in court. The trial chamber consented to the prosecution's request to amend the indictment to include these charges, and the prosecution's case reopened with five additional witnesses heard.[66] This, as discussed more in Chapters 3 and 4, led to the tribunal's much-heralded finding that rape could be considered an act of genocide. In this sense, despite Akayesu's relatively minor role in the genocide, the case against him ended up being relatively extensive, including a total of fifteen counts, and was a landmark in the development of important aspects of jurisprudence.

---

[63] See CONTRA001175, Akayesu – Transcript of 9/1/1997, 9 January 1997, 8–73.
[64] ICTR–96–4–0003; and CONTRA001175.
[65] ICTR–96–4, ICTR–96–4–0555, Akayesu – Leave to Amend the Indictment, 17 June 1997.
[66] ICTR–96–4, ICTR–96–4–0459/1, Akayesu – Judgement, 2 September 1998, 37.

Overall, over forty-three trial days, forty-one witnesses took to the stand, in a trial that, from arrest to appeals judgment, took five years and eight months.[67] Ultimately, the trial chamber found (as upheld on appeal) Akayesu guilty of all counts in the indictment.[68]

Cyangugu

Cyangugu resulted from the merging of an indictment against Samuel Imanishimwe, Emmanuel Bagambiki and Yussuf Munyakazi with one against André Ntagerura.[69] Munyakazi, a local businessperson in Cyangugu, was severed from the proceedings after he continued to evade the tribunal (he was finally captured in 2004 and convicted in 2010). Ntagerura, a Cyangugu native, was the Minister for Transport and Communication during the genocide; Bagambiki was the *préfet* of Cyangugu; and Imanishimwe was the commandant of the Cyangugu military barracks (Karambo camp). The trial marked the second phase in the OTP's indictment policy, which, after the failure of a mega-indictment against twenty-nine individuals (including Ntagerura) in 1999, saw smaller multi-accused indictments clustered around an institution (such as military or government) or region (such as Cyangugu and Butare). This move to more collective trials was motivated by both notions of efficiency, but also a desire to present an accurate picture of the genocide. In many ways, *Cyangugu* was typical of how the OTP ultimately came to see the genocide play out as it saw a member of government (Ntagerura) take responsibility for the genocide in their home region, working with local and regional military and political personalities (Bagambiki and Imanishimwe) and other people of significance (Munyakazi) to ensure the success of the plan.[70]

The trial hinged on a number of accusations.[71] The first was that Ntagerura was the person responsible overall for the genocide in Cyangugu. To this end he convened meetings with local political and military personalities (such as Bagambiki and Imanishimwe) to incite the population to violence prior to the genocide and also ensured, by working with the military (including Imanishimwe) and utilising his

[67] *Ibid.*, 17, 23–24.
[68] *Ibid.*, 293.
[69] *Prosecutor v. André Ntagerura et al.*, Case No. ICTR–96–10 (hereafter ICTR–96–10), ICTR–99–46–0018, *[Cyangugu] – Bagambiki – Ntagerura et al – Decision on the Prosecutor's Motion for Joinder*, 11 October 1999.
[70] ICTR–96–10, TRA000207/01, *[Cyangugu] – Ntagerura et al – Redacted Transcript of 18/09/2000*, 18 September 2000, 1–63.
[71] See ICTR–96–10, ICTR–96–10A–0311, *Ntagerura Amended Indictment*, 1 November 1999.

access to large vehicles, that the *Interahamwe* were adequately trained. Once the genocide began it was up to Bagambiki and Imanishimwe to make sure that the violence continued as planned. This resulted in a number of large massacres at Mibilizi, Shangi and Nyamasheke Parishes, as well as on Gashirabwoba football field. This happened along with a sustained attack against refugees in the Kamarampaka stadium, where Bagambiki and Imanishimwe, on a number of occasions, took refugees out of the stadium in order to execute them. This included one occasion (particularly important during the trial) when seventeen refugees were extracted, killed and then buried in a latrine. In addition, Imanishimwe was accused of rounding up civilians and murdering them in the military camp, and both Bagambiki and Imanishimwe were accused of being responsible for attacks in Kamembe town and in the Nyarushishi refugee camp towards the end of the genocide.[72] Unlike the charges against Akayesu, for many of these acts of violence the accused were not believed to be present during their commission. Rather, they were accused of creating the conditions whereby the violence could occur and directing this from behind the scenes.[73]

The trial took 111 trial days, during which 123 witnesses were heard, and lasted, from the date of Ntagerura's arrest until the provisional appeals judgment, just under ten years.[74] For the OTP, the trial was an unmitigated disaster. Due to a number of factors discussed more in Chapter 5 the trial chamber found Ntagerura and Bagambiki innocent of all charges and Imanishimwe guilty of only one instance of genocide and one of crimes against humanity (murder).[75] Things got worse on appeal as, due to additional issues with the prosecution's charging, Imanishimwe was acquitted of genocide.[76] As such, not one of the indictees was found to have participated in the genocide, which caused considerable anger in Cyangugu specifically, and Rwanda more generally.[77] As will be discussed in Chapter 5, the prosecution's failure

---

[72] See also TRA000207/01, 1–63.
[73] ICTR–96–10, ICTR–96–10A–0272, *Ntagerura – Prosecutor Request for Leave to File an Amended Indictment*, 2 December 1999.
[74] ICTR–96–10, ICTR–99–46–0599/1, *Trial Judgement – the Prosecutor v. André Ntagerura Emmanuel Bagambiki Samuel Imanishimwe*, 25 February 2004, 1–4.
[75] *Ibid.*, 208–14.
[76] ICTR–99–46, TRA003809/1, *[Cyangugu] – Ntagerura et al – Redacted Transcript of 07/07/2006 – Appeals Judgement*, 7 July 2006, 54.
[77] Interview with Member of ICTR OTP 6 (June 2015); African Rights and Redress, *Survivors and Post-genocide Justice in Rwanda: Their Experiences, Perspectives and Hopes* (November 2008).

prompted, in part, a shift in the archive's strategy, as trial management and efficiency came to be the metrics against which success was judged.

Gatete

Jean-Baptiste Gatete was a minster within the Ministry of Family Welfare at the time of the genocide and was previously the *bourgmestre* of Murambi commune from 1987 until 1993, at which point he was removed from his post amidst accusations that he had assisted in a series of attacks against the Tutsis within the region. Gatete's trial was one of the last trials to occur, with the trial judgment being delivered in 2011, after forty-nine witnesses were heard over just thirty trial days. Whilst Gatete's trial was amongst the quickest (with the substance of the trial over in under five months), it took nearly ten years from his arrest for the tribunal to deliver his appeals judgment.[78]

The main accusation against Gatete was that once the genocide had started he returned to Murambi where, from 7 April onwards, he organised and incited the locality to participate in the genocide. This included his role in a number of large-scale massacres at Kiziguro and Mukarange Parishes where he personally directed the killing and provided weapons, as he contributed to a 'joint criminal enterprise' (JCE) that was designed to wipe out the Tutsis within the region.[79]

The case against Gatete was the most compact out of the three trials considered, and over the course of a series of amendments to the indictment a number of charges against Gatete were dropped as the OTP pursued increasingly streamlined and efficient trials.[80] Gatete was found guilty of all remaining charges, mostly for his role in the JCE.[81]

As this already begins to suggest, the tribunal's approach to the trials did not remain consistent throughout but shifted over time. This had important consequences for both what accounts of violence were produced within the archive, but also what imagining of the international community subsequently emerged. Excavating what these shifting

---

[78] *Prosecutor* v. *Jean Baptiste Gatete*, Case No. ICTR–00–61 (hereafter ICTR–00–61), ICTR–00–61, ICTR–00–61–0240/1, *Gatete – Judgement and Sentence*, 31 March 2011, 1 and 177–78.

[79] ICTR–00–61, ICTR–00–61–0036/1, *Gatete – Amended indictment*, ICTR–00–61, 10 May 2005; and ICTR–00–61, TRA001643/1, *Gatete – Redacted Transcript of 20/10/2009*, 20 October 2009.

[80] ICTR–00–61–0036/1; ICTR–00–61, ICTR–00–61–0074/1, *Gatete – the Prosecutor's Submission Complying with the Decision on Defence Motion Concerning Defects in the Amended Indictment Dated 3 July 2009*, 7 July 2009.

[81] ICTR–00–61–0240/1, 169–70.

notions of community were, and the rules that underpinned it, is a central aspect of the analysis that follows.

As this also alludes to, throughout its existence, the tribunal witnessed numerous successes and many failures. The tribunal saw the first head of state prosecuted and found guilty of genocide; it ruled that rape could constitute an act of genocide and was crucial in development jurisprudence on command responsibility, joint criminal enterprise and hate speech.[82] It also took judicial notice that what had happened in Rwanda constituted genocide, declaring, as such, that 'no reasonable person' could refute that this crime had taken place.[83] Against this, however, lie numerous criticisms. The relationship with Rwanda never recovered from the initial dispute over the legitimacy of the court,[84] and over time the tribunal became known as an incredibly costly, slow and inefficient organisation.[85] Prosecutorial failures like *Cyangugu* also raised a number of questions about the quality of some of the trial work. Some trials took nearly two decades to complete, raising questions about due process. This was only exacerbated by the fate of those acquitted by the tribunal, many of whom, without any third country to offer them residency, remain stuck in a safe house in Arusha in a permanent state of purgatory.[86]

THE ARCHIVE

This narrative of the changing nature and function of the court also applies to the archive itself. At the outset of the archive, as with the tribunal as a whole, a lack of resources severely limited its work, as even basic facilities like photocopiers remained in short supply.[87] Under-resourced, the

---

[82] Tim Gallimore, 'The Legacy of the International Criminal Tribunal for Rwanda (ICTR) and Its Contributions to Reconciliation in Rwanda', *New England Journal of International and Comparative Law* 14:2 (2007): 242–50.

[83] ICTR–98–44, ICTR–98–44–2411/1, *[Government 1] – Karemera et al – Decision on Prosecutor's Interlocutory Appeal of Decision on Judicial Notice*, 16 June 2006, 13–15.

[84] See Paul Magnarella, *Justice in Africa: Rwanda's Genocide, Its Courts, and the UN Criminal Tribunal* (Aldershot: Ashgate, 2000); Victor Peskin, 'Courting Rwanda: The Promises and Pitfalls of the ICTR Outreach Programme', *Journal of International Criminal Justice* 3:4 (2005): 950–61.

[85] A/51/PV.78, 18; UNSC, *4429th Meeting*, S/PV.4429, 27/11/2001, 7; UNSC, S/PV.5453, *5453rd Meeting*, 7 June 2006, 23; UNSC, S/PV.5697, *5697th Meeting*, 18 June 2007, 22–23 and 28; and UNSC, S/PV.7192, *7192nd Meeting*, 5 June 2014.

[86] Chine Labbé et al., 'Rwanda Court's Forgotten Men Pose Challenge to International Justice', found: www.reuters.com/article/us-un-justice-insight-idUSKCN0HN0NK20140928 (last accessed 19 February 2019).

[87] Nigel Eltringham, '"We Are Not a Truth Commission": Fragmented Narratives and the Historical Record at the International Criminal Tribunal for Rwanda', *Journal of Genocide Research* 11:1 (2009): 69–71.

archive struggled to even meet the immediate needs of trials. This meant that throughout the early years of the archive there was no long-term strategy in place, and a retention policy was not formed until 2008.[88] As will be discussed in more detail in Chapter 7, this had important consequences for the archive, both in terms of what was preserved and how it can be used. However, one such consequence of this lack of planning was an insufficient amount of storage for administrative records. This, in turn, led to a significant number of administrative records being left to rot in temporary storage containers. Here, the materiality of the archive speaks volumes for how the archive was seen within the institution. This ad hoc approach also meant, for instance, that digitisation of the archive was not planned in advance, which had serious knock-on effects. One of these was that once it became clear that all audio-visual (AV) records were an important source that should be made publicly available, these had to be retrospectively redacted to remove sensitive information – an incredibly slow process that is still not yet complete.

The status of the archive improved over time. As the tribunal began to wind down (albeit slowly) from 2003, thoughts started turning to its legacy. The archive increasingly featured as a prominent aspect of this legacy, seen as holding a crucial record of the ICTR's existence and of the genocide.[89] This saw an influx of personnel and financial support – including for the digitisation of the archive[90] – and ultimately the need for a long-term solution for the archive acted, as discussed in Chapter 7, as a key factor in the UN's decision to build a new complex for the MICT and a new state-of-the-art archive in Arusha.[91]

As this book will show, the record that the archive has produced is unquestionably both an extensive and significant record of the violence in Rwanda. Whilst the *Gacaca* archive (a traditional form of conflict resolution used in Rwanda) might rival the ICTR's archive in terms of size, and might be considered superior in terms of depth and breadth of coverage of the genocide,[92] unlike *Gacaca*, the ICTR's archive has

---

[88] Interview with Former ICTR archivist, June 2015.
[89] Ibid.
[90] Interview with MICT archivists (Arusha, Tanzania: August 2019).
[91] UNSC, S/2009/258, *Report of the Secretary-General on the Administrative and Budgetary Aspects of the Options for Possible Locations for the Archives of the International Tribunal for the Former Yugoslavia and the International Criminal Tribunal for Rwanda and the Seat of the Residual Mechanism(s) for the Tribunals*, 21 May 2009.
[92] For discussion of Gacaca, see Phil Clark, 'The Rules (and Politics) of Engagement: The Gacaca Courts and Post-Genocide Justice, Healing, and Reconciliation in Rwanda', in *After Genocide:*

retained full transcripts from each trial, providing a verbatim record of witness testimony (*Gacaca* records often only contained summaries). As discussed in Chapter 7, whilst these records remain underutilised by researchers and practitioners, these have the potential – as with the *Nuremberg* archive – to underpin an in-depth exploration of the violence in Rwanda and help shape a historical consciousness about that violence.

CONCLUSION

It is not, however, the purpose of this book to determine the extent to which the tribunal was a legal success, or whether or not the archive should be considered, either in archival or historical terms, a 'good' record of the violence. It is, rather, to examine the vast records produced within the archive, to determine how and why they were created as they were, and to understand how this led to certain imaginings of community. This outline of the genocide, the UN's involvement in Rwanda, and the history of the court and the archive is, however, crucial to examining these questions. The shifting emphasis on the importance and role of the archive, and the final decision to build a new archive in Arusha, was important in determining what role the archive was to play in Rwanda's transition and ultimately the question of who and what the archive was for. Similarly, the tribunal's drive to do more than administer retributive justice, but to contribute to peace and security through the construction of a verified account of the violence and providing witnesses a space to testify, played, as the following chapters explore, a crucial part in determining what account of violence was produced within the archive and consequently what image of the international community was constructed.

It is to these questions that the book now turns. In applying the analytical and methodological approach set out in Chapter 1, along with the understanding of the archive's strategies developed in this chapter, it provides a detailed account of what exactly has been recorded in the tribunal's archive, why it was recorded so and by whom, and how this links to the construction of a particular idea about what the international community is, and should be. First in this exploration is an analysis of how the legal framework of the court

Transitional Justice, Post-Conflict Reconstruction and Reconciliation in Rwanda and Beyond, eds. Phil Clark and Zachery Kaufman (New York: Columbia University, 2009), 297–319.

affected the production of knowledge. For, whilst a myriad of different ideas about what the tribunal was for emerged, the ICTR remained a legal institution that was tasked with delivering legal verdicts. As the following chapter will make clear, however, this is not to say that this legal framework was devoid of political consequence.

CHAPTER THREE

THE FORCE OF LAW

This chapter examines how the discourse and practice of international criminal law structured the ICTR's archive. This feeds into, and builds on, the scholarly work on the relationship between courts and knowledge production, which has tended to emphasise how the legal process limits what accounts can be told.[1] However, this chapter adds greater depth to these insights by, as was set out in Chapter 1, not just focusing on what appears to be *lacking* within these records, but instead thinking more systematically about how legal discourse and practice produces particular accounts of violence. Returning to the methodological approach outlined in Chapter 1, the analytical focus of this chapter is on the concepts and objects that occupy, and constitute, the archive. As will become clear, international criminal law is built up of an array of interconnected concepts, and the drive to divide, categorise and decide between these is one of the principal functions of international courts. In this sense, whether or not an act of violence falls within a court's jurisdiction, and should be considered genocide, crimes against humanity or war crimes – or an act of violence which forms an accepted part of war and the community – is at the heart of the trial process and the way in which knowledge is produced. This is the focus of the first part of the chapter. The discourse of international criminal law, however, also 'refracts light' in particular ways to reveal particular objects that it takes to be its domain of responsibility and authority. This is central to understanding why the archive's account of violence

---

[1] See Chapter 1, 8–11.

appeared as it did. Two such objects discussed at greater length towards the end of the chapter are 'perpetrators' and 'victims'.

LAW AS FRAMEWORK

Despite the extrajudicial goals associated with the ICTR, as discussed in Chapter 2, the tribunal's primary responsibility was to deliver verdicts against those deemed responsible for the Rwandan genocide and other violations of international humanitarian law. The absence of a *Nuremberg*-style paper trail produced by – and then used against – the perpetrators meant that, with few exceptions, both the prosecution and defence relied on witnesses to establish their cases. Any other non-oral evidence used (which for the most part were submissions of investigation documents, such as photos, diagrams, etc.) was largely supplementary to witness testimony.[2] In contrast to the approach adopted at *Nuremberg* – which had viewed witness testimony with a deep scepticism[3] – at the ICTR's outset, the reliance on witnesses was seen as positively adding to the trials' potential impact on Rwanda's transition towards peace. This meant that the trials, as discussed in Chapter 2, could both secure justice whilst providing the witnesses with a moment of cathartic relief as they were given space to tell their story.[4] The centrality of witnesses at the ICTR also differed from ICTY prosecutions. Whilst witnesses certainly played a significant role at the ICTY too, the ICTY also had greater access to a wider array of other types of evidence, from intercepted cables, government and military communiques, and forensic evidence.

The records of the witnesses' testimony make it clear that the courts' drive towards a legal verdict very much structured how testimony was recorded. Whilst Chapter 4 examines how the witnesses also shaped and resisted this process, the rest of this chapter considers how the force of law attempted to constrain this testimony. This section deals first

---

[2] The two partial exceptions to this that I have found were the 'Media trial' (which drew on transcripts of the radio broadcasts and copies of *Kangura* newspaper) and *Government 1* (which used government directives). *Prosecutor v. Édouard Karemera et al,* Case No. ICTR–98–44, ICTR–98–44–4803/1, *Judgement and Sentence,* 2 February 2012, 181–92; *Prosecutor v. Ferdinand Nahimana et al,* Case No. ICTR–99–52, ICTR–99–52–1323/1, *Judgement and Sentence,* 3 December 2003, 39–80.

[3] For an interesting account of courts', and more generally society's, relationship with witness testimony, see Annette Wieviorka, *Era of the Witness* (New York: Cornell University Press, 2006).

[4] Richard Goldstone, 'Justice as a Tool for Peace-Making: Truth Commissions and International Criminal Tribunals', *Journal of International Law and Politics* 28 (1995): 487–89.

with the role of the indictments, before looking at how the main articles of the statute shaped the archive's records.

The Indictment

During each of the trials, witness testimony was directed to unfold in particular ways based on the parameters of the prosecution's case against the accused. The indictment was crucial in this respect; the concept of a 'fair trial' meant that the prosecution's account, and consequently the defence's, was limited to crimes that had been charged in the indictment. The principle of a fair trial was a central organising concept within the archive and was mobilised particularly by the defence as they contested the scope and nature of the prosecution's case. Frequently, then, the defence would challenge the scope of the indictment prior to trial, accusing the prosecution of relying on vague indictments that prevented them from preparing their case. The judges often sided with the defence and demanded further specificity from the prosecution in their indictments, which, in turn, meant that the parameters within which the accounts were to be produced at trial were narrowed further.[5] Similarly, as a trial got underway, the defence often urged the judges to prevent certain records from being produced when the information contained (allegedly) exceeded the perimeter of the indictment. For example, during *Cyangugu*, the defence intervened as Witness LBH began to tell the court how on a number of occasions *Interahamwe*, under the supervision of Bagambiki and Imanishimwe,

---

[5] *Prosecutor v. Jean-Paul Akayesu*, Case No. ICTR–96–4 (hereafter ICTR–96–)4, ICTR–96–4–0028, *Akayesu – Inter-Office Memo Transmitting a Brief in Response to a Preliminary Motion*, 4 September 1996; ICTR–96–4, ICTR–96–4–0531, *Akayesu – Decision on the Preliminary Motion Submitted by the Prosecutor for Protective Measures for the Witnesses*, 27 September 1996; ICTR–96–4, ICTR–96–4–0160, *Akayesu – Decision on the Preliminary Motions Presented by the Prosecution and the Defence*, 17 February 1997; ICTR–96–10, ICTR–96–10A–0072, *Ntagerura – Brief in Response to the Preliminary Motions*, 29 July 1997; ICTR–96–10, ICTR–96–10A–0208, *Ntagerura – Decision on the Preliminary Motion Filed by the Defence Based on Defects in the Form of the Indictment*, 28 November 1997; *Prosecutor v. Emmanuel Bagambiki*, Case No. ICTR–97–36 (hereafter ICTR–97–36), ICTR–97–36–0039/1, *Imanishimwe Preliminary Motions*, 28 January 1998; ICTR–97–36–0043, *Preliminary Motions*, 18 February 1998; ICTR–97–36, ICTR–97–36–0048, *The Prosecutor's Brief in Reply to the Defence Preliminary Motions on Behalf of Samuel Imanishimwe*, 24 March 1998; *Prosecutor v. André Ntagerura, Emmanuel Bagambiki and Samuel Imanishimwe*, Case No. ICTR–99–46 (here after ICTR–99–46), ICTR–99–46–0072, *[Cyangugu] – Bagambiki – Ntagerura et al – The Prosecutor's Preliminary Pre-Trial Brief*, 24 May 2000; *Prosecutor v. Jean Baptiste Gatete*, Case No. ICTR–00–61 (hereafter ICTR–00–61, ICTR–00–61–0025, *Gatete – Defence Preliminary Motions, Under Rule 72 of the Rules of Procedure and Evidence*, 12 April 2003; ICTR–00–61, ICTR–00–61–0022, *Gatete – Prosecutor's Response to the Defense Preliminary Motion Challenging Defects in the form of the indictment Pursuant to Rule 72*, 9 May 2003; and ICTR–00–61, ICTR–00–61–0029, *Gatete, Decision on Defence Preliminary Motion*, 29 March 2004.

took women from Kamarampaka stadium in Cyangugu town and raped them:[6]

> Mr So'o [Defence counsel for Imanishimwe]: Mr President, Your Honour. The Defence is rather worried that these matters of rapes are put on record because the rapes do not appear in the indictment served on us. So we feel rather concerned that they are being included in the record.[7]

Whilst the prosecution contested this interpretation,[8] the judges sided with the defence, and this testimony was consequently prevented from entering the archive.[9]

As this suggests, the indictment was an important instrument for determining which records would be produced. The indictment was in turn structured by the tribunal's statute, which governed its parameters geographically, temporally, and in terms of subject-matter and personal jurisdiction. When combined the statute's articles provided a checklist of the evidence needed for a trial chamber to find the defendant guilty of each crime.[10] Each article will now be considered in turn.

Article 1: Temporal and Geographic Jurisdiction
Article 1 provided the ICTR with the power

> to prosecute persons responsible for serious violations of international humanitarian law committed in the territory of Rwanda and Rwandan citizens responsible for such violations committed in the territory of neighbouring States between 1 January 1994 and 31 December 1994.[11]

This, as such, limited the archive geographically and temporally. Geographically, the statute worked to construct an account that became narrowly focused on the violence in Rwanda. This was heightened by judicial rulings which explicitly prohibited the submission of

---

[6] ICTR–99–46, CONTRA002340, [Cyangugu] – Ntagerura et al – Redacted Transcript of 13/02/2001, 13 February 2001, 88–90.

[7] Ibid., 89.

[8] During the opening statement the prosecution stated: 'Many witnesses will say that they saw him committing or allowing other individuals to commit other acts of violence against Tutsis especially against women, Tutsi women who were every day kidnapped so that they would be raped.' This, as will be discussed in Chapter 6, allegedly – for the prosecution – meant that the defence had been warned of the intent to pursue sexual violence at trial. ICTR–99–46, TRA000207/01, [Cyangugu] – Ntagerura et al – Redacted Transcript of 18/09/2000, 18 September 2000, 53.

[9] ICTR–99–46, TRA000433/2, [Cyangugu] – Ntagerura et al – Redacted Transcript of 14/02/2001 – Decision, 14 February 2001, 11–13.

[10] UNSC, S/RES/955, ICTR Statute, 8 November 1994.

[11] S/RES/955, Article 1.

evidence that pointed to the 'international' nature of the conflict. During Cyangugu, in this respect, the judges ruled against the defence's attempts to introduce evidence of the international nature of the conflict.[12] Pointing to the inclusion of Additional Protocols 2 in the statute (Article 4), which only covered non-international conflicts, the judges argued:

> The Security Council has said it is an internal conflict and not international. It goes further than us taking judicial notice. The Security Council, itself, has said that this conflict was an internal conflict and not international. So, we don't have to go and adjudicate that.[13]

Here, then, the UNSC's decision became legally binding, and different concepts, through the interaction between the concept of war crimes and geographic jurisdiction, worked to limit the archive's scope. In *Gatete*, the judges reaffirmed this point and officially took judicial notice of the non-international nature of the conflict. This rendered this a 'notorious fact of common knowledge' and made it absolutely clear that there was no room in the court (or the archive) for evidence that would suggest otherwise.[14] As discussed in Chapter 6, the exclusion of the international nature of the violence in Rwanda had significant consequences for the type of community imagined within the archive.

The ICTR's temporal jurisdiction posed a number of difficulties for the tribunal, especially for the prosecution when attempting to establish the accused's responsibility for planning the genocide. It was clear that much of the planning occurred prior to the commencement of the tribunal's jurisdiction, which only began on 1 January 1994.[15] The

---

[12] ICTR–99–46, TRA001851/2, *[Cyangugu] – Ntagerura et al – Redacted Transcript of 20/01/2003*, 20 January 2003, 19; TRA001610/2, 26–27; ICTR–99–46, TRA001618/02, *[Cyangugu] – Ntagerura et al – Redacted Transcript of 02/10/2002*, 2 October 2002, 78–79; and ICTR–99–46, TRA001293/2, *[Cyangugu] – Ntagerura et al – Redacted Transcript of 22/07/2002*, 22 July 2002, 46 and 48.

[13] ICTR–99–46, TRA001278/2, *[Cyangugu] – Ntagerura et al – Redacted Transcript of 29/05/2002*, 29 May 2002, 129.

[14] *Prosecutor v. Jean Baptiste Gatete*, Case No. ICTR–00–61, ICTR–00–61–0086/1, *Gatete – Decision on Prosecution's Motion for Judicial Notice of Facts of Common Knowledge*, 21 August 2009.

[15] As will be recalled, a fear that the temporal jurisdiction would negatively affect the prosecution had contributed towards Rwanda's decision to vote against the creation of the tribunal. S/PV.3453, 3453rd Meeting, 8 November 1994, 14. Barrie Sander interestingly argues that the ICTR's findings about whether or not the genocide was preplanned were inconclusive, with different trial chambers reaching different decisions. Barrie Sander, 'History on Trial: Historical Narrative Pluralism within and beyond International Criminal Courts', *International & Comparative Law Quarterly* 67:3 (2018): 555–59.

potential impact on the archive was significant. Adhering to this jurisdiction would have meant, for instance, that the prosecution would not have been allowed to submit most editions of the *Kangura* newspaper – often seen as crucial to spreading ethnic hatred in the 1990s – as evidence against its editor Hassan Ngeze during the *Media Trial*, because all but two issues were published prior to 1994.[16] Similarly, the time limit would have prevented the prosecution from presenting evidence of Ntagerura's, Bagambiki's and Gatete's roles in preparing the terrain for genocide within their respective regions.

Significantly, however, the archive's rules ended up accommodating evidence relating to events that occurred prior to 1 January 1994. In this respect, the genocide was interpreted as an inchoate crime,[17] meaning that the tribunal's temporal jurisdiction could be partially stretched.[18] As such, the prosecution in *Cyangugu* was allowed to offer evidence of Ntagerura's and Bagambiki's presence at a series of rallies in 1993 which were used to stir up hatred against the Tutsis, and they were also allowed to consider Ntagerura's role in training the *Interahamwe* during 1993.[19] This also meant that each edition of *Kangura* was added into the archive at the *Media Trial*.[20]

This was not, however, a blanket provision, and these rulings attached limits to what pre-1994 evidence was permissible. Indeed, pre-1994 evidence was only allowed into the archive when the evidence went to establish: conspiracy;[21] a component of a crime where all

---

[16] ICTR–99–52–1323/1, 39; and Jean-Marie Biju-Duval, '"Hate Media" – Crimes against Humanity and Genocide: Opportunities Missed by the International Criminal Tribunal for Rwanda', in *The Media and the Rwandan Genocide*, ed. Allan Thompson (London: Pluto Press, 2007): 346–47.

[17] This is where the commission of a crime constitutes a step towards the commissioning of another crime – and so in effect forms part of that crime. Under this logic, an act of preparing to commit genocide prior to the actual genocide, and even if prior to the start of the court's jurisdiction, could therefore be seen as part of a crime committed *within* the jurisdiction.

[18] This was particularly heavily litigated during Gatete. ICTR–00–61, ICTR–00–61–0025, *Gatete – Defence Preliminary Motions, Under Rule 72 of the Rules of Procedure and Evidence*, 12 April 2003, 5; ICTR–00–61, ICTR–00–61–0088, *Gatete – Defence Motion Raising Defects in the Prosecution Pre-Trial Brief of 19 August 2009*, 30 September 2009; ICTR–00–61, ICTR–00–61–0100, *Gatete, Decision on Defence Motion Raising Defects in the Prosecution Pre-Trial Brief of 19 August 2009*, 2 October 2009; ICTR–00–61, ICTR–00–61–0188, *Gatete, Decision on Defence Motion for Exclusion of Evidence and Delineation of the Defence Case*, 26 March 2010; ICTR–00–61, ICTR–00–61–010, *Gatete, Motion on Admissibility of Allegations outside the Temporal Jurisdiction of the Tribunal*, 15 October 2009.

[19] ICTR–99–46, TRA000124/01, *[Cyangugu] – Ntagerura et al – Redacted Transcript of 10/10/2000*, 10 October 2000, 63; and ICTR–99–46, TRA000131/1, *[Cyangugu] – Ntagerura et al – Redacted Transcript of 21/11/2000*, 21 November 2000, 22–44.

[20] ICTR–99–52–1323/1, 338–39.

[21] ICTR–00–61, ICTR–00–61–0029, *Gatete – Decision on Defence Preliminary Motion*, 29 March 2004, 3.

the elements were *also* present in 1994;[22] or a historical context that either made the accused's behaviour or the violence *in* 1994 more intelligible.[23] As a result, the archive's account very much remained focused on events that occurred in 1994.

As this shows the archive is a dynamic site as different actors contest the rules to reshape what is allowed into the archive. This shift in the archive's rules to allow for pre-1994 evidence to be submitted is also an example of what Stoler refers to as 'false-starts' of the archive, as it struggled to make sense of the world it was recording, and adapted to bring order to the archive.[24]

Substantive Jurisdiction: Articles 2 (Genocide), 3 (Crimes against Humanity) and 4 (War Crimes)

The tribunal's statute covered three crimes: genocide (article 2), crimes against humanity (article 3) and war crimes (article 4). These functioned as important structuring concepts within the archive and produced three different overarching frameworks within which records would be constructed.[25] Each crime came, in turn, with three distinct elements that had to be established or contested: *mens reas, actus reus* and a contextual *in chapeau* element (which limited each crime's applicability to a particular context). Records had to go towards evidencing these elements to meet the relevance threshold that governed what was, and what was not, allowed to enter the courtroom, and therefore the archive.[26]

To prove that genocide had occurred, for instance, records had to establish that one of the crimes recognised as genocide in the statute had been committed (such as causing 'serious bodily or mental harm') against a group protected by the Genocide Convention (which were limited to: religious, national, ethnic or racial groups) to establish the *actus reus*; that it had been committed with intent, establishing the *mens rea*; and that it was committed with the intent to destroy that protected group 'in whole or in part', establishing the *dolus specialis* (special intent), which formed the *in chapeau* element here.[27] For war

[22] *Ibid.*, 3; ICTR–00–61–010, 5; and S/2004/601, 10–11.
[23] ICTR–00–61–0029, 3.
[24] Ann Stoler, *Along the Archival Grain: Epistemic Anxiety and Colonial Common Sense* (Princeton: Princeton University Press, 2010), 1 and 97.
[25] Articles 2–4 ICTR Statute.
[26] *Prosecutor v. Andre Ntagerura et al*, Case No. ICTR–99–46 (hereafter ICTR–99–46), TRA000434/2, *[Cyangugu] – Ntagerura et al – Redacted Transcript of 14/02/2001*, 14 February 2001, 8.
[27] Article 2 of ICTR Statute.

crimes or crimes against humanity, records had to show that a crime recognised as such in the statute (such as murder) had been committed intentionally against individual non-combatants within the context of a non-international armed conflict (for war crimes) or a group on political, racial, religious, ethnic, or national grounds in an attack that targeted a civilian population (for crimes against humanity).[28]

As will become clear throughout this book, the exact definition of the crimes covered in the statute was highly contested, and the way in which particular definitions emerged had significant bearings for the account of violence and community produced within the archive. An example of this would be the emergence of rape as an act of genocide in *Akayesu*. Finding that rape could constitute genocide is widely heralded as a significant moment in the development of jurisprudence concerning gender-based crimes and seemingly opened up the possibility of the tribunal addressing the widespread gender-based violence that underpinned the Rwandan genocide. In doing this, a strong statement was made both about the international community's objection to this type of violence and, seemingly, its affirmation of the rights of women. That this potential was never realised, as discussed in Chapter 6, is instructive about what type of community was constituted within the archive.

Articles 5 and 6: Responsibility

As specified under Article 6 of the court's statute, to find a defendant guilty of a crime, the prosecution also had to establish the accused's individual criminal responsibility. There were two modes of liability that could be used to frame the record in this respect. The accused were either directly responsible under Article 6(1) for the violence because they had planned, instigated, ordered, committed (later incorporating Joint Criminal Enterprise – JCE), or otherwise aided and abetted a crime, or they were responsible under Article 6(3) as a superior for failing to prevent or punish their subordinates for committing a crime (as limited by Articles 2–4).[29] Article 5 of the statute gave the tribunal jurisdiction over 'natural persons' – as opposed to states or organisations. These two articles when combined meant records focused on the accused as conscious and rational actors and their discrete role in the violence. As will be recalled from Chapter 2, the individualisation of

---

[28] Articles 3 and 4 of ICTR Statute.
[29] See Allison Danner and Jenny Martinez, 'Guilty Associations: Joint Criminal Enterprise, Command Responsibility, and the Development of International Criminal Law', *California Law Review* 93:1 (2005): 75–169.

these crimes was one of the reasons why the ICTR was seen as a useful response to the genocide, and as a result, the archive projected a distinctly liberal understanding of community.

These articles also had a significant bearing in determining the form and content of the tribunal's account of violence. Reading the trial transcripts for the three cases analysed here gave the impression that the accused and their reach of influence acted as a spotlight that illuminated particular aspects of the violence in Rwanda. During *Akayesu* the occurrence of genocide outside Taba commune, where Akayesu was *bourgmestre*, was, for the most part, an irrelevance *except* when this violence was linked to Akayesu. Hence the spotlight shifted to Murambi commune on 19 April when Akayesu pursued the Inspector of Police in Taba, Emphrem Karangwa, and his brothers, who were subsequently murdered under Akayesu's orders.[30] When the accused was not present directly, it was only those sites where the accused's responsibility and authority left a lingering presence that accounts of violence could be given. Hence, whilst most witnesses claimed that Bagambiki and Imanishimwe were not present during the massacre of refugees on the Gashirabwoba football field in Cyangugu prefecture by soldiers on 12 April 1994,[31] Imanishimwe's authority over soldiers within the region and Bagambiki's prior presence and promise to send soldiers (who arrived only to kill the refugees) meant that witnesses were permitted to present their evidence concerning that episode of violence:[32]

WITNESS: During the attacks [at the football field] we saw a vehicle arrive and in that vehicle, was the director of the Shagasha Tea Factory, who was called Callixte Nsabimana [. . .] accompanied by Emmanuel Bagambiki. They arrived where we were and asked us to explain what our situation was.

We told them that we had problems, that for four days we had not eaten or drank anything. They promised that they were going to send soldiers to protect us in that area.

---

[30] See testimonies from Witness S (ICTR–96–4, CONTRA001197, *Akayesu – Transcript of 5/2/1997*, 5 February 1997), Witness Q (ICTR–96–4, CONTRA001190, *Akayesu – Transcript of 4/2/1997*, 4 February 1997, 1–81) and Witness D (ICTR–96–4, CONTRA001198, *Akayesu – Transcript of 6/2/1997*, 6 February 1997).

[31] ICTR–99–46, ICTR–99–46–0599/1, *Trial Judgement – the Prosecutor v. André Ntagerura Emmanuel Bagambiki Samuel Imanishimwe*, 25 February 2004, 118.

[32] ICTR–99–46, TRA000122/01, *[Cyangugu] – Ntagerura et al – Redacted Transcript of 09/10/2000*, 9 October 2000.

PROSECUTION: I'd like you to be more specific and tell Their Lordships who of the two addressed you or if both of them, that is Nsabimana and Bagambiki addressed you?

WITNESS: We were talking to Bagambiki.[33]

Where the seniority of the accused led to accusations of their involvement in the planning and execution of the genocide at a national level, or where the mobilisation of JCE[34] as the mode of liability attached them to a broader collective of perpetrators, then narratives of violence across whole regions and swaths of the country were possible, *but only because of the reach of the accused's authority*.[35]

A Framework

When these articles were combined they produced a grid of intelligibility, within which evidence was recorded and contested. One example of this was the sexual violence charge against Akayesu. The allegation here was that Akayesu had overseen, instigated, and aided and abetted the mass perpetration of sexual violence at the bureau communal (the commune's main administrative building) by the *Interahamwe*. The following extracts from the prosecution's examination-in-chief of Witness JJ highlights how this framed the witnesses' testimony.

PROSECUTION: Witness JJ, when we left off you were explaining to us how you were taken by some Interahamwe and brought to the cultural center [*sic*] [. . .] At this time, how many of these men were escorting you to the cultural center?

WITNESS: There were many, there were very many at that time. In fact we did not have the presence of mind to be able to count them.

PROSECUTION: At this time, you mentioned to us that Akayesu was in the yard, the courtyard, of the compound. Can you tell us exactly where he was at the time that you passed him?

---

[33] TRA000122/01, 35–36. More direct evidence of their participation was established through the accomplice witness testimony of Witness LAI, but this was ultimately rejected by the court. See ICTR–99–46, TRA000254/2, [*Cyangugu*] – *Ntagerura et al – Redacted Transcript of 24/01/2001*, 24 January 2001, 1–49.

[34] A joint criminal enterprise is a group of individuals that, broadly, shared an agreement – whether implicit or explicit – to engage in a form of criminal activity. As discussed more in Chapter 5, how this was defined shifted over time at the tribunal.

[35] See for instance the findings in *Government 1* about widespread occurrence of violence (including sexual violence) in regions far from the accused. ICTR–98–44–4803/1, 201–58. See also *Prosecutor v. Jean Baptiste Gatete*, Case No. ICTR–00–61 (hereafter ICTR–00–61), TRA005506/2, *Gatete – Redacted Transcript of 02/11/2009*, 2 November 2009, 46.

WITNESS: He was standing there in front of the bureau communal of Taba.[. . .]

PROSECUTION: I may have asked you this before, and forgive me for reasking if I did, but at the time you saw Akayesu, was he there alone or with someone?

WITNESS: He was with policemen and some Interahamwes who met him there.[. . .]

PROSECUTION: When you were being taken to the [cultural centre], were you being taken was this voluntary, or were you being taken by force?

WITNESS: They dragged us by force.[. . .]

PROSECUTION When you entered into the cultural center, what did you see upon entering into the room?

WITNESS: When we entered the house, the Interahamwe pounced on us and started raping us.[. . .]

PROSECUTION: Do you know whether or not at that time or after you were raped [Akayesu] ever came to the area of the cultural center?

WITNESS: I remember one time he came in front of the center and he addressed the Interahamwe and told them, 'So, never ask me what a Tutsi woman is like.'[36]

This string of questioning established the location of the crime, those that were responsible, the presence of Akayesu, the ethnicity of the victims and also that, as captured in the final exchange, women were targeted *because* of their ethnicity. Combined with other witness testimony, which demonstrated Akayesu's authority over the communal police, the *Interahamwe* and, more generally, the population, this established Akayesu's responsibility for the violence. Authority over the police and *Interahamwe* meant that under Article 6(3) he had a responsibility to prevent or punish the commission of a crime, and further that his presence whilst these crimes occurred (and without condemning their occurrence) gave active consent to, and 'encouraged', the commission of the crime.[37]

---

[36] ICTR–96–4, CONTRA001181, *Akayesu – Transcript of 23/1/1997*, 23 January 1997, 67–75.
[37] For examples, see ICTR–96–4, CONTRA001175, *Akayesu – Transcript of 09/1/1997*, 9 January 1997; ICTR–96–4, CONTRA001187, *Akayesu – Transcript of 28/1/1997*, 28 January 1997, 102–3; ICTR–96–4, CONTRA001178, *Akayesu – Transcript of 14/1/1997*, 14 January 1997, 92; and ICTR–96–4, CONTRA001180, *Akayesu – Transcript of 22/1/1997*, 22 January 1997, 39.

As such – and as would be expected – law, and contestations over what the law was, played a fundamental part in determining the contours of the archive's account of violence. Even at this very early point of the enquiry it is also apparent on how this led to particular imaginings and orderings of community. One example here would be the decision in *Akayesu* to find that rape could be considered an act of genocide. This seemingly challenged the patriarchal nature of community, and the, then still common, sense that rape was just an unfortunate by-product of war. Another example would be the effect of the concept of a 'fair trial', which was important in shaping the court's account but was also suggestive of the types of community produced. For this principle exists as a means of protecting the defendant, and more generally the citizen, from the excesses and arbitrary use of sovereign power. This both suggests a particular relationship between citizen and sovereign and establishes law as a crucial mechanism in the governance, and protection, of the community.

CONSTRUCTING ACTORS

The legal discourse underpinning the tribunal's work also played an important role in shaping the archive's understanding of perpetrators and victims. The following section examines this and shows that the way these were constituted had significant bearings for the type of community imagined within the archive.

Perpetrators

Within the archive relatively specific and detailed understandings of each of the defendants emerged, which looked to capture their personality and motivations for engaging in the genocide. During *Akayesu*, for instance, the prosecution's narrative structure captured the political nature of Akayesu's actions in a plotline that bore resemblance to Arendt's notion of the banality of evil.[38] Akayesu was not, the prosecution emphasised, an ideological zealot whose participation in the genocide made sense due to some form of inner evil. He was, rather, a politician: a rational thinker that craved power and authority. This meant that Akayesu resisted the violence against the Tutsis when it politically benefitted him, as a member of the main opposition party,

---

[38] Hannah Arendt, *Eichmann in Jerusalem: A Report on the Banality of Evil* (London: Penguin, 2006).

the *Mouvement Démocratique Républicain* (MDR), to do so.[39] When, however, it suited him politically to support the genocide he became a willing genocidaire. The turning point, the prosecution argued, was an interim government meeting held in Gitarama on 18 April 1994, where the government called for unity between the various political parties to pursue the genocidal policy that could ensure that they could *all* retain power.[40] Akayesu's choice here was either to participate in the violence (having spent two weeks defending his commune from external attacks) or face political ostracisation. Akayesu chose to retain his power and authority and became a willing participant in the genocide. This framework also helped to explain why Akayesu spent a number of days in crazed pursuit of prominent local figures (such as Emphrem Karangwa, the Inspector of Police) all over the Gitarama region.[41] This was, the prosecution explained, because they had challenged Akayesu's authority, and so to secure his political authority within the commune, and also to take *ownership* over the violence (and the political capital that came with this), he had to pursue and kill them.[42]

During *Cyangugu* the emphasis was slightly different as the prosecution presented the defendants as being more pre-disposed to participating in the genocide than Akayesu had been. Each was portrayed as a person closely linked to the *Akazu* (roughly translated as 'the President's House', and a group strongly linked to the leadership of the genocide), who had advanced in their careers by supporting those in power and their intentions to commit genocide. Bagambiki was *préfet* of Kigali-Rural during the orchestrated violence against Tutsis in the Bugesera region in 1992, and he was promoted to the position of *préfet* of Cyangugu because of his continued loyalty to the regime.[43] The prosecution presented Ntagerura as a figure who maintained a hostility towards the Arusha Peace Accords, blocked the introduction of the transitional government, and was hostile towards all opposition parties, because these processes would mean that he and his *Akazu* friends would

---

[39] CONTRA001180, 75–76; and ICTR–96–4, CONTRA001193, *Akayesu – Transcript of 18/2/1997*, 18 February 1997, 59–73.

[40] ICTR–96–4, Akayesu, *Audio Recording: Interview of Jean Paul Akayesu in Zambia*, 10 April 1996, Tape I, Side A; and CONTRA001175, 36–40.

[41] CONTRA001198, 42–118; CONTRA001197, 5–57; CONTRA001180, 21–64 and 143–56; and ICTR–96–4, ICTR–96–4–0459/1, *Akayesu – Judgement*, 2 September 1998, 97–106.

[42] CONTRA001175, 42–45; CONTRA001198, 97–100; and CONTRA001193, 61–70.

[43] ICTR–99–46, TRA001774/1, *[Cyangugu] – Ntagerura et al – Redacted Transcript of 24/09/2001*, 24 September 2001, 206.

have to relinquish power.[44] For Imanishimwe, whilst he had no prior track record of hostility towards the Tutsis before his alleged training of the *Interahamwe* in 1993, he also craved power and authority, was close to the *Akazu* and even had General Nsabimana – a key figure in the genocide – as a military 'godfather'.[45] He, like Akayesu, would do anything for more authority.

There were similar stories of power and authority in the prosecution's construction of Gatete as a perpetrator – albeit tinged more strongly with an inner willingness to commit violence.[46] Indeed, as the trials went on, it became clear that underneath the seemingly specific accounts of the accuseds' characters lay similar understandings of what type of person they were and what motivated them to participate in the violence. The prosecution presented each defendant as being intelligent persons, conscious and rational actors, in positions of responsibility who had the ability to decide between right and wrong.[47] However, instead of 'doing the right thing', they *chose* to commit violence in order to retain authority and power. During Akayesu's sentencing hearing the prosecution argued:

> Akayesu *consciously chose* to participate in the systematic killings that followed in Taba. He publicly incited people to kill in Taba. He also ordered the killing of a number of persons some of whom were killed in

---

[44] ICTR–99–46, ICTR–99–46–0130, *[Cyangugu] – Bagambiki – Ntagerura et al – The Prosecutor's Pre-Trial Brief*, 3 July 2000, 5; and ICTR–99–46, TRA000207/01, *[Cyangugu] – Ntagerura et al – Redacted Transcript of 18/09/2000*, 18 September 2000, 43–45, 48–50 and 54–58.

[45] TRA000207/01, 55–57.

[46] What was also notable about the prosecution's case against Gatete is that, unlike the other cases examined here, there was the least attempt by the prosecution to tell some thicker narrative about Gatete that made his actions make sense. This was, in part, because of the need to quicken the pace of the trials, as will be discussed more in Chapter 6. Tellingly, the prosecution's opening and closing statements (where much of this detail was normally provided) during Gatete, and unlike those in Cyangugu or Gatete, did not even occupy a whole trial day session. ICTR–00–61, TRA001643/1, *Gatete – Redacted Transcript of 20/10/2009*, 20 October 2009; and ICTR–00–61, TRA005592, *Gatete – Redacted Transcript of 08/11/2010*, 8 November 2010.

[47] The tribunal prosecuted two different types of persons: those in positions of authority, and those who had committed particularly egregious acts of violence – people such as Yussuf Munyakazi. Even these latter types of defendants, however, were still presented as knowing, purposeful and conscious individuals, even if there was a greater sense of the accused's 'inner evil'. During the *Munyakazi* opening statement the prosecution both said that Munyakazi was 'a villain; the devil who stripped his victims of everything it meant to be human', but also that he 'was not a stranger to the criminal enterprise and that he executed its objectives with great efficiency, in person and in concert with other members of the criminal enterprise with whom he shared the intent to commit genocide and extermination'. ICTR (Press Release), 'Trial of Yussuf Munyakazi Starts', 22 April 2000.

THE FORCE OF LAW

his presence and he participated in the killings. He also cautioned and supported through his presence and acts, the rape of many women at the bureau communal. (emphasis added)[48, 49]

Moreover, in abusing their position of responsibility they convinced otherwise innocent members of the (Hutu) population to commit acts of violence:

[Akayesu] *used innocent people* to commit crimes, the motive of which *they were perhaps not fully aware* of or *were afraid to* disobey him [. . .]. Akayesu had *choices*. He rather became a willing, indeed an enthusiastic participant in the killing and the persecution of Tutsis by *choice*. Therefore, his responsibility is very severe. (emphasis added)[50]

In many respects, Akayesu's ability to choose was heightened by the populations seeming inability to refuse the calls to violence. As will be discussed more subsequently, with the archive's ethnocentric understanding of the violence this introduced a problematic notion of the Hutu population as inevitable supporters of the genocide.[51]

The roots of these narratives lie with the criminal law's liberal and enlightenment-driven understanding of individuals as conscious and rational actors. The accuseds' ability to *choose* to act, along with the calculations that they made about how their interests were best served, meant that they demonstrated that they were the conscious and rational actors that law required to find them guilty of wrongdoing. This is central to the very possibility of criminal justice and the righteousness of punishing wrongdoers. As Hegel argued, the intentional actor is so central to criminal law *that the act of punishment also becomes the perpetrator's choice*:

Punishment is the *right* of the criminal. It is an act of his own will. The violation of right has been proclaimed by the criminal as his own right.

---

[48] ICTR–96–4, CONTRA001233, *Akayesu – Transcript of 28/09/1998 – Sentencing Hearing*, 28 September 1998, 15.

[49] 'The other side of Akayesu is the side of him as an individual. We see him and we saw him in court as an articulate man, an intelligent man, a good public speaker. He is also a politician. He knows how to view and weigh the political scene. He's able to make the right political decision, at least that's what he believes, until the decision he made on the 18th of April 1994.' ICTR–96–4, CONTRA001235, *Akayesu – Transcript of 19/03/1998*, 19/ March 1998, 20, 59 and 63; ICTR–99–46, TRA002053/1, *[Cyangugu] – Ntagerura et al – Redacted Transcript of 11/ 08/2003*, 11/08/2003, 2; and ICTR–96–4–0003, 2–3.

[50] CONTRA001175, 58.

[51] This plot line was further emphasised during *Akayesu* when the prosecution presented evidence of another *bourgmestre* from Akayesu's region who did manage to resist the violence throughout the genocide, showing that it was possible to resist. CONTRA001187, 6–113.

His crime is the negation of right. Punishment is the negation of this negation, and consequently an affirmation of right, solicited and forced upon the criminal by himself.[52]

This emphasis on the conscious and rational actor, with a clear set of responsibilities and rights, places a liberal vision of community at the very centre of the archive, discussed more in Chapter 6.

This way of viewing the world not only affected how the accused were understood, but it also determined how the violence itself was presented, having, as such, a significant impact on the archive. Violence within these narratives was never the result of chance. Rather, the violence was always the result of careful planning, instigation, an organised attack, intentional deceit, or *knowing* carelessness:[53] behind each attack there was always an individual that could be found responsible. In *Gatete* the prosecution argued:

> Forensic enquiry and the judgments of this tribunal in the aftermath of this slaughter have established that what occurred in Rwanda cannot be simply wished away as the kind of spontaneous communal bloodletting that often goes with a violent transition of power, but that it was a genocide of the Tutsi organised at the highest levels of state which relied for its efficient execution on the local administration, political party functionaries, all supported by government troops, party militia and ordinary Hutu peasants mobilised for that purpose.[54]

The genocide was, then, presented as being organised, highly coordinated and controlled. As such, the accused's exact, and discrete, contribution to that violence could be discerned through the trial process.

Even the defence's accounts of violence – which tried to achieve a fundamentally different outcome to the prosecution – reinforced this account of perpetratorhood. De facto acknowledging the idea of the perpetrator as a rational, conscious and powerful actor, the defence contested the prosecution's accounts by arguing that the defendants did not have anything like the power or authority that

---

[52] Hegel, *Philosophy of Right*, quoted on www.marxists.org/archive/marx/works/1853/02/18.htm (last accessed 25 May 2017).

[53] During the *Gatete* closing arguments, for instance, the prosecution also argued that part of Gatete's guilt came from his 'managerial like' organisation and overseeing of the violence in Byumba and Murambi. TRA005592, 10.

[54] TRA001643/1, 2.

the prosecution alleged.[55] The most persistent of these narratives came from Imanishimwe in *Cyangugu*.[56] He argued that despite the prosecution's claims, not only was he not closely tied with the *Akazu* and did not have Colonel Nsabimana as his military godfather, he was not even in charge of an important military camp. Wounded in 1991, Imanishimwe was kept away from the front line and the top posts in the military when he was transferred to Cyangugu – an insignificant station, far away from the front line that was staffed by the war-wounded and otherwise immobile persons, like him. These soldiers were not even capable of serving the military in the war with the RPF, let alone starting a genocide.[57] One witness noted:

DEFENCE: You name Captain Kazabavaho, Second Lieutenant Dusenguremyi, and Lieutenant Samuel Imanishimwe as being commanders of the Karambo camps [. . .]. Was there anything special, peculiar about these three officers?

WITNESS: The three officers had many common characteristics and characteristics that were peculiar to them. In fact, the Cyangugu camp mainly comprised soldiers who had been wounded at the front. And if my memory serves me right, I think Captain Kazabavaho had scars on his face and also on – near his ribs. As concerns Dusenguremyi, he was one-eyed, he could only see with one eye. And as regards Samuel,

---

[55] Both Bagambiki and Akayesu in this respect argued that their authority had diminished since the advent of multiparty democracy in Rwanda in 1992, as they were no longer considered the direct representative of the president within the commune or prefecture; similarly, for Ntagerura this meant that the MRND – his party – was no longer the biggest within the region. ICTR–99–46, TRA000437/2, [Cyangugu] – Ntagerura et al – Redacted Transcript of 20/02/2001, 20 February 2001, 35; ICTR–99–46, TRA002063/1, [Cyangugu] – Ntagerura et al – Redacted Transcript of 13/08/2003, 13 August 2003, 23–26; ICTR–99–46, TRA001907, [Cyangugu] – Ntagerura et al – Redacted Transcript of 21/01/2003, 21 January 2003, 9; TRA001918/1, 2–4; CONTRA001207, 12–17; CONTRA001231, 7–34; and TRA000525/1, 32–33. ICTR–99–46, TRA002000/1, [Cyangugu] – Ntagerura et al – Redacted Transcript of 11/02/2003, 11 February 2003, 12–16. The main narrative during Gatete in this regard was to allege that Gatete was not one of the ringleaders of the genocide in the Murambi commune, as evidenced by the frequency with which witnesses mentioned other personalities in the region. TRA005152/1, 40; ICTR–00–61, TRA005145/1, Gatete – Redacted Transcript of 10/3/2010, 10 March 2010, 54; ICTR–00–61, TRA005153/1, Gatete – Redacted Transcript of 16/03/2010, 16 March 2010, 42, 61 and 64–66; and ICTR–00–61, TRA005157/1, Gatete, Redacted Transcript of 22/3/2010, 22 March 2010, 53.

[56] See all of his own testimony. TRA001851/2.

[57] ICTR–99–46, TRA001615/1, [Cyangugu] – Ntagerura et al – Redacted Transcript of 25/03/2002, 25 March 2002, 30–33; and TRA001618/02, 77–79. See also ICTR–99–46, TRA001782/1, [Cyangugu] – Ntagerura et al – Redacted Transcript of 16/10/2002, 16 October 2002, 28; and ICTR–99–46, TRA001799/1 [Cyangugu] – Ntagerura et al – Redacted Transcript of 30/10/2002, 30 October 2002, 12–17.

he had sustained or suffered an accident during which a mine exploded as he passed by, and this made him suffer complications in his lower leg.[58]

Similarly, the defence tried to further diminish the defendant's ability to intervene and stop the genocide or rebuke the idea that they had organised this by emphasising the spontaneous and chaotic nature of the violence. A defence witness in *Cyangugu* claimed:

> Well, in this country where disorder was rife, where there was fighting everywhere, where the RPF was advancing, where infiltrators were being hunted down, *people running helter-skelter, dying of accidents*, people killed at roadblocks, Bagambiki saved as many people as he could. If Mr. Karegyesa [chief prosecutor] had been in that country, would he have been able to do more? (emphasis added)[59]

This suggested that against this outpouring there was little that the defendants could have done to re-introduce peace within the region.[60]

DEFENCE: Witness, can you tell this Court whether between the 9th of April 1994 and the 12th of April 1994 – the date when the government fled – whether the said government was in a position to take any governmental – plausible governmental action?

WITNESS: It was impossible for the simple reason that this government was under siege. It was at war. And we realised that as soon as it was installed, the first thing it did was to prepare its flight, and under those circumstance, this flight did not mean that this government was making progress.[61]

Blame, then, shifted away from the interim government and towards the RPF. During *Cyangugu* the defence argued that after the Rwandan government's army (FAR) had successfully defeated the RPF in a conventional war in 1992, the RPF turned instead to guerrilla tactics.[62] At this point the

[58] ICTR–99–46, TRA001619/2, [Cyangugu] – Ntagerura et al – Redacted Transcript of 03/10/2002, 3 October 2002, 39–40.
[59] ICTR–99–46, TRA002003/1, [Cyangugu] – Ntagerura et al – Redacted Transcript of 18/02/2003, 18 February 2003, 33.
[60] ICTR–99–46, TRA001293/2, [Cyangugu] – Ntagerura et al – Redacted Transcript of 22/07/2002, 22 July 2002, 102; ICTR–00–61, TRA005147/1, Gatete – Redacted Transcript of 09/03/2010, 09 March 2010, 60; ICTR–00–61–0240/1, 73; and ICTR–99–46, TRA000546/2, [Cyangugu] – Ntagerura et al – Redacted Transcript of 20/09/2001, 20 September 2001, 37, 41 and 44.
[61] ICTR–99–46, TRA001277/2, [Cyangugu] – Ntagerura et al – Redacted Transcript of 28/05/2002, 28 May 2002, 55.
[62] TRA001851/2, 24–5; TRA001618/02, 80–1; and TRA001619/2, 38–40.

RPF, the defence alleged, began to recruit young Tutsis, who were trained in Uganda before being sent back to Rwanda to commit acts of terrorism and sabotage.[63] This violence rendered places like Cyangugu, miles from the front line, as effective 'passive war fronts', producing considerable tension within the region in the build-up to the genocide, as the population became increasingly suspicious of each other.[64] When the president's plane was shot down, the built-up tension spilled over into 'spontaneous' acts of violence.[65] This argument also rendered some of the Tutsis within the region as 'legitimate' targets of the violence, meaning, for instance, that Bagambiki and Imanishimwe had been correct in their decision to remove seventeen suspected RPF infiltrators from Karamapaka stadium (these persons were later killed).[66] These records even implied that some Tutsis brought the violence upon themselves as they attacked Hutus, committed acts of terrorism and exacerbated tensions as they celebrated the death of President Habyarimana or the arrival of the RPF.[67] Chaos reigned, then, which made any notion of individual responsibility meaningless.[68]

This point was reinforced by showing instances, prior to 1994, where the defendants had successfully maintained the peace. During *Cyangugu*, Bagambiki emphasised this by pointing to his successful intervention in the chaos that had enveloped Cyangugu in the wake of Martin Bucyana's death – the former head of the CDR – in February 1993.[69] At that time Bagambiki convened security meetings and conducted 'pacification tours' and successfully reintroduced peace

---

[63] ICTR–99–46, TRA000527/2, *[Cyangugu] – Ntagerura et al – Redacted Transcript of 13/03/2002*, 13 March 2002, 75; ICTR–99–46, TRA001288/2, *[Cyangugu] – Ntagerura et al – Redacted Transcript of 11/07/2002*, 11 July 2002, 32–33 and 46; ICTR–99–46, TRA001800/1, *[Cyangugu] – Ntagerura et al – Redacted Transcript of 04/11/2002*, 4 November 2002, 32; TRA001907, 21 January 2003, 5–10; and ICTR–99–46, TRA002002/2, *[Cyangugu] – Ntagerura et al – Redacted Transcript of 17/02/2003*, 17 February 2003, 5–6.

[64] TRA001907, 8.

[65] TRA002000/1, 14; and ICTR–99–46, TRA001912/1, *[Cyangugu] – Ntagerura et al – Redacted Transcript of 11/03/2003*, 11 March 2003, 39.

[66] TRA001920/1, 25.

[67] *Ibid.*, 52–53; and ICTR–99–46, TRA001795/1, *[Cyangugu] – Ntagerura et al – Redacted Transcript of 22/10/2002*, 22 October 2002, 48; TRA001618/02, 1. See also ICTR–99–46, TRA001796/1, *[Cyangugu] – Ntagerura et al – Redacted Transcript of 23/10/2002*, 23 October 2002, 40; and TRA001909/1, 10–11.

[68] This was underscored by the testimony of expert witness Lucien Houkpatin. They argued that *no one* was responsible for the genocide, since (drawing on 'ethno-psychiatry' – a discipline strongly linked with colonialism) the violence was the consequence of the 'collective insanity' that resulted from the death of the father of the nation, Habyarimana. *Ibid.*, 2; and ICTR–99–46, TRA001286/2, *[Cyangugu] – Ntagerura et al – Redacted Transcript of 08/07/2002 – Motion*, 8 July 2002, 25 and 36.

[69] ICTR–99–46, TRA001919/1, *[Cyangugu] – Ntagerura et al – Redacted Transcript of 31/03/2003*, 31 March 2003, 4–6.

and security within the region.[70] Bagambiki used exactly the same tactics during the genocide: He held three prefecture security council meetings within the first two weeks, and held pacification meetings, including one with President Sindikubwabo and Ntagerura.[71] However, unlike in 1993, during the genocide these actions failed.[72]

Throughout, defence counsels also argued that the defendants 'did what they could' to prevent the violence, but to no avail. From this perspective, the accused became simply victims of circumstance, and a number of the defendants indeed made claims to their victim status during the genocide. Bagambiki, for example, testified:

> I do regret that I was not able to save all of those I would have liked to save, and I ask for forgiveness and understanding from those who were disappointed by my lack of power, by the fact that I was not able to save everyone. It was my dearest hope, my wish. *I did what I could* and I spared no effort. And I want to thank those who helped me, who assisted me with their advice, who helped me by accompanying me during the pacification campaign, who helped me by intervening where I sent them to intervene, and those who helped me with their prayers.
>
> I thank my family. We spent some very difficult times together, nights that were endless, sleepless nights. Our life was in danger and they comforted me; they encouraged me; they supported me. I thank my wife and my children because they were at my side during these difficult times. *It was a nightmare for everyone, for them and for me.* (emphasis added)[73]

As this suggests, a similar set of rules underpinned both prosecution and defence accounts. Both demonstrated the close association between levels of agency and perpetratorhood. Whilst the prosecution

---

[70] ICTR–99–46, TRA002001/1, *[Cyangugu] – Ntagerura et al – Redacted Transcript of 13/02/2003*, 13 February 2003, 11–15.

[71] TRA001918/1, 33–35.

[72] A similar narrative was presented in Akayesu:

> Akayesu, with the assistance of other persons, struggled against the Interahamwe and then the reinforcement became unfavourable to Akayesu and they were overwhelmed by the Interahamwe. This witness continues that the killings became widespread between the 23rd and the 24th of April in Taba, because Taba was the only commune that had been spared thus far from the killings. CONTRA001238, 23.

See also ICTR–96–4, Akayesu, *Audio Recording:* Interview of Jean Paul Akayesu in Zambia, 10 April 1996, Tape I, Side A; CONTRA001180, 14–15; CONTRA001207, 31–32; see also CONTRA001208, 34–35; ICTR–96–4, CONTRA001214, *Akayesu – Transcript of 19/11/1997*, 19 November 1997, 19–20 and 43–44; and ICTR–96–4, CONTRA001217, *Akayesu – Transcript of 9/2/1998*, 9 February 1998, 50–53.

[73] TRA001921/1, 20.

throughout their accounts constructed an understanding of the accused as hyper-conscious and rational perpetrators seeking power at all costs, and with this attributing a considerable amount of agency to them, the chaos argument *removed* any sense of agency; the accused were simply unable to act any differently and therefore could not be punished. Similarly, the defence presented the Tutsis within Cyangugu as poten- tial threats due to their alleged acts of terrorism and sabotage. This attributed agency to these actors, which both legitimised certain forms of violence against them and prevented them from being seen as victims. As explored in the following section, this sense of the passivity of victims formed a crucial part of the archive's constitution of victimhood.

Victims

The archive also constructed distinctive notions of victimhood. Part of how victims were imagined in the archive was due, again, to the tribunal's statute; each of the statute's three crimes (as a result of a combination of the *actus reus* and *in chapeau* element) came with a stipulation as to the type of victim that needed to be targeted to be recognised as a crime within the court's statute.[74] As Campbell has noted, victims in international law are defined by their membership of a broader group who are seen as being the primary target of the crime *rather* than the individual.[75] At the ICTR, this fundamentally altered both who the archive acknowledged as a victim, but also, and crucially, why the account of the violence, constructed *through* the witnesses (often victims) and deposited within the archive, appeared as it did.

To be a victim of a crime against humanity, the individual had to have been targeted as part of a widespread or systematic attack against a group on political, national, ethnic, religious, or racial grounds.[76] This was, for the most part, established by demonstrating the breadth of the violence at a national level committed against the Tutsis as an ethnic group and moderate Hutus as a political group. By drawing links between this national-level violence and the violence locally, the prosecution was able to argue that the local violence was part of a broader strategy to eliminate or target a particular group. As they stated during *Akayesu*:

---

[74] Articles 2–4 of ICTR Statute.

[75] Kirsten Campbell, 'Victims and Perpetrators of International Crimes: The Problem of the "Legal Person"', *International Humanitarian Legal Studies* 2:2 (2011): 340–45.

[76] Article 3 of ICTR Statute.

Your Honors, the isolated attacks or the isolated crimes that were alleged Akayesu had performed or committed, by themselves, alone, would not constitute crimes against humanity [. . .]. Akayesu's isolated acts become crimes against humanity only when they are part of the systematic and widespread attack that has been taking place during the temporary jurisdiction that this Court has.[77]

For it to be a war crime, the victim had to be a civilian or a prisoner of war, and the act of violence had to be committed in the context of a non-international armed conflict.[78] As such, it was in the prosecution's interests to establish the non-combatant status of the victims of the crimes where possible.[79] When asking Witness S about the murder of Karangwa's brothers, the prosecution asked:

PROSECUTION: Do you know how they were dressed; were they in, I guess, normal civilian clothes or some sort of military uniform?

WITNESS: Yes. They were wearing civilian clothes.

PROSECUTION: And were they carrying any weapons, guns or anything like that?

WITNESS: Are you talking about Ephrem's brothers?

PROSECUTION: Yes?

WITNESS: They had no arms – no weapons.[80]

In the majority of incidents, however, the very fact that attacks took place at sites of refuge, such as churches – one of the most common sites of violence during the genocide – seemed sufficient to remove any doubt that the victims were non-combatants. The very site of the killing seemed to ensure that those attacked were seen as innocent victims, as this contributed towards establishing the actor's innocent and largely *passive* nature. Indeed, the passivity of the victims became an important signifier of victimhood, in contrast with the purposeful perpetrator. The archive's discomfort with more active victims was seen when the judges exonerated refugees that did fight back against the attackers. During the *Nizeyimana* judgment the judges, for example, argued: '[T]he defensive efforts against attacks on the primarily displaced Tutsis at the parish [did

---

[77] ICTR–96–4, CONTRA001184, *Akayesu – Transcript of 16/1/1997*, 16 January 1997, 49.

[78] Article 4 of ICTR Statute.

[79] ICTR–96–4, CONTRA001182, *Akayesu – Transcript of 24/1/1997*, 24 January 1997, 12; ICTR–96–4, CONTRA001222, *Akayesu – Transcript of 23/10/1997*, 23 October 1997, 7 and 34.

[80] CONTRA001197, 14. See also TRA000254/2, 12; and ICTR–00–61, TRA005158/1, *Gatete – Redacted Transcript of 17/03/2010*, 17 March 2010, 49.

not turn] them into combatants.'[81] As stated earlier, the defence attempted to use the claimed agency of some Tutsis to justify the violence directed against them.

The most important framing of victimhood came from the provisions of the Genocide Convention, which underpinned the statute's definition of genocide. This only afforded protection to those targeted because of their race, ethnicity, nationality or religion (with the additional criteria that they were targeted with the intention to wipe out the wider group, in whole or in part). Whilst in *Akayesu* the court had some difficulty establishing which type of group the Tutsis represented, discussed more in Chapter 4, ultimately it was accepted they were an ethic group and so fell within the parameters of the Genocide Convention.[82]

Hutu victims of the genocide were, however, not covered by the Genocide Convention. This was because those Hutus killed were clearly targeted because of their political identity as opponents of Hutu power. Importantly, as the Genocide Convention was being drafted, the USSR deliberately excluded political groups from the convention as they feared this might open them up to accusations of genocide due to their treatment of 'class traitors'. In the ICTR's archive, this both meant that Hutu victims were excluded from the genocide narrative, and, moreover, that the violence in Rwanda was misconstrued as 'ethnic'. Whilst it is true that the majority of victims were Tutsis, the genocide was, fundamentally, a political act which, whilst pursued at a local level for a variety of different reasons, was designed and executed to ensure that a small political clique could retain political control of the country. Moreover, in the genocidal discourse that swept through Rwanda, the Tutsis were presented as *political* threats to the status quo, as suspected affiliates with the invading RPF forces, and as the unjust beneficiaries of the colonial past.[83] Emphasising the ethnic nature of the violence flattened this out and essentially *depoliticised* the violence.

---

[81] *Prosecutor v. Ildéphonse Nizeyimana*, Case No. ICTR–00–55, ICTR–00–55C–0536/1, *Judgement and Sentence*, 19 June 2012, 437.

[82] CONTRA001175, 67; ICTR–96–4–0459/1, 209–10 and 281.

[83] René Lemarchand, 'The 1994 Rwanda Genocide', in *The Genocide Studies Reader*, ed. Samuel Totten et al. (Abingdon: Routledge, 2009), 484; Helen Hintjens, 'Explaining the 1994 Genocide in Rwanda', *The Journal of Modern African Studies* 37:2 (1999), 247–8 and 261; Gérard Prunier, *The Rwanda Crisis: History of Genocide* (London: Hurst & Company,1995), 159–64; Lee Fujii, *Killing Neighbours: Webs of Violence in Rwanda* (London: Cornell University Press, 2009), 5, 46, 50, 76–7 and 89; Alison Des Forges, 'Leave None to Tell the Story: Genocide in Rwanda,' (Human Rights Watch, 1999); Lee Fujii, *Killing Neighbours: Webs of Violence in Rwanda* (London: Cornell University Press, 2009); and Scott Straus, *The Order of Genocide: Race, Power and War in Rwanda.* (London: Cornell University Press, 2006), 128–40.

As a result, the prosecution repeatedly focused in on the ethnicity of the victims being attacked. When Witness K testified to the murder of refugees at the Taba communal office, the prosecution followed up by asking: 'Do you know whether or not these people were Hutu or Tutsi?'[84] The centrality of the witnesses' ethnicity to the prosecution's strategy was such that even when a witness attempted to resist answering the question they were forced to comply:

PROSECUTION: How old are you?
WITNESS: I'm 30 years old.
PROSECUTION: What's your ethnic group?
WITNESS: I am Rwandan.
PROSECUTION: How were you considered in 1994?
WITNESS: In 1994 I was Tutsi. But today in Rwanda there is no distinction between the ethnic groups; so, I am Rwandan.[85]

This exchange also reveals a tension between the ICTR's and Rwanda's conceptions of the post-conflict process. For the witness's response signified the RPF government's attempts to *eradicate* ethnicity as an organising principle in Rwandan society in the aftermath of the genocide, instead emphasising that all citizens were Rwandan. In contrast, ethnicity was very much the central pillar around which the ICTR's archive built up its understanding of the violence. Indeed, as time went on, the ethnocentricity of the archive's understanding of violence increased. The strength of this association can be seen in this following extract:

PROSECUTION: Do you know why they were killed? Or maybe let me rephrase the question. What was the ethnic group of the victims, of those three victims that night?
WITNESS: They were Tutsi.[86]

---

84 ICTR–96–4, CONTRA001176, *Akayesu – Transcript of 10/1/1997*, 10 January 1997, 55 and 60; CONTRA001222, 21 and 24; CONTRA001195, 117; ICTR–96–4, CONTRA001224, *Akayesu – Transcript of 27/10/1997*, 27 October 1997, 13; CONTRA001227, 17; ICTR–99–46, TRA000218/1, *[Cyangugu] – Ntagerura et al – Redacted Transcript of 25/10/2000*, 25 October 2000, 57; ICTR–99–46, TRA000750/01, *[Cyangugu] – Ntagerura et al – Redacted Transcript of 06/06/2001*, 6 June 2001, 4–57; TRA000122/01, 12; and ICTR–00–61, TRA005491/2, *Gatete – Redacted Transcript of 03/11/2009*, 3 November 2009, 84.
85 ICTR–99–46, TRA000443/1, *[Cyangugu] – Ntagerura et al – Redacted Transcript of 02/05/2001*, 2 May 2001, 4. See also ICTR–99–46, TRA000444/2, *[Cyangugu] – Ntagerura et al – Redacted Transcript of 03/05/2001*, 3 May 2001, 32.
86 ICTR–99–46, TRA000251/2, *[Cyangugu] – Ntagerura et al – Redacted Transcript of 18/01/2001*, 18 January 2001, 81.

In this exchange, the prosecution realised that their original question would be objected to, because it would produce a speculative answer from the witness, and so reformulated the question to extract an answer that would prove that the act of violence was part of the genocide within the tribunal's ethnocentric discourse of victimhood.

This ethnocentric narrative was, to a degree, contested by the defence as they tried to muddy who exactly was a victim of the violence.[87] However, on the whole, the defence's records also tacitly supported this ethnocentric framing of victimhood. In particular, a dominant narrative trope within the defence's account, which was aimed at attacking the prosecution's *mens rea* and *dolus specialis* claims, was that the accused lacked genocidal intent. To this end, the defence's records emphasised the accused's lack of animosity towards the Tutsis, suggesting by extension their inability to have been involved with the planning or execution of the genocide. During each trial, witnesses came forward to declare that the defendants had never treated Tutsis unfairly, nor made any anti-Tutsi statements.[88] Their disposition in this regard was particularly emphasised by showing that the defendant had relatives or, even better, spouses, who were Tutsis.[89]

This allocation of victimhood to Tutsis alone was made more problematic by the flipside of this; Hutus as a group became increasingly associated with perpetratorhood.[90] When Witness JJ described the attackers without being prompted, she noted that they were 'our neighbors'.[91] It was only after the prosecution's intervention that the violence became reframed in ethnic terms.

---

[87] TRA002003/1, 33; TRA000122/01, 69; TRA002001/1, 22–23; and TRA002003/1, 58. There were also the more politicised defence lawyers that either tried to argue that there was no genocide or that the Hutus were the main victims of violence. Nigel Eltringham, *Genocide Never Sleeps: Living Law at the International Criminal Tribunal for Rwanda* (Cambridge: Cambridge University Press, 2019), 49–50.

[88] For examples see ICTR–96–4, CONTRA001207, *Akayesu – Transcript of 17/11/1997*, 17 November 1997, 17; hereafter ICTR–99–46, TRA000525/1, *[Cyangugu] – Ntagerura et al – Redacted Transcript of 19/03/2002*, 19 March 2002, 7; and ICTR–00–61, ICTR–00–61–0240/1, *Gatete – Judgement and Sentence*, 31 March 2011, 40.

[89] ICTR–99–46, TRA000528/2, *[Cyangugu] – Ntagerura et al – Redacted Transcript of 11/03/2002*, 11 March 2002, 28; and TRA000525/1, 4.

[90] For an example of this see TRA000218/1, 62 and 71; and TRA005145/1, 64.

[91] CONTRA001222, 20.

PROSECUTION: These people who destroyed your home and ate your livestock, your neighbors, do you know whether or not they were Hutu or Tutsis?

WITNESS: They were Hutus.[92]

Another example of this understanding of perpetratorhood can be seen in this exchange during *Gatete* where the court required clarification for why a Hutu might have felt victimised:

MADAM PRESIDENT: And why were you afraid? In view of your ethnicity?

WITNESS: Madam President, I would like to point out to you that the killings were not committed by all the Hutus. Hutus who refused to kill people were characterised as accomplices, and they could very easily be killed for that.[93]

In this case it should also be noted that during *Gatete* the court's focus was on crimes committed in the north-east of the country, which quickly fell under RPF control, and where a substantial number of Hutus were deliberately targeted by RPF forces.[94] However, with the addition of the inevitable compliance of the masses to the leaders' calls to participate in the violence, noted earlier, within these accounts *all* Hutus seemingly became always already perpetrators of violence – complicit in the crime by default. As with the association between Tutsis as an ethnic group and victimhood, this flattened out the meaning of the violence in Rwanda, as will be discussed more in Chapter 4.

Again, this division between Hutu/perpetrators and Tutsi/victims has implications for the governance of community. First it reproduces and reifies these categories as the natural basis around which society is organised. But within the specific context of Rwanda, such a division has also helped to justify the state's reliance on autocratic governance techniques driven in part by a suspicion (and despite the government's claims to have eradicated ethnicity) of the Hutu population. This can be seen through the use of 're-education' programmes aimed at Hutus thought to support the genocide ideology, and also in the narrative adopted by the state which presents the Hutu population as having

---

[92] *Ibid.*, 21.

[93] ICTR–00–61, TRA005507/2, *Gatete – Redacted Transcript of 10/11/2009*, 10 November 2009, 32.

[94] Chris McGrail, 'Genocide Tribunal Ready to Indict First Tutsis', *The Guardian*, 5 April 2002.

been easily led astray by Hutu-power advocates during the genocide. The drive to divide the population between victim and perpetrator was also seen in the RPF's official renaming of the genocide to the 'Genocide against the Tutsi'. Whilst the desire to claim a particular narrative of the violence is understandable in the face of the widespread suffering that it caused, largely amongst Tutsis, this move further solidified and naturalised this divide between Tutsi victims and Hutu perpetrators.

CONCLUSION

This chapter has demonstrated the way in which international criminal law framed the archive's account of violence in particular ways. This resulted in records which were constrained – temporally, geographically and substantively – and which revolved around the actions of the accused. This already began to show some of the ways in which this produced specific imaginings of different types of actors and community. The constitution of perpetrators as rational actors, and the individualisation of the violence, reproduced a distinctly liberal understanding of community. This also placed criminal justice as a central tool for the governance of community, as the court helped decide which acts of violence were to be punished whilst also protecting citizens from the abuse of sovereign power. As Eltringham argued in this respect, the constitution of the victim as innocent, passive and, ultimately, 'abject' legitimises law as a governance tool, rendering courts such as the ICTR as 'saviour' to the victim's plight.[95]

This chapter has also pointed to some of the tensions that exist between the tribunal's different goals and priorities. The law's ethnocentric framing of genocide and its Manichean division of actors into innocent victims and guilty perpetrators and the repeated emphasis on the *identities* of those that participated in the violence jointly concealed the fluidity and *political* (and therefore contestable) nature of these identities and rendered them fixed and stable.[96] In this very important way, then, the account as produced within the archive works contrary to the goal of reconciliation, as within this way of understanding

---

[95] Eltringham, *Genocide Never Sleeps*, 124–25; and Clarke, 'Affective Justice', 246–52.
[96] Ruti Teitel, 'The Universal and the Particular in International Criminal Justice', *Columbia Human Rights Law Review* 30:285 (1998): 288; and Kris Brown and Fionnuala Ni Aolain. 'Through the Looking Glass: Transitional Justice Futures through the Lens of Nationalism, Feminism and Transformative Change', *International Journal of Transitional Justice* 9:1 (2015): 127–49.

Rwandan society, there is little chance of bringing these 'two sides' together when they appear as always, and inevitably, opposed to each other.[97] This sense of an ingrained victimhood is, moreover, often politically mobilised to violent ends. This much was seen in the build-up to the Rwandan genocide when the Hutu extremists constructed a strong collective memory of the Hutus' past status as victims under the Tutsis' monarchical rule to legitimise the genocide against them.[98]

However, as has already been suggested in this chapter, the law itself is not static, but changes over time, seen, for instance, in the expansion of the definition of genocide to include rape. The following chapters examine why these shifts occurred and to what effect. As will be argued across Chapters 4 and 5, numerous actors had a vested interest in contesting the ways and means through which the archive structured knowledge, and this also meant that the archive's understanding of international criminal justice, the violence in Rwanda, and of the international community shifted over time. Chapter 4 begins this exploration by looking at the role of witnesses in the production of the archive. As this shows, whilst undoubtedly constrained by the force of law, witnesses played a much more significant role in structuring the archive's account of violence than is usual noted.

---

[97] See also Michael Humphrey, 'International Intervention, Justice and National Reconciliation: The Role of the ICTY and ICTR in Bosnia and Rwanda', *Journal of Human Rights* 2:4 (2003): 502.

[98] Mahmood Mamdani, *When Victims Become Killers: Colonialism, Nativism, and the Genocide in Rwanda* (Oxford: Princeton University Press, 2014), 189–96.

CHAPTER FOUR

CONTESTING THE ARCHIVE

Chapter 3 examined the role that international criminal law played in shaping the archive's records and vision of community. As that chapter argued, however, what constituted 'the law', and rules of the archive, evolved over the course of the tribunal, whether this was the partial expansion of the tribunal's temporal jurisdiction or the definition of what constituted genocide. Indeed, as the following chapters will demonstrate, the archive was a highly contested space where different actors brought different versions of justice and community to bear and tried to restructure the archive's rules accordingly. This, then, turns to the different enunciative modalities – or subject positions – that were made possible within the archive. It also considers how these enunciative modalities interacted with the archive's objects (such as victims and perpetrators), concepts (such as genocide) and strategies (such as the realisation of truth, justice and reconciliation) as discussed in Chapters 2 and 3.

This part of the enquiry continues across Chapters 4 and 5. Chapter 4 focuses on the witnesses' role in shaping the archive. As this chapter shows, witnesses played a more significant role in constructing the archive than scholars normally credit. Whilst it is the case that the legal actors and discourse attempted to constrain the witnesses' records, as discussed in Chapter 3, witnesses also contested these parameters both in terms of which crimes would be addressed by the tribunal and how the law was to account for violence. This contestation also destabilised many of the objects and subjects that the legal discourse tried to produce, such as what constituted a victim or perpetrator. In exploring this, the chapter traces the witnesses' engagement in the production of records from pre-trial investigations through to the judgment.

INVESTIGATIONS AND INDICTMENTS

As discussed in Chapter 1, scholars often present courtrooms as sites that silence witnesses due to a clash of interests between the witness's desire to tell *their* story and the courts' need for a *legal* story.[1] This sentiment was also expressed to me in a number of the interviews I conducted with legal actors at the tribunal.[2] However, as this chapter argues, this does not necessarily mean that witnesses were passive in the production of knowledge within the archive. This will show that these notions of silence and passivity conceal the important role witnesses played throughout the trials.[3] This role can be traced all the way back to how witnesses helped build the trials' narrative and legal frameworks during the prosecution's initial investigations.

As Eltringham argues, witnesses substantially contributed to the pre-trial investigations, and when this is considered, witnesses' in-trial testimony becomes something less forced upon them (as the work of scholars such as Marie-Bénédicte Dembour and Emily Haslam suggests), but, rather, a re-performance of a narrative that had been *co-produced* by the witnesses and prosecution.[4] This was most clearly seen in the counsel's interjections when a witness skipped ahead of a crucial aspect of their account, essentially directing them to 'get their lines right':

---

[1] See Chapter 1 *supra note* 36.

[2] Interview with Member of ICTR Victim and Witness Support Section (June 2015); and Interview with Reviser – ICTR Registry (June 2015). This conflict also seems to underpin the defence's perception of the relationship between the court and witnesses. Indeed, taking this further, it appears that many defence counsels saw that the tactics needed to defend their clients' interests would almost inevitably have adverse consequences for the witnesses. See Jenia Turner, 'Defense Perspectives on Law and Politics in International Criminal Trials', *Virginia Journal of International Law* 48:3 (2007): 529–93.

[3] It is also perhaps important to note that this statement about (victim) witnesses' passivity mirrors the dominant understanding of victimhood within transitional justice more generally, discussed later in this chapter. See Kieran McEvoy and Kirsten McConnachie, 'Victims and Transitional Justice: Voice, Agency and Blame', *Social and Legal Studies* 22:4 (2013): 492–95; Nicola Henry, 'The Impossibility of Bearing Witness: Wartime Rape and the Promise of Justice', *Violence against Women* 16:10 (2010): 1107–10.

[4] Nigel Eltringham, '"We Are Not a Truth Commission": Fragmented Narratives and the Historical Record at the International Criminal Tribunal for Rwanda', *Journal of Genocide Research* 11:1 (2009): 65–67; Nigel Eltringham, *Genocide Never Sleeps: Living Law at the International Criminal Tribunal for Rwanda* (Cambridge: Cambridge University Press, 2019), 187.

WITNESS: [. . .] after he told me that people began to be killed here in this courtyard.

PROSECUTION: Before we get to the killing, after he said this to you did Akayesu call for Etienne?

WITNESS: Yes. He called that person.[5]

The archive's account of the violence in Rwanda was, then, primarily constructed through the witnesses' voices. It was the witnesses' voices that constructed the case against the accused, and witnesses played an important role in identifying what happened in each locality and who was responsible.[6] These initial acts of testimony not only affected how individual trial narratives were constructed, but also helped shape the prosecution's understanding of the violence in Rwanda more generally.[7] As was noted during *Cyangugu* when the prosecution questioned one of their investigators:

PROSECUTION: Now, can you tell this Court any common denominator you have established in the course of your inquiries as an investigator with the OTP?

WITNESS [OTP investigator]: It gradually, perhaps, it goes to the background here, when we originally started doing investigations in various areas, we focused on geographical locations. So a team would go to Cyangugu, a team would go to Kibuye, a team may go to Butare, Gisenyi and so on. And those teams would simply take statements from witnesses, from victims and survivors as to what happened. It gradually emerged that there was, there was a pattern in the sense that you had a connection, as we have here, between the Government member, Mr. Ntagerura, and between the *prefet*, Mr. Bagambiki, between the military commander [. . .]. And [subsequent to follow–up investigations

---

[5] *Prosecutor v. Jean–Paul Akayesu*, Case No. ICTR–96–4 (hereafter ICTR–96–4), CONTRA001176, *Akayesu – Transcript of 10/1/1997*, 10 January 1997, 51. For another example, see ICTR–99–46, TRA000131/1, *[Cyangugu] – Ntagerura et al – Redacted Transcript of 21/11/2000*, 21 November 2000, 99.

[6] Interview with ICTR OTP Investigator (June 2015).

[7] *Prosecutor v. André Ntagerura*, Case No. ICTR–96–10 (hereafter ICTR–96–10), ICTR–96–10A–0272, *Ntagerura – Prosecutor Request for Leave to File an Amended Indictment*, 2 December 1999, 11–12.

and], obviously, once our legal advisers had a chance to see these various connections, [this led to the] kind of situation, as we have now, where various people were indicted together.[8]

This model of genocide governance, whereby national was connected to local and the various organs of state were brought together, became the prosecution's narrative framework that was deployed at each trial.

This is not, however, to claim that the witnesses' influence within the investigations was boundless. As Kirsten Campbell has argued, the potential scope of a witness's testimony was always already limited by the legal frameworks at play and the need for these testimonies to speak of a crime that the tribunal recognised as such.[9] The investigators, then, did not enter these encounters with witnesses blind, but were influenced by prosecution strategies that were also structured by (in addition to the witnesses' testimony) the tribunal's statute and information about the violence that had been provided in reports from the UN – such as those by the Expert Commission and the Special Rapporteur – human rights organisations and the RPF.[10] Combined, this gave the investigators an indication of what had occurred and what type of evidence they should be looking for, and consequently it also excluded some evidence from the outset.[11] For instance, the ICTR's temporal jurisdiction meant that there were to be no investigations into (and therefore no accounts of) the RPF's violations of international law in Rwanda that occurred after 1994.

The archive contains evidence of these constraints. Frequently, for example, when the defence attacked the prosecution witnesses' credibility on the grounds that their in-court testimony was

---

[8] *Prosecutor v. André Ntagerura et al.*, Case No. ICTR–99–46 (hereafter ICTR–99–46), TRA000209, *[Cyangugu] – Ntagerura et al – Redacted Transcript of 20/09/2000*, 20 September 2000, 94–96.

[9] Kirsten Campbell, 'The Laws of Memory: The ICTY, Archive, and Transitional Justice', *Social and Legal Studies* 22:2 (2013): 251–53.

[10] UNSC, S/1994/1125, *Preliminary Report of the independent Commission of Experts Established in Accordance with Security Council Resolution 935* (1994), 4 October 1994, 9–17; UNESC, E/CN.4/1995/7, *Question of the Violation of Human Rights and Fundamental Freedoms in Any Part of the World, with Particular Reference to Colonial and Other Dependent Countries and Territories: Report on the Situation of Human Rights in Rwanda Submitted by Mr. R. Degni–Ségui, Special Rapporteur of the Commission on Human Rights, Under Paragraph 20 of Commission Resolution E/CN.4/S–3/1 of 25 May 1994*, 28 June 1994, 7–8; UNSC, S/PV.3400, *3400th Meeting*, 1 July 1994, 4–6 and 8–10; and Investigator (2015).

[11] Interview with Member of ICTR OTP 2 (June 2015).

different from their pre-trial statement, witnesses responded that they had not been asked questions about certain matters by the investigators but were using their appearance in court to add to their account.[12] During *Cyangugu*, to protect against these allegations, the prosecution called one of their investigators as a witness. The investigator explained that whereas Witness LAM had mentioned the defendant Bagambiki during the trial, he would not have done so during the initial investigations:

> In this case it is notable that the witness statement was taken in 1997 when the Prosecutor was investigating military involvement in the genocide in Cyangugu, and it was taken before Bagambiki was arrested.[13]

On one occasion the defence even called a prosecution investigator as a witness to put questions about a shift in a prosecution witness's testimony. Similarly, the investigator responded:

> I found a name which suggested to me – and this was [Witness] LAB. And I thought if I spoke to him – I had gone actually to find out about what had happened at the stadium. And so my intention was to find prisoners in the prison, talk to them and see whether there was any good information I could get about the stadium. So, before I left Kigali, I had this name at the back of my mind and, therefore, I wanted to just find out. So, I – when I was sure I had gotten this person, I began to talk with him and *to check whether I could get anything about what I wanted. But I realised that this person, LAB, was only talking about events of the factory which I was not interested in. And, therefore, at a certain point, I halted the Interview.* (emphasis added)[14]

The investigations, then, limited what statements a witness could make for the archive.[15] Consequently, it is important to retain the notion of

---

[12] ICTR–99–46, TRA000217/1, *[Cyangugu] – Ntagerura et al – Redacted Transcript of 24/10/2000*, 24October 2000, 16 and 38; and ICTR–99–46, TRA000438/1, *[Cyangugu] – Ntagerura et al – Redacted Transcript of 21/02/2001*, 21 February 2001, 44.

[13] ICTR–99–46, TRA000409/2, *[Cyangugu] – Ntagerura et al – Redacted Transcript of 07/05/2001*, 7 May 2001, 56.

[14] ICTR–99–46, TRA001616/1, *[Cyangugu] – Ntagerura et al – Redacted Transcript of 26/03/2002*, 26 March 2002, 18–19.

[15] Investigator (2015). Interview with Member of ICTR OTP 5 (June 2015); E/CN.4/1998/54/Add.1, *Further Promotion and Encouragement of Human Rights and Fundamental Freedoms, Including the Question of the Programme and Methods of Work of the Commission Alternative Approaches and Ways and Means within the United Nations System for Improving the Effective Enjoyment of Human Rights and Fundamental Freedoms Report of the Special Rapporteur on Violence against Women, Its Causes and Consequences, Ms. Radhika Coomaraswamy Addendum Report of the Mission to Rwanda on the Issues of Violence against Women in Situations of Armed Conflict*, 4 February 1998, 12–18; and A/51/789,

co-construction, with the witnesses working within the rules of the archive to produce the narrative frameworks that governed the trials without overstating the witnesses' agency.[16] Indeed, what is perhaps important here is the *relationship* between the witnesses and the lawyers. In accounts, such as Dembour and Haslam's that see courts as spaces filled with silence, agency seems like a zero-sum game where ultimately the witnesses lose out.[17] In contrast, as Foucault's understanding of power suggests, agency and power are *relational*, existing between subjects or objects. These relations are, therefore, dynamic and subject to contestation and resistance.

EXPANDING THE SCOPE

When analysing the trial transcripts from the archive, it became apparent that witnesses continued to shape, contest and expand the trials' frameworks when taking the stand. For example, during *Akayesu*, whilst testifying to other crimes charged within the indictment, two witnesses, Witnesses J and H, also testified to the occurrence of rape within the Taba commune. Witness J testified that her six-year-old child had been raped, whilst Witness H testified that she herself had been raped.[18] These statements sat uneasily within the courtroom at this point of the trial due to absence of sexual violence charges in the indictment. This meant that the defence had not been pre-warned of the allegations and so this testimony undermined their fair trial rights.[19] However, the testimony along with an *amicus curie* from a human rights organisation and the presence of Judge Pillay on the bench – who is said to have been particularly attentive to issues of gender-based violence – [20] led the prosecution to introduce six new counts relating to sexual violence in

---

Financing of the International Criminal Tribunal for the Prosecution of Persons Responsible for Genocide and Other Serious Violations of International Humanitarian Law Committed in the Territory of Rwanda and Rwandan Citizens Responsible for Genocide and Other Such Violations Committed in the Territory of Neighbouring States between 1 January and 31 December 1994: Report of the Secretary-General on the Activities of the Office of Internal Oversight Services, 6 February 1997, 2–3 and 17–20.). See also Interview with Member of ICTR OTP 2 (June 2015); Interview with Member of ICTR OTP 3 (June 2015); and Interview with Member of ICTR OTP 4 (June 2015).

[16] See also Eltringham, *Genocide Never Sleeps*, 143.

[17] Marie–Bénédicte Dembour and Emily Haslam, 'Silencing Hearings? Victim-Witnesses at War Crime Trials', *European Journal of International Law* 15:1 (2004): 151–77.

[18] ICTR–96–4, CONTRA001186, *Akayesu – Transcript of 27/1/1997*, 27 January 1997, 101–2; and ICTR–96–4, CONTRA001195, *Akayesu – Transcript of 6/3/1997*, 6 March 1997, 106–7.

[19] This, again, demonstrates the important interconnection between an archive's enunciative modalities and concepts.

[20] Interview with Appeals Judge (May 2016).

an amended indictment.[21] The judges, despite the fact that the prosecution's case had effectively come to a close, accepted this new indictment, and as a result a further five witnesses were called to testify. As discussed more shortly, the judges subsequently found that rape had occurred in Taba, and, in a ground-breaking ruling, that it was part of the genocide.

This is important for a number of reasons. First, this opened up a pathway for records relating to sexual violence to form a legitimate part of the archive. Moreover, soon after Witness H's and Witness J's testimonies, a special investigation unit tasked solely with investigating sexual violence crimes was created, which would (in theory at least) mean that an increasing volume of evidence pertaining to sexual violence would make it into the archive.[22]

Second, the expansion of the trial in this way at the close of the prosecution's case demonstrates that against the fair trial rights of the defendant were a sea of other considerations that were to determine the course of a case, including the rights of the victim.[23] As Allison Danner and Jenny Martinez argue, the early years of the ICTR and ICTY saw the intrusion of human rights discourse and practice into the workings of the courtroom.[24] This, in many respects, pulled in a different direction to the practice of criminal justice, as this discourse centred the victims' interests, rather than the defendants'. This injected a different notion of what 'justice' meant and represented the hope of the early 1990s that the end of the Cold War meant the realisation of a rights-based liberal internationalism within the international community.[25]

Whilst not downplaying the significance of these developments, it must be stressed that the additional sexual violence charges in *Akayesu*

---

[21] ICTR–96–4, ICTR–96–4–0183, *Akayesu – Amicus Brief Respecting Amendment of the Indictment and Supplementation of the Evidence to Ensure the Prosecution of Rape and Other Sexual Violence within the Competence of the tribunal*, 28 May 1997; Moore, 'The Story a UN Court Didn't Want Three Rape Survivors to Tell'; and ICTR–96–4, CONTRA001212, *Akayesu – Transcript of 17/6/1997 – Motion*, 17 June 1997, 8–12.

[22] UNGA, A/53/429, *Report of the International Criminal Tribunal for the Prosecution of Persons Responsible for Genocide and Other Serious Violations of International Humanitarian Law Committed in the Territory of Rwanda and Rwandan Citizens Responsible for Genocide and Other Such Violations Committed in the Territory of Neighbouring States between 1 January and 31 December 1994*, 23 September 1998; and E/CN.4/1998/54/Add.1.

[23] This idea of the rights of victims was taking hold in municipal courts at around the same time and can be seen in changes such as the introduction of victim statements during sentencing. Carolyn Hoyle and Leila Ullrich. 'New Court, New Justice? The Evolution of "Justice for Victims" at Domestic Courts and at the International Criminal Court', *Journal of International Criminal Justice* 12:4 (2014): 682–83; and OTP 5 (2015).

[24] Allison Danner and Jenny Martinez, 'Guilty Associations: Joint Criminal Enterprise, Command Responsibility, and the Development of International Criminal Law', *California Law Review* 93:1 (2005): 103–20, 132–39 and 145–46.

[25] This will be discussed at greater length in Chapters 5 and 6.

still maintained a legal quality and value. Even here the inclusion of sexual violence in *Akayesu* was only possible because Witnesses J's and H's statements captured acts of violence that were recognisable as crimes that could then be linked to the accused. It was notable that one of the prosecution's explanations for why these charges were not brought about earlier was that they previously had insufficient evidence to link the perpetration of sexual violence crimes specifically to Akayesu.[26] As such, the idea of co-construction retains its importance.

Further evidence of the witnesses' ability to (re)shape the trials' framework was seen in other instances when the witness testimony exceeded the boundaries of the indictment but was nonetheless allowed to form part of the archive. This was permitted when the content of the testimony was seen as sufficiently related to charges in the indictment so as not to endanger the defendants' rights to a fair trial. For example, on one occasion during *Cyangugu* when the defence attempted to exclude evidence about a weapons-drop that Bagambiki and Ntagerura had allegedly participated in, the judges responded:

> Mr President: Mr. Henry [defence counsel for Ntagerura], isn't there a distinction between a situation where there is no charge in the indictment and facts to be led to establish that charge, as against a situation where there is a charge in the indictment, and then facts to be led to establish that charge.[27]

And subsequently:

> Mr President: In paragraph 13 of the indictment there is some reference to arms and ammunition being distributed.
>
> Granted that this is not in Cyangugu proper with regard to the facts, but as part of the process of continuing acts. And in those circumstances we will overrule the objection, and we'll allow the evidence to be led.[28]

Similarly, during *Cyangugu* and *Gatete* the defence also tried to exclude witnesses' evidence on the grounds that it contained information that exceeded the parameters of their pre-trial statements and therefore violated the rights of the defendant. On a number of occasions, however, these

---

[26] Investigator (2015).

[27] ICTR–99–46, TRA000404/1, *[Cyangugu] – Ntagerura et al – Redacted Transcript of 11/09/2001*, 11 September 2001, 13.

[28] *Ibid.*, 18–19. For other examples see ICTR–99–46, TRA000750/01, *[Cyangugu] – Ntagerura et al – Redacted Transcript of 06/06/2001*, 6 June 2001, 79–85; TRA000404/01, 11 September 2001, 7–20; and ICTR–99–46, TRA000324/2, *[Cyangugu] – Ntagerura et al – Redacted Transcript of 04/03/2002 – Motion*, 4 March 2002, 69–70.

arguments failed, and the judges allowed the evidence to be heard. When, for example, the defence objected repeatedly to Witness NL's testimony that he had witnessed Ntagerura speak at meetings in Bushenge and Cyimbogo in 1993, the judges responded variously:

> Mr President: I would like to recall that what your Chamber several times explained to the Defence; that is, a witness statement cannot contain everything, no rule of procedure obliges an investigation to make sure that the witness says everything, because no witness is capable of saying everything that he has to say.[29]

[. . . .]

> Mr President: In addition to that, we have Rule 89, General Provisions, which says that 'The Chamber may admit any relevant evidence which it deems to have some probative value.'[30]

The judges' response here suggests that there was an accepted untameable quality about witness testimony, which meant that space had to be provided for witnesses to testify during the trial and that witnesses were not to be restricted solely to the evidence provided during the investigations. This implicitly underlined a similar argument utilised by the prosecution to rebut the defence's objection over a similar issue during *Gatete*:

PROSECUTION: Madam President, Your Honours. My response is, this is information which has just come out in evidence. We did not – prior to today – know about this [. . .].

JUDGE MUTHOGA: Counsel for the Prosecution has said it is not something she planned to put to you so that she could give you notice. She didn't know it herself [. . .]. It has come spontaneously from the witness.[31]

---

[29] TRA000438/1, 27.

[30] *Ibid.*, 31. In another particularly clear example of this a witness who was only scheduled to testify about an exhumation of a mass grave ended up testifying to a story about the extraction of his father from Karamapaka stadium at the orders of Bagambiki, noting that this was the last time that he had seen him before seeing his body exhumed. What is more, unlike the examples detailed subsequently, this evidence was clearly led by the prosecution rather than arising spontaneously. ICTR–99–46, TRA000533/1, *[Cyangugu] – Ntagerura et al – Redacted Transcript of 14/05/2001*, 14 May 2001, 69–73.

[31] *Prosecutor v. Jean Baptiste Gatete*, Case No. ICTR–00–61 (hereafter ICTR–00–61), TRA005458, *Gatete – Redacted Transcript of 22/10/2009*, 22 October 2009, 39–40; ICTR–00–61, TRA005461, *Gatete – Redacted Transcript of 13/11/2009*, 13 November 2009, 15. See also CONTRA018137, *Gatete – Redacted Transcript of 04/11/2009*, 4 November 2009, 42; and ICTR–00–61, TRA005507/ 2, *Gatete – Redacted Transcript of 10/11/2009*, 10 November 2009, 56.

Even when the defence intervened again to argue that the testimony was 'prejudicial' the judges responded:

MR PRESIDENT: You can't stop the witness. You can't prevent the witness from giving answers.

[...]

WITNESS: I must say this. When I was interviewed, I did not provide these details. I answered the questions as they were put to me and as they are being put to me here before the Chamber.[32]

In-trial testimony could, then, significantly add to the information collected during the pre-trial stage. As such, what was a pre-trial statement that might only consist of a handful of notes (which might be either verbatim testimony or a summary of the statement) could turn into a lengthy testimony once the witness took to the stand.[33] One former investigator noted an instance when a pre-trial statement of three pages became an in-court testimony that took up a whole trial session (about fifteen days).[34] The ability of witnesses to expand the scope of the indictments was, undoubtedly, also aided by the vague nature of the prosecution's indictments, especially in the early years. This increased the scope through which the judges could decide that a witness's testimony, even if loosely, aligned with charges in the indictment.

The dynamic relationship between the witnesses and the court was evident in other ways too, particularly in terms of who was to testify in court. For instance, changes within Rwanda at around the turn of the century, including the advent of *Gacaca* and the increased pace of domestic trials, meant that perpetrators became increasingly willing to act as ICTR witnesses. These changes meant that perpetrators had already been legally processed domestically and so no longer faced the danger of potentially incriminating themselves whilst testifying to crimes they had participated in. This resulted in a shift in the prosecution's investigation strategy as they began to rely on 'insider' or 'accomplice' witnesses, rather than victim witnesses, which meant that the prosecution could more easily connect

---

[32] TRA005458, 43.
[33] Eltringham notes that in 2004 there was a shift to the sole use of verbatim (or what he calls dialogic) statements. Eltringham, *Genocide Never Sleeps*, 138–40.
[34] Investigator (2015).

the genocide's leaders to the acts of violence committed on the ground,[35] which also resulted in an increased use of superior responsibility charges.[36] This also fundamentally altered what types of accounts were created, and from which vantage point these were told, as the episodes of violence would now be narrated from the position of the perpetrators.[37]

THE MEANING OF VIOLENCE

The witnesses' records also produced much 'messier' accounts of the violence than the legal discourse sought, as outlined in Chapter 3. In places these records undermined the discourse's construction of particular ideas about victimhood and perpetratorhood, as well as its attempts to extract what was generalisable about the episodes of violence and the witnesses' experience.[38]

Within the witnesses' testimonies, the narrative tropes of resistance and survival, for instance, pushed back against the notion of victims' inherent passivity. Traces of this can be found first of all in the accounts that documented the victims' resistance against the attackers in those places the victims had sought refuge.[39] This resistance was often only overcome after the local authorities intervened with reinforcements for the attackers; as occurred in Mukarange Parish, in Kibungo, when Gatete provided grenades to the attackers, and Nyange Parish, in Kibuye, where local officials resorted to destroying the church completely with the refugees inside after they determined that this was the only way to

---

[35] A similar impact was seen with the guilty pleas made by former Prime Minister Jean Kambanda and a senior figure in the Interahamwe, Omar Serushago, which provided firm evidence of the existence of a conspiracy and helped demonstrate that what happened across Rwanda was part of the same genocidal plan. ICTR–99–46–0001, Prosecutor's Motion for Joinder of the Accused (Ntagerura, ICTR–96–10A–T0, Bagambiki ICTR–97–36–T, Imanishimwe ICTR–97–36–I, and Munyakazi ICTR–97–36–I), 2 April 1999, 3.

[36] Investigator (2015). I would surmise that this can be seen in Cyangugu, where at trial only ten of forty-one witnesses who appeared had been included in the initial witness list submitted in 1997 – and the vast majority of those called were 'insider witnesses'. ICTR–99–46, TRA002960, [Cyangugu] – Ntagerura et al – Redacted Transcript of 06/02/2006 – Appeals Hearing, 6 February 2006, 73–74.

[37] Investigator (2015). ICTR–96–10, ICTR–96–10A–0006, Ntagerura – Request for Extension of Detention, 18 June 1996, 6; ICTR–97–36, ICTR–97–36–00189, Bagambiki – Audio Recording of 08/09/97 – AM, 8 September 1997; and ICTR–99–46, TRA000434/2, [Cyangugu] – Ntagerura et al – Redacted Transcript of 14/02/2001, 14 February 2001, 30.

[38] This drive to extract what is generalisable is, for Payam Akahavan, fundamental to the practice of law. Payam Akahavan, Reducing Genocide to Law: Definition, Meaning, and the Ultimate Crime (Cambridge: Cambridge University Press, 2012), 174.

[39] ICTR–99–46, TRA001796/1, [Cyangugu] – Ntagerura et al – Redacted Transcript of 23/10/2002, 23 October 2002, 9–11; ICTR–99–46, TRA000122/01, [Cyangugu] – Ntagerura et al – Redacted Transcript of 09/10/2000, 9 October 2000, 13–34; and TRA005458, 46–48.

overcome the refugees' resistance.[40] Resistance came in other forms also: during *Akayesu* Witness N testified how she continued to withhold information about the location of her daughter-in-law, Alexia, despite Akayesu torturing her.[41] Witness N told Akayesu, '[I]f you continue hitting me with all the strength that it left in me I will bite you with my teeth.'[42] After this, Akayesu and the *Interahamwe* he was with stopped questioning her. Being a victim did not, then, necessarily signify passivity.

The symbolism attached to the act of testifying itself could also signify survival and resistance. By giving a voice to victimised groups, testimony defied the attempt to wipe out all traces of that group.[43] Here, moreover, the witnesses' testimony could help to determine the criminality of an accused's action and so afforded them a chance to invert the power dynamics of the violence and contribute to deciding the accused's fate. A particularly powerful example of this was when the witnesses' testimony captured the accused's voice, such as Witness JJ's evidence that Akayesu, having authorised the mass rape of women at the bureau communal, uttered the words, 'Never ask me again what a Tutsi tastes like.'[44] This unequivocally showed Akayesu's discriminatory intent against the Tutsi and significantly contributed towards proving Akayesu's genocidal intent both generally and in relation to the sexual violence charges.

The inversion of the genocide's power dynamics was particularly apparent during Witness N's testimony in *Akayesu*. Importantly, at this point in the trial the judges permitted Akayesu to personally cross-examine the

---

[40] ICTR–00–61, ICTR–00–61–0240/1, *Gatete – Judgement and Sentence*, 31 March 2011, 4, 9 and 90; and *Prosecutor v. Grégoire Ndahimana*, Case No. ICTR–01–68, *Trial Judgement*, 30 December 2001), 143–53.

[41] ICTR–96–4, CONTRA001183, *Akayesu – Transcript of 15/1/1997*, 15 January 1997, 106–19.

[42] *Ibid.*, 115–16.

[43] Shoshana Felman, 'Fire in the Archive: The Alignment of Witnesses', in *The Future of Testimony: Interdisciplinary Perspectives on Witnessing*, eds. Anthony Rowland and Jane Jun (Florence: Routledge, 2014), 50–51.

[44] ICTR–96–4, CONTRA001222, *Akayesu – Transcript of 23/10/1997*, 23 October 1997, 77. Another particularly good example of this was Witness C's testimony that he had heard Akayesu say, 'I do not think that what we are doing is proper. We are going to have to pay for this blood that is being shed.' TRA001178, *Akayesu – Transcript of 14/1/1997*, 14 January 1997, 154.

PROSECUTION:	You confirm that you did not see Akayesu kill?
WITNESS:	That depends on what you call kill, because if Akayesu had wanted to, nobody would have been killed.
PROSECUTION:	Well, I am asking you a question. Please answer the question the tribunal is asking. Did you see Akayesu kill a person with his own hands? I want to be clear on this?
WITNESS:	No, he had killed by orders.

ICTR–96–4, CONTRA001180, *Akayesu – Transcript of 22/1/1997*, 22 January 1997, 149.

witnesses whilst they rendered a decision on Akayesu's request to change defence counsel for a second time. In the following extract, Witness N was in no doubt of Akayesu's responsibility for her suffering:

MR PRESIDENT: As regards the death of these people, did you see this, did you witness their death, or did you hear that these people had been killed by Akayesu, or are you just deducing this based on the fact that they were taken away by Akayesu? There are three scenarios here.

THE WITNESS: *Ask [Akayesu] where he took them.* I maintain that *he* is the one who killed them. *I will persist in saying that he is the one who killed them.* I have not seen them since *he* took them away. (emphasis added)[45]

This tension peaked when Akayesu cross-examined Witness N directly:

AKAYESU: You said that the only time Akayesu came to your house he killed and went back. Who did he kill?

THE WITNESS: *You* started by killing Ntereye, after that *you* killed his wife Alexia. In fact, *you* killed the entire Ntereye family on that same day. (emphasis added)[46]

The witness's accusations were incessant, and every time she mentioned a crime or violent act she stated that 'you' (i.e. Akayesu) were responsible for it.[47] This also challenges the notion that these courts produce generalised accounts of violence that are abstracted to the point of irrelevance for the witnesses; Witness N was very much aware of who they felt was responsible for the crimes they had suffered.

Witnesses' accounts of violence, then, defied a notion of a universal victim experience. For some, the violence suffered and survived was worse than dying or a disembodied moment of unimaginable trauma;

---

[45] CONTRA001183, 132–33.

[46] ICTR–96–4, CONTRA001184, *Akayesu – Transcript of 16/1/1997*, 16 January 1997, 4.

[47] See the whole of this exchange: *Ibid.*, 4–52. Another example is:

PROSECUTION: And can you tell the judges how you knew Jean-Baptiste Gatete?

WITNESS: I know him. I know him in particular, because during the war of 1994, he attacked us and exterminated members of our families. He attacked us in the churches where we had sought refuge and in other places. Many people were killed. So those are the circumstances in which I know him. I know him as a result of his acts.

ICTR–00–61, TRA005459, *Gatete – Redacted Transcript of 05/11/2009*, 5 November 2009, 14. See also CONTRA018137, 49; and TRA005507/2, 60. See also CONTRA001176, 54; and ICTR–96–4, CONTRA001178, *Akayesu – Transcript of 14/1/1997*, 14 January 1997, 154.

for others, the inflicted injuries still affected their lives in the present; and for others still the final moments before a massacre were moments of religious reflection.[48] It was even possible for the court to accept two distinct understandings of the same episode of violence by different witnesses. In the following example witnesses variously described refugees singing a death march as they were forced out of a church to be murdered as a final act of resistance or humiliation.

> The Interahamwe got us out of the church. They asked the refugees to get out of the church. Some refugees were saying that we should accept to be killed inside the church whereas others had accepted to go out in order to be killed outside the church. So we linked hands and went out of the church singing the song, 'We Were Created to Go to Heaven'.[49]

A different witness, however, testified:

> When I came back inside the church with my children, shortly thereafter, I believe it was around 10 a.m., I went near the altar, then I saw soldiers enter the church and people started going out. A soldier asked us to sing the funeral dirge which was titled 'We were created to go to heaven.' When we started singing that song, the soldiers made us get out of the church and brought us to the courtyard.[50]

The idea of the deontological and generalisable nature of legal accounts of violence was further challenged by the way that local contexts and personal relationships clearly influenced the violence captured in the records.[51] Witness NN stated, for example, how the person that raped her told her, just before assaulting her, that whilst she had rejected him before the war she now could not, capturing both the locally situated nature of the violence and also the centrality of patriarchal structures within the genocide.[52] In other instances prior encounters could lead to survival.

48
    PROSECUTION: [W]hat was going through your mind, Witness?
    WITNESS: I cannot describe exactly what was going on in my mind. I thought I was going to die. But it was not just ordinary death, it was as if the air was breaking loose on us. It was the end of the world to us.

ICTR–99–46, TRA000218/1, [Cyangugu] – Ntagerura et al – Redacted Transcript of 25/10/2000, 25 October 2000, 74. See also CONTRA001183, 119; ICTR–00–61, TRA005158/1, Gatete – Redacted Transcript of 17/03/2010, 17 March 2010, 63; ICTR–00–61, TRA001643/1, Gatete – Redacted Transcript of 20/10/2009, 20 October 2009, 23–24; and CONTRA001222, 59–62.

49 ICTR–00–61, TRA005490/2, Gatete – Redacted Transcript of 21/10/2009, 21 October 2009, 56.
50 TRA005458, 5.
51 TRA000218/1, 62; CONTRA001222, 20; and ICTR–00–61, TRA005491/2, Gatete – Redacted Transcript of 03/11/2009, 3 November 2009, 16.
52 ICTR–96–4, CONTRA001227, Akayesu – Transcript of 3/11/1997, 3 November 1997, 20.

During *Gatete* a witness noted how, after regaining consciousness in a mass grave, an *Interahamwe* saw that she was alive, recognised her, and took her out of the pit to his home.[53] Witness PP, in *Akayesu*, noted how the persons that came to kill her stopped when an *Interahamwe*, Rafiki, recognised her as someone that had been kind to him in the past because she had given him a sandwich.[54] Nevertheless, Rafiki subsequently kept Witness NN captive for days on end during which time he repeatedly raped her.[55]

As this also suggests, the witnesses' testimony presented different understandings of what it meant to be a perpetrator during the genocide; as the examples mentioned earlier show, 'perpetrators' could, as well as committing horrendous acts of violence, also be 'saviours' and 'resisters'. These accounts particularly came through after the prosecution turned to perpetrator witnesses in the early 2000s, which introduced the possibility that formerly concealed elements of the genocide (such as the planning of the violence) could come into view.[56] These captured the myriad ways and reasons that people came to participate in the killing. There were statements that showed that witnesses participated out of a sense of obligation, noting the work-like nature of the violence,[57] or that the violence was seen as a service to the community.[58] Elsewhere, witnesses stated that participating in the genocide was just a way to make money.[59] Other witnesses suggested that violence committed as part of the genocide became something that was understood by the population as being de facto legal:

PROSECUTION: Mr. Witness, I'm still interested in this meeting with Félicien, when he gives you instructions to kill. When he told you that, you knew that killing was a crime; right?

WITNESS: I knew that killing was a crime, but after Habyarimana was killed, no one considered killing to be a crime. It is only later that I confessed to the crimes that I committed and asked for forgiveness. But at the beginning of the events, I did not consider killing to be a crime.

---

[53] TRA005458, 8.

[54] ICTR–96–4, CONTRA001205, *Akayesu – Transcript of 4/11/1997*, 4 November 1997, 141.

[55] CONTRA001227, 46–47.

[56] Having 'insiders' also made it easier – in theory – to link senior figures in the genocide with crimes committed on the ground. Interview with ICTR Investigator (June 2015).

[57] See also ICTR–00–61, TRA005152/1, *Gatete – Redacted Transcript of 08/03/2010*, 8 March 2010, 64.

[58] During another testimony, a witness similarly noted the communal nature of the violence, as represented by the killing and eating of cows after participating in the violence. CONTRA001178, 107.

[59] ICTR–99–46, TRA000126/02, *[Cyangugu] – Ntagerura et al – Redacted Transcript of 23/10/2000*, 23 October 2000, 66 and 101.

PROSECUTION: And you considered that killing was not a crime because you were told by the authorities to go and kill.

WITNESS: Yes. That is correct.

PROSECUTION: So you considered that you were acting in compliance with the directions of the local authorities.

WITNESS: Yes. That is correct, because that's what happened.

PROSECUTION: And you wouldn't have killed, except for the fact that you were told.

WITNESS: If I had not been – if I had not been given the orders to kill, I would not have killed anyone.[60]

This is not to say that this worked *against* the archive's legal interests nor undermined the legal value of the record. The extract mentioned earlier, which notes the authorities' involvement, for instance, helped to establish the local authorities' (such as Gatete) responsibility for the violence and as such advanced the prosecution's case. This type of testimony could also counter the defence's (ironic) contention that a witness's perpetrator status meant that their credibility should automatically be suspected, as this helped to contextualise their reasons for participation and so challenged the idea that perpetrator witnesses were sadistic killers that could not be trusted.[61] The same was true for the victims' narratives noted earlier, whereby as long as the legal criteria were also met there was nothing detrimental about these fuller accounts of the violence. In many respects this made the testimony more compelling and therefore arguably *increased its probative value*. The most pertinent example of potential overlap here was, again, the symbolism attached to witnesses' capturing of the accused's own voice and hence inverting the power dynamics of the genocide – such as Witness PP's statement that Akayesu had declared 'Never ask me again what a Tutsi tastes like' – and the *legal* role that this played in establishing the accused's intent. This, therefore, continues to support the notion of the co-construction of the archive.

EXPERT WITNESSES

In addition to 'perpetrator' and 'victim' witnesses, 'expert' witnesses also significantly shaped the archive.[62] The notion of 'expertise' was, as

---

[60] TRA005152/1, 85.

[61] See, for example, ICTR–99–46, TRA002063/1, [*Cyangugu*] – *Ntagerura et al – Redacted Transcript of 13/08/2003*, 13 August 2003, 27–30.

[62] For discussion of expert witnesses see Fergal Gaynor, 'Uneasy Partners – Evidence, Truth and History in International Trials', *Journal of International Criminal Justice* 10 (2012): 1262;

with all aspects of the archive, constituted in particular ways.[63] To be heard as an expert, the parties had to establish the prospective witness's experience and qualifications in a relevant field and the probative value of their evidence. I would argue, however, following Eltringham, that the lack of clarity in the rules of evidence and procedure on what constituted a legitimate expert afforded the judges' considerable leeway when deciding if a particular expert was relevant and in possession of the necessary expertise. As such, what was defined as 'expert knowledge' was relatively broadly interpreted at the ICTR.[64] This, for instance, covered academics that were, indisputably, leaders of their fields – such as Alison Des Forges, discussed more subsequently. But these rules also allowed testimony from disciplines that have been highly criticised, such as 'ethno-psychology' – a practice that has strong links to colonialism.[65] From the trials examined here, experts made two clear contributions to the archive. First, these expert witnesses provided statements that helped the tribunal to better understand the historical background to the genocide. Second, they influenced how the tribunal interpreted the evidence being presented.[66]

The best example of the first type of expert was the aforementioned Des Forges, who featured prominently in almost all of the early trials and also acted as an advisor to the prosecution more generally.[67] Des Forges testified in *Akayesu* and her importance was evident by the length of her testimony, which lasted for eight trial days (eight times as long as any other witness's testimony) as she provided a history of Rwanda, beginning in the pre-colonial era and continuing all the way through to the genocide itself.[68] This was extremely detailed testimony,

Ruti Teitel, *Transitional Justice* (Oxford: Oxford University Press, 2000), 69–75; Gerry Simpson, *Law, War and Crime: War Crimes Trials and the Reinvention of International Law* (Cambridge: Polity Press, 2007), 79–80; Richard Wilson, *Writing History in International Criminal Trials* (Cambridge: Cambridge University Press, 2010), 12–20, 69–86, 112–13 and 121–28; and Nigel Eltringham, 'Illuminating the Broader Context: Anthropological and Historical Knowledge at the International Criminal Tribunal for Rwanda', *Journal of the Royal Anthropological Institute* 19:2 (2013): 342.

[63] Eltringham, 'Illuminating the Broader Context', 350–52.

[64] *Ibid.*, 342–44.

[65] ICTR–99–46, TRA001286/2, *[Cyangugu] – Ntagerura et al – Redacted Transcript of 08/07/2002 – Motion*, 8 July 2002, 25 and 36.

[66] Eltringham, 'Illuminating the Broader Context', 350.

[67] Interview with Member of ICTR OTP 8 (June 2015).

[68] ICTR–96–4, CONTRA001199, *Akayesu – Transcript of 11/2/1997*, 11 February 1997; ICTR–96–4, CONTRA001200, *Akayesu – Transcript of 12/2/1997*, 12 February 1997; ICTR–96–4, CONTRA001191, *Akayesu – Transcript of 13/2/1997*, 13 February 1997; ICTR–96–4, CONTRA001192, *Akayesu – Transcript of 14/2/1997*, 14 February 1997; ICTR–96–4, CONTRA001193, *Akayesu – Transcript of 18/2/1997*, 18 February 1997; ICTR–96–4, CONTRA001209, *Akayesu – Transcript of 22/5/1997*, 22 May 1997;

which at points was more like a lecture than an in-court witnesses statement, as Des Forges spoke almost completely uninterrupted for hours at a time. This testimony provided the main content for the judgment's historical context section in *Akayesu* and most subsequent trials and was also key in the judges' determination that what occurred in Rwanda was genocide.[69]

Des Forges also provided a framework which helped to explicate Akayesu's actions, as her history of Rwanda (especially its political history) overlapped with the prosecution's explanation of how Akayesu came to be involved in the genocide. This captured the historic use of violence against Tutsis as a means to secure local patronage, and the importance of the shifting political landscape in Rwanda for understanding the genocide – both crucial in the prosecution's explanation for how Akayesu came to participate in the genocide.[70] In particular, Des Forges highlighted the significance of the introduction of multiparty politics, the growth of the MDR party (Akayesu's party) as the main opposition to the MRND, and the use of ethno-nationalism by Hutu extremists as a tool to unify what was a fractured political landscape around a common cause: genocide against the Tutsi and the eradication of all dissident voices.[71] This testimony explained why Akayesu, as a member of the opposition party, would resist the violence in the first weeks of the genocide (as discussed in Chapter 3) and then become a willing participant when the interim government called, on 18 April, for a cross-party alliance so that all of those in positions of privilege could retain political power by executing a genocidal policy nationwide against all those that threatened the status quo (whether this threat was real or imagined), and particularly the Tutsi. Through Des Forges's testimony the genocide in Taba became a microcosm of the genocide at a national level.[72]

---

[69] ICTR–96–4, CONTRA001210, *Akayesu – Transcript of 23/5/1997*, 23 May 1997; and ICTR–96–4, CONTRA001211, *Akayesu – Transcript of 24/5/1997*, 24 May 1997.

[70] ICTR–96–4, ICTR–96–4–0459/1, *Akayesu – Judgement*, 2 September 1998, 27–39.

[71] CONTRA001200, 42–44.

[72] CONTRA001191, 24–28, 121–24 and 132–34; and CONTRA001193, 59–60 and 101–3.

This type of testimony was also seen during *Cyangugu*, where Professor Guichaoua testified as an expert witness, and not only provided a similar framework through which the violence could be understood, but even more explicitly detailed the guilt of the accused. ICTR–99–46, TRA000543/01, *[Cyangugu] – Ntagerura et al – Redacted Transcript of 19/09/2001*, 19 September 2001, 47; ICTR–99–46, TRA000546/2, *[Cyangugu] – Ntagerura et al – Redacted Transcript of 20/09/2001*, 20 September 2001; and ICTR–99–46, TRA001774/1, *[Cyangugu] – Ntagerura et al – Redacted Transcript of 24/09/2001*, 24 September 2001.

There were, of course, limits to how this type of testimony was able to contribute to the trials and archive. In particular, expert testimony was, unlike fact witnesses' testimony, unable to directly contribute towards establishing the factual case against the accused – as it was treated, essentially, as 'hearsay'. This could have significant consequences. In *Cyangugu*, for instance, the expert witness André Guichaoua provided evidence that clearly demonstrated that the so-called pacification meetings held by Ntagerura and Bagambiki were really convened to organise the genocide.[73] However, under the archive's rules the judges were unable to rely on this in their factual findings against Bagambiki and Ntagerura, and the failure to do so significantly contributed to the defendant's acquittal. If the court had accepted Guichaoua's evidence, this would have unequivocally demonstrated the pair's genocidal intent, their authority in the local area and their contribution to the planning and execution of the genocide.[74]

The second type of expert witness, which also featured in *Akayesu*, was introduced to explain Rwandan culture, both to help with the court's understanding of the violence and also to assist it with interpreting Rwandan witnesses' evidence. The OTP drew on this form of testimony to help address several difficulties that the witnesses' testimonies had created for them.[75] Particularly problematic, from the prosecution's perspective, was the witnesses' evasive style of answering during examination and difficulties in ascertaining the source of the witnesses' knowledge, as the witnesses often seemed to confuse what they had seen and heard (i.e. hearsay evidence – which carried less probative value according to the courts rules).[76] As such, a Rwandese cultural and linguistic expert, Professor Mathias Ruzindana, was called to explain some of these 'issues'.[77] His testimony stated that the

---

[73] Bagambiki admitted that the message of the meeting was 'to incite citizens to continue to track the enemy, regardless of where he is hiding and wherever he is hiding weapons without, however, threatening or mistreating innocent persons'. Within the discourses circulating within Rwanda during the genocide, and the equation of the Tutsis with the enemy, then this was a clear directive to continue the genocide. ICTR–99–46, TRA001918/1, *[Cyangugu] – Ntagerura et al – Redacted Transcript of 27/03/2003*, 27 March 2003, 34–36.

[74] ICTR-99–46–0609/1, *[Cyangugu] – Ntagerura et al – Prosecutor's Notice of Appeal*, 25 March 2004; ICTR–99–46–0599/1, 31 and 47.

[75] As discussed in Chapter 6, this is not to 'essentialise' Rwandan culture, nor to present it as the obstacle to the 'truth'. What becomes apparent, however, was that legal actors very much saw it in this way. Eltringham, *Genocide Never Sleeps*, 121–24.

[76] Ruzindana (2015).

[77] See generally Ruzindana's testimony on ICTR–96–4, CONTRA001189, *Akayesu – Transcript of 30/1/1997*, 30 January 1997, 105–165. See also ICTR–96–4, CONTRA001190, *Akayesu – Transcript of 4/2/1997*, 4 February 1997; and Carla Del Ponte, 'Investigation and Prosecution of

witnesses' defensiveness during examination could be explained by Rwandan's suspicion of unfamiliar persons in positions of authority, and because they were unaccustomed with the criminal justice process.[78] He also stated that because Rwandan society was rooted in an oral culture witnesses did not always distinguish between what they saw and heard. Whilst Rwandans could, of course, tell the difference, the court would need to ask specifically about the source of their information if they wished to be sure of this.[79] As discussed subsequently, this testimony significantly shaped how the tribunal approached the witnesses' testimony.

It is, as such, possible to see how historical, anthropological, linguistic and social science discourses interwove with legal ones to determine the rules of the archive. This further resonates with Richard Wilson's argument that history, along with other academic disciplines, became legally relevant at the ad hoc international criminal tribunals, shaping both the prosecution's overall strategy, and setting the context through which the court could understand the accounts of violence produced by fact witnesses.[80]

SETTING THE RULES AND JUDGING GENOCIDE

With perhaps greater consequence, analysing the archive, and particularly the trial judgments, demonstrates that witnesses' influence extended beyond shaping the factual account of the violence, but also what was considered a crime and, building on the findings mentioned earlier, how the court assessed the evidence that came before it.

The judgments were, in many respects, the records most marked by the legal discourse. At this point, bits of testimony could be dismissed if, for instance, they sat beyond the boundaries of the indictment and were seen to infringe the defendant's rights.[81] In the *Akayesu* judgment, the judges decided that the prosecution had failed to properly charge Akayesu under Article 6(3) of the statute (command responsibility) for the sexual violence crimes committed by the *Interahamwe* in the Taba commune, which meant that swaths of witness testimony was disregarded at this moment. In the end, only those instances where

Large-Scale Crimes at the International Level', *Journal of International Criminal Justice* 4:3 (2006): 553.
[78] CONTRA001189, 164–71.
[79] Ibid., 172–76.
[80] Wilson, *Writing History in International Criminal Trials*, 12–20, 69–86, 112–13 and 121–28.
[81] For example, see ICTR–96–4–0459/1, 184.

Akayesu was actually present during the perpetration of sexual violence were allowed to contribute to Akayesu's guilt.[82] It was also in the judgment that the judges decided on the witnesses' credibility.[83] This was determined by the judges' assessment of how 'convincing' a witness's performance was, shaped by particular imaginings of how a credible witness would testify. This was based on a witness's ability to tell a story that was internally coherent; told in a clear and orderly way, with as little emotion as was possible; and aligned with other accounts of the events given by other witnesses. It was, furthermore, important that the witness answered any questions during the cross-examination directly and quickly.[84]

Yet the witnesses' mark on the archive was also clear in the judgments.[85] An interesting phenomenon at the ICTR in this respect was the way that the judges seemingly tried to make 'allowances' for the cultural specificity of the Rwandan witnesses and their traumatic experiences when judging their testimony.[86] Evidence of the court's adaptation was seen in the *Akayesu* judgment where the judges explicitly drew on Ruzindana's expert testimony, discussed earlier, when explaining how they interpreted the witnesses'

---

[82] ICTR–96–4–0459/1, 168–70. Other narratives were also rejected in the final judgment, such as the repeated sexual assaults suffered by Witness NN at her home with her sister (Witness JJ) in front of her mother. CONTRA001227, 3 November 1997, 16–48. It must also be remembered that many of the narratives constructed during the trial find *no* place within the final judgment at all. For instance, during *Cyangugu*, all the evidence regarding the tension within the community – and the claims of RPF infiltration – produced during the trial were completely absent from the judgment. ICTR–99–46–0599/1.

[83] ICTR–96–4, CONTRA001183, *Akayesu – Transcript of 15/1/1997*, 15 January 1997; ICTR–99–46, TRA001288/2, *[Cyangugu] – Ntagerura et al – Redacted Transcript of 11/07/2002*, 11 July 2002, 79–80. Interview with Member of ICTR OTP 3 (2015); ICTR–96–4, ICTR–96–4–0459/1, *Akayesu – Judgement*, 2 September 1998, 36; ICTR–99–46–0599/1, 27, 30, 34 and 84; and ICTR–00–61, ICTR–00–61–0240/1, *Gatete – Judgement and Sentence*, 31 March 2011, 103. The judges' assessment was also influenced by decisions over the different levels of reliability of different types of witness and about the different possible contributions that they were permitted to make to the court's final 'truth'. Some of these factors that particularly affected the trials' outcomes were the prioritisation of witnesses that had seen a crime, over those that had heard about it; and a general scepticism of perpetrator witnesses. ICTR-99–46–0609/1, *[Cyangugu] – Ntagerura et al – Prosecutor's Notice of Appeal*, 25 March 2004; ICTR–99–46–0599/1, 31 and 47.

[84] ICTR–96–4, CONTRA001183, *Akayesu – Transcript of 15/1/1997*, 15 January 1997; ICTR–99–46, TRA001288/2, *[Cyangugu] – Ntagerura et al – Redacted Transcript of 11/07/2002*, 11 July 2002, 79–80. Head of Appeals (2015); ICTR–96–4, ICTR–96–4–0459/1, *Akayesu – Judgement*, 2 September 1998, 36; ICTR–99–46–0599/1, 27, 30, 34 and 84; and ICTR–00–61, ICTR–00–61–0240/1, *Gatete – Judgement and Sentence*, 31 March 2011, 103. ICTR, 'Testifying before the International Criminal Tribunal for Rwanda', 06FB002 (Arusha: 2005).

[85] ICTR–96–4–0459/1, 41.

[86] Interview with ICTR Judge (June 2015).

testimonies.[87] Having accepted Ruzindana's explanation as to why witnesses did not always distinguish between what they had seen and heard, the judges stated:

> According to the testimony of Dr. [sic] Ruzindana, it is a particular feature of the Rwandan culture that people are not always direct in answering questions, especially if the question is delicate. In such cases, the answers given will very often have to be 'decoded' in order to be understood correctly. This interpretation will rely on the context, the particular speech community, the identity of and the relation between the orator and the listener, and the subject matter of the question. The Chamber noted this in the proceedings.[88]

And went on to note that

> cultural constraints were evident in [the witnesses] difficulty to be specific as to dates, times, distances and locations. The Chamber also noted the inexperience of witnesses with maps, film and graphic representations of localities, in the light of this understanding [sic], the Chamber did not draw any adverse conclusions regarding the credibility of witnesses based only on their reticence and their sometimes circuitous responses to questions.[89]

Another issue was accounting for the changes between witnesses' pre-trial and trial statements, which, as aforementioned, the defence regularly argued undermined their credibility.[90] However, here the witnesses' traumatic experience was drawn on to explicate these shifts, and whilst there were instances where witnesses were successfully challenged because of this, the judges in *Akayesu* set a clear marker for how this issue was to be dealt with:

> Many of the eyewitnesses who testified before the Chamber in this case have seen atrocities committed against their family members or close friends, and/or have themselves been the victims of such atrocities. The possible traumatism [sic] of these witnesses caused by their painful experience of violence during the conflict in Rwanda is a matter of particular concern to the Chamber. The recounting of this traumatic experience is likely to evoke memories of the fear and the pain once

---

[87] Indeed, I have not found any instances where a witness was deemed not to be credible solely on their inability to 'accurately' recall dates, times and distances. The only instances where this was the case was where subsequent site visits or measurements indicated that the witness could not have seen or heard what they claimed to be able to. ICTR–99–46–0599/1, 46.

[88] ICTR–96–4–0459/1, 76–77.

[89] *Ibid.*, 77.

[90] For an example see *Ibid.*, 79.

inflicted on the witness and thereby affect his or her ability fully or adequately to recount the sequence of events in a judicial context. The Chamber has considered the testimony of those witnesses in this light [. . .]. *Inconsistencies or imprecisions in the testimonies, accordingly, have been assessed in the light of this assumption, personal background and the atrocities they have experienced or have been subjected to.* (emphasis added)[91]

Overall, this significantly affected how evidence was assessed at the ICTR[92] and meant that the judges, at times, overlooked relatively serious issues with the witnesses' testimony.[93] For example, when Witness LAW during *Cyangugu* stated that they could not personally identify Bagambiki in court as a result of the traumatic nature of their experience, the court still accepted that the witness had encountered Bagambiki during the genocide, as claimed during LAW's trial testimony.[94] In *Akayesu*, a particularly serious shift in testimony, which the judges nonetheless accepted as credible, occurred during Witness D's testimony. Whilst Witness D's pre-trial statement claimed that he had buried his brothers after Akayesu had killed them, during

---

[91] ICTR–96–4–0459/1, 42. The prosecution also specifically drew on the level of trauma and destruction experienced throughout Rwanda as part of their justification for why their evidence perhaps did not meet the standards that would usually be expected, such as their inability often to name specific victims of the massacres. ICTR–99–46, TRA000446/2, *[Cyangugu]* – *Ntagerura et al – Redacted Transcript of 09/05/2001*, 9 May 2001, 82–83. See also TRA002053/1, 2.

[92] There was, more generally, a relatively broad approach towards evidence at the tribunal from the very outset. This meant, for instance, that hearsay evidence was permitted, and uncorroborated testimony was also allowed to form the basis of judicial decisions, unlike in most common-law systems (which formed the basis of the court's rules). The rules clearly specified, moreover, that this was the case with sexual violence testimony, demonstrating, it appeared, a departure from the deep scepticism that this type of testimony normally was subjected to in courts. ICTR Rules of Procedure and Evidence, Rule 96(i); Gideon Boas, 'Creating Laws of Evidence for International Criminal Law: the ICTY and the Principle of Flexibility', *Criminal Law Forum* 12:1 (2001): 51. What is also notable here is that the level of specificity *expected* of the prosecution altered depending on the magnitude of the violence. With crimes like murder, the names of the victims and perpetrators, as well as the date, time and location of the crime were expected. With large-scale massacres, however, less specificity was required. ICTR–96–10, ICTR–96–10A–00347, *Ntagerura – Audio Recording: Defence Motion*, 19 March 1999.

[93] The defence considered this to be a serious issue and during *Rutaganda* the defence counsel unsuccessfully lodged an appeal against the trial chamber's decision to make 'allowances' for discrepancies in witness testimony due to the 'cultural specificity' of the witnesses. Eric Stover, *The Witnesses* (Philadelphia: University of Pennsylvania Press, 2005), 10.

[94] ICTR–99–46–0599/1, 160; TRA000441/1, 105; ICTR–00–61–0240/1, 78. This was not, however, always enough as the manner in which a narrative was told could mean that the judges did reject the credibility of a witness. 'In addition, the Chamber found Witness AIK's evidence confusing and inconsistent. While the Chamber acknowledges the impact of trauma on a witness's memory, in this instance, these ambiguities raise further questions about his reliability. In sum, the Chamber finds Witness AIK's evidence insufficient to support findings beyond reasonable doubt.' ICTR–00–61–0240/1, 51.

the trial Witness D claimed that he *hadn't* buried them.[95] The judges, however, ruled that this shift could be explained by Witness D's traumatic experience, and consequently his testimony that Akayesu had killed his brothers was accepted.[96] This shows the significant effect that the judges' 'allowances' could have on the archive.[97]

Witnesses also significantly affected how substantive law evolved at the tribunal. A good example of this was the way that witnesses influenced the tribunal's interpretation of sexual violence in *Akayesu*. It was because of the witnesses' testimony that the judges found that rape could not 'be captured in a mechanical description of objects and body parts' and instead found that it was 'a physical invasion of a sexual nature, committed on a person under circumstances which are coercive'.[98] This definition allowed for the incorporation of acts not typically seen as legally constituting sexual violence, as captured by Witness KK's testimony of how she had seen *Interahamwe* 'thrusting a piece of wood into the sexual organ of a woman as she lay dying'.[99] Drawing on the witnesses' experiences the judges also, in a particularly important ruling, determined that the environment surrounding the genocide was such that a lack of consent should be presumed.[100] The judges also drew on the witnesses' testimonies when they made their landmark ruling that the rape could be considered an act of

---

[95] *Ibid.*, 106. See also ICTR–96–4, CONTRA001198, *Akayesu – Transcript of 6/2/1997*, 6 February 1997, 171.

[96] ICTR–96–4–0459/1, para 408.

[97] These 'issues' appeared to feed into other courtroom practices as well. First, over time, the manner in which the witnesses would be questioned on matters of distance and time changed, as witnesses, for instance, could be asked to demonstrate distance by using marker points within the courtroom (which would be subsequently measured). Reviser (2015); Akayesu, 15 January 1997, 36–37; and Mathias Ruzindana, 'The Challenges of Understanding Kinyarwanda Key Terms Used to Instigate the 1994 Genocide in Rwanda', in *Propaganda, War Crimes Trials and International Law*, ed. Predrag Dojcinovic (Abingdon: Routledge, 2012), 150. Second, there also appeared to be a shift within the courtroom away from a focus on the more minute details of the crimes that had occurred, towards the broader, or perhaps cruder, accounts of the violence, even though the law concerns itself with exactly such precision. It therefore became possible for the court to accept as truths relatively vague facts, such as that a particular massacre occurred in, for example, 'late April'. *Prosecutor v. Pauline Nyiramasuhuko et al (Butare)*, Case No. ICTR–98–42, *Trial Judgement*, 24 June 2011, at unictr.unmict.org (last accessed 15 July 2017), 512. See also ICTR–99–46, TRA000258/2, *[Cyangugu] – Ntagerura et al – Redacted Transcript of 31/01/2001*, 31 January 2001, 10–11.

[98] ICTR–96–4–0459/1, 240–1, 274–6. See also S/2015/884, *Letter Dated 17 November 2015, From the President of the International Criminal Tribunal for Rwanda Addressed to the President of the Security Council: Report on the Completion of the Mandate of the International Criminal Tribunal for Rwanda as at 15 November 2015*, 17 November 2015, 7 and 16.

[99] They drew here on the broader notion of torture to support this definition as an act intended to cause 'intimidation, degradation, humiliation, discrimination, punishment, control or destruction of a person'. ICTR–96–4–0459/1, 275.

[100] *Ibid.*, 275.

genocide.[101] With this there is evidence of law shaping itself *around* the violence – *around the witnesses' experiences*.

Once more, these examples should not be read as working contrary to the archive's interests and purpose. Indeed, the tribunal's expansion into areas such as gender-based violence is also representative of the archive's drive to command control and authority over a wider set of objects and subjects. As Foucault argues, all discourses and apparatuses seek to expand their sphere of influence in this way.[102] Whilst showing a certain adaptability, these shifts in the archive's rules were also, then, required for the archive to retain a sense of legitimacy. During *Akayesu*, for instance, it was significant that there was pressure for the court to address gender-based crimes from both outside the courtroom (from human rights groups) and inside the courtroom (principally from Judge Pillay).[103] The *need* for the archive to adapt was, however, most clearly seen in the decision discussed in Chapter 3 regarding the protected status of the Tutsis in accordance with the groups covered in genocide convention – limited to racial, ethic, national and religious. Here, the judges sidestepped what they saw as the difficulty of establishing which type of protected group the Tutsis were by simply stating that the intention of the UNGC's drafters had been to protect all stable and permanent groups. This logic is more than questionable, as whilst all of these categories could be considered as social constructions, even a positivist understanding of the social world would recognise there is little, necessarily, permanent about religious or national groups.[104] Rather, I would argue that the curious logic used by the *Akayesu* bench is suggestive of the *necessity* that the archive alter its rules in

---

[101] *Ibid.*, 282 and 290. Similar shifts in the jurisprudence could be seen in, for instance, the evolution of JCE jurisprudence used in order to capture the collective nature of the genocide.

[102] Michel Foucault, 'The Confession of the Flesh: An Interview with Michel Foucault', in *Power/ Knowledge: Selected Interviews and Other Writings 1972–1977*, ed. Colin Gordon (New York: Pantheon Books, 1980), 195; Colin Koopman, 'Foucault's Historiographical Expansion', *Journal of the Philosophy of History* 2:3 (2008): 338–62. See also John Hagan and Ron Levi, 'Crimes of War and the Force of Law', *Social Forces* 83:4 (2005): 1504.

[103] There is also the importance here again of the idea of the introduction of 'human rights methodologies' as argued by Allison Danner and Jenny Martinez, 'Guilty Associations: Joint Criminal Enterprise, Command Responsibility, and the Development, and the Development of International Criminal Law', *California Law Review* 93:1 (2005): 103–20, 132–39 and 145–46.

[104] The difficulty here came from the extent to which both groups: shared a cultural, religious and linguistic heritage; the fluidity, at various points in history, of the division between Hutus and Tutsis; a lack of distinct physical or 'hereditary' traits; and the level of inter-marriage between the groups. Most of this problem, however, came from the judges' conservative reading of ethnicity and race, as they looked for 'objective' markers of these identities that could prove their fixed and permanent existence. ICTR–96–4–0459/1, 209–210 and 281; and Wilson, *Writing History*, 170–91.

this instance: without adapting in this manner, the judges would have been unable to find that genocide had occurred in Rwanda – exactly what the ICTR was set up to do.

Highlighting these shifts in the law, then, is not to state that the witnesses gained control over the archive. Indeed, as will be discussed in Chapter 6 some of these more expansive definitions of law were restricted with time and in a way that very much worked against the interests of the victims. This is, rather, to once more emphasise the idea of the role of the witnesses in co-constructing of the archive.

CONCLUSION

This chapter has outlined how witnesses worked with the archive's rules and at times reformulated what those rules were, as they helped to co-construct the archive. This showed that witnesses helped to establish the trials' frameworks and that, whilst testifying, witnesses could expand these boundaries further. I also demonstrated that witnesses retained control over the meaning of the violence, as their testimony captured the personal and local nature of the genocide in the face of law's deontological drive. Of great significance, and pointing to the interaction between the archive's enunciative modalities and concepts, was that the witnesses' experiences shaped how international humanitarian law evolved at the tribunal. It was, similarly, possible to see that, at least in the tribunal's early years, the idea of the 'rights of victims' came to influence how the archive was constructed and that they counterbalanced criminal justice's more traditional focus on the defendant's rights. With this, a distinct understanding of what justice would look like materialised. This was also, as such, demonstrative of how the archive's strategies worked to maintain a sense of coherence within the archive, as the amorphous notion of delivering 'justice' allowed for both the more traditional focus on the rights of the defendant *and* a need for these courts to engage in more expansive readings of the law in order to satisfy the needs and rights of the victims.

The shifts in the archive's rules identified here are also suggestive of the power relations and imaginings of community imbedded within archive. For this points to the post-colonial nature of the archive as the international, as a 'distinct juridical space' and framed by epistemologies rooted in Western culture, being contested and reshaped through encounters with the post-colonial subject.[105] Whilst, as the following chapters demonstrate, over time these shifts to accommodate the subaltern revealed themselves to be relatively superficial, this nonetheless shows how the archive's rules and imaginings of community are resisted and contested and, further, pushes back against the notion of the witness as a passive subject when confronted with the force of law.

This is also, then, revealing about questions of voice and about whether or not these archives inevitably silence the subaltern.[106] As has been suggested here, whilst it would be too much to see the ICTR's archive as a site of unconstrained subaltern speech – if such as thing could ever exist – the influence that Rwandan witnesses had on this archive suggests that it would also be too much to see the archive as a site where their voice is eradicated completely. Reading, then, both the moments where these voices cut through the discourse's noise to become audible, but remaining consonant of the ways in which it is always already shaped in particular ways by the archive's rules, is important.[107]

This is not, then, to give a distorted account of the archive, and international courts more generally, as spaces that 'empower' witnesses or the subaltern. Rather, this looks to better understand how knowledge is produced within these courts and with what effect. As will be discussed in the following chapter, the witness's ability to shape these rules was contingent on a number of other factors and actors, and as such when these contexts changed, the witnesses' role in constructing the archive was weakened. Indeed, the witnesses were not the only actors that influenced how the archive's rules evolved. As will become clear, the archive was a site where numerous actors staked a claim to determine the archive's rules, who and what the archive was for and, ultimately, what vision of community was constituted. It is to these other actors that the book now turns.

---

[105] Jabri, 'Peacebuilding', 11–15.

[106] This resonates with Dianne Otto's understanding of how to approach the subaltern's speech in contexts so heavily framed by hegemonic, colonial power. Dianne Otto, 'Subalternity and International Law: The Problems of Global Community and the Incommensurability of Difference', *Social & Legal Studies* 5:3 (1996): 355–58.

[107] Arlette Farge, *The Allure of the Archive*, trans. Thomas Scott-Railton (London: Yale University Press, 2013).

CHAPTER FIVE

RECONSTITUTING JUSTICE

The previous chapter examined how witnesses co-constructed the archive. Drawing on the idea of enunciative modalities, this began to explore how different subjects contested the terms on which knowledge was produced at the ICTR. This chapter continues this line of enquiry as it examines how other actors tried to fix and alter the archive's rules. This is concerned with the prosecution, defence, judges and external political actors, including those from the UNSC and the Rwandan government. Continuing the ideas developed in Chapter 4, this Chapter looks to highlight the human and sociological nature of courts, as different individuals brought different world views and visions of justice to bear on the practice of international law and the construction of the archive.[1]

This chapter shows that over time, as a result of shifting relations between these actors, the very concept of justice that underpinned the archive evolved from a broader, more restorative, understanding – where the tribunal was seen as pursuing multiple goals for multiple stakeholders – to a more strictly retributive model. As such, this also continues to show the importance of understanding the interaction between different categories of statements, as here shifts in the archive's enunciative modalities had a bearing on the strategies underpinning the archive. This chapter also focuses more closely on the

---

[1] Nigel Eltringham, 'A War Crimes Community? The Legacy of the International Criminal Tribunal for Rwanda beyond Jurisprudence', *New Eng. J. Int'l & Comp. L.* 14 (2008): 309–14; Richard Goldstone, *For Humanity: Reflections of a War Crimes Prosecutor* (London: Yale University Press, 2000), 74–120.

tribunal's relations with the Rwandan government, which further point to how archive's rules were fractured as incompatible ideas about what and *who* the archive was for emerged. The chapter begins by setting out the notion of justice that underpinned the archive at the tribunal's outset and how this changed, before looking more closely at why this occurred.

IN PURSUIT OF TRUTH, JUSTICE AND RECONCILIATION

Chapter 2 examined the archive's strategies at the tribunal's outset. Under the broad goal of securing international peace and security, these strategies were focused on delivering impartial justice, establishing a verified account of the genocide, and, when combined with giving the witnesses a space to testify, contributing to reconciliation in Rwanda and the Great Lakes region more generally. More clearly directed at the international community as a whole, the tribunal would also contribute to the establishment of international criminal justice as a tool of governance and reaffirm the values (and indeed existence) of the international community.[2] In so doing, an albeit weak form of restorative justice emerged within the archive that went beyond the strict retributive sense of balancing wrongs through punishment, as the tribunal became a site that could restore relationships and values within Rwanda and the international community and assist those affected by the violence to confront and overcome their trauma.[3]

This emphasis on truth, justice and reconciliation, at both a local and international level, fed through to shape the records in a number of ways in the tribunal's early years.

First, these records, and particularly those of the prosecution, contain traces of the attempts to define, and expand the parameters of, international law.[4] Important examples here include pursuing: rape as an act

---

[2] Richard Goldstone, 'Justice as a Tool for Peace-Making: Truth Commissions and International Criminal Tribunals', *Journal of International Law and Politics* 28 (1995): 485–504.

[3] See Kieran McEvoy, 'Beyond Legalism: Towards a Thicker Understanding of Transitional Justice', *Journal of Law and Society* 34: 4 (2007): 411–40.

[4] Interview with Member of ICTR OTP 3 (June 2015). UNGA, A/60/229–S/2005/534, *Report of the International Criminal Tribunal for the Prosecution of Persons Responsible for Genocide and Other Serious Violations of International Humanitarian Law Committed in the Territory of Rwanda and Rwandan Citizens Responsible for Genocide and Other Such Violations Committed in the Territory of Neighbouring States between 1 January and 31 December 1994*, 15 August 2005, 11. For a good discussion of this see Allison Danner and Jenny Martinez, 'Guilty Associations: Joint Criminal Enterprise, Command Responsibility, and the Development, and the Development of International Criminal Law', *California Law Review* 93:1 (2005), 75–169.

of genocide; the applicability of superior responsibility to non-military organisations; and, along with the ICTY, joint criminal enterprise (JCE) as a mode of liability.[5] The motivation behind these expansions of the law varied. As suggested in Chapter 4, this was partly so as to be able to capture the types of violence and criminality that occurred in the genocide. This was perhaps most clearly seen with the emergence of JCE which, whilst only very tenuously based on customary international law, allowed for the more amorphous nature of collective violence to be captured, as an individual's actions and contribution to a crime were interpreted in the context of a broad network of collective criminal action.[6] As Alison Danner and Jenny Martinez argue, such expansions of the law represented the intervention of human rights methodologies into the courtroom, whereby more expansive interpretations of the law were deemed permissible, so as to protect the interests and rights of victims.[7]

This was also, clearly, for the prosecution about trying to help establish their cases against the accused across multiple trials. In the *Akayesu* appeals, for example, the prosecution argued that the trial chamber had erred in law by deciding that for non-military personnel to be found guilty of war crimes they had to have held a position in government that led to an obligation to have supported the war effort (referred to as the 'government test').[8] Whilst, they noted, this had no bearing on *Akayesu*, it had negatively impacted other prosecutions, including *Kayishema and Ruzindana*, *Musema*, and *Rutaganda*.[9] The appeals chamber agreed with the prosecution and so redefined the tribunal's understanding of war crimes. This, however, meant a significant expansion of court's statute, as this forced the appeals

---

[5] *Prosecutor v. Alfred Musema*, Case No. ICTR–96–13, *Judgement and Sentence*, 27 January 2000, 49; ICTR–98–44–4803/1, 2 February 2012, 261–72; Martha Walsh, 'Gendering International Justice: Progress and Pitfalls at International Criminal Tribunals', in *Gendered Peace: Women's Struggle for Post-War Justice and Reconciliation*, ed. Donna Pankhurst (Abingdon: Routledge, 2009), 40.

[6] Carla Del Ponte, 'Investigation and Prosecution of Large-Scale Crimes at the International Level', *Journal of International Criminal Justice* 4 (2006), 540 and 552; Susanna SáCouto, Leila Sadat, and Patricia Sellers, 'Collective Criminality and Sexual Violence: Fixing a Failed Approach. *Leiden Journal of International Law*, 33:1 (2020): 207–12. One of the first uses of JCE at the ICTR was in *Karemera et al.*, and this was deployed so as to be able to link the accused – seen as principal actors at the national level – to crimes committed in localities throughout Rwanda. Interview with Member of ICTR OTP 5 (June 2015).

[7] Danner and Martinez, 'Guilty Associations,' 132–37.

[8] ICTR–96–4, CONTRA000050, *Akayesu – Transcript of 2/11/2000 – Appeals Hearing*, 2 November 2000, 22; and ICTR–96–4, ICTR–96–4–0868/1, *Akayesu – Appeal Judgement*, 1 June 2001, 129–34.

[9] CONTRA000050, 22.

chamber to reinterpret Article 24 of the statute, which strictly *prohibited* the appeals chamber from deciding on matters that did not affect the outcome for the case at hand.[10] This reinterpretation, and transformation, of the tribunal's rules as such gave the appeals judges greater scope and power to determine the state of the law.[11]

In other instances, parties would look to challenge particular legal interpretations when it was thought to be 'just wrong as a matter of public policy'.[12] The fleshing out of law, and ensuring that it reflected good 'public policy', was, then, also about securing the legitimacy of international criminal justice and demonstrating that it *could work*. It should not be forgotten that the ICTR was only the third institution to apply international humanitarian law, and so a vital part of its role was demonstrating that it could work and could have a positive impact in securing international peace and security.[13]

The prosecution, particularly under Goldstone, additionally used trials didactically, as sites of history and reconciliation.[14] Goldstone noted:

> This link between peace and justice, between the work of the Criminal Tribunals and stability in Yugoslavia and Rwanda is, jurisprudentially speaking, extremely interesting. The link clearly shows that, in the international realm, the criminal law has a different focus from that in the domestic arena. National criminal law function primarily to punish perpetrators for violating societal norms encapsulated in the common law and in statutes, and thereby provide satisfaction to the parties most directly injured by the crime. ... On the international level, however, the crucial link between criminal prosecution and the preservation of

---

[10] Article 24 clearly states that appeals are only allowed in instances where the error at trial level has impacted on the trial's outcome: ' The Appeals Chamber shall hear appeals from persons convicted by the Trial Chambers or from the Prosecutor on the following grounds: (a) An error on a question of law invalidating the decision; or (b) An error of fact which has occasioned a miscarriage of justice.' UNSC, 'Statute of the International Criminal Tribunal for Rwanda', found: http://legal.un.org/avl/pdf/ha/ictr_EF.pdf (last accessed 25 October 2019).

[11] ICTR–96–4, CONTRA000049, *Akayesu – Transcript of 1/11/2000 – Appeals Hearing*, 1 November 2000, 41.

[12] This was in reference to the appeals launched against Ngirabatware for the trial chamber's ruling that he was not responsible for the crimes committed by subordinates prior to taking up his post. This was despite the fact that Ngirabatware knew about these crimes after he assumed control and still failed to punish those responsible. OTP 3 (2015).

[13] Richard Goldstone, 'Interview: Obstacles in International Justice: The Establishment and Efficacy of International Courts', *Harvard International Review* 30:4 (2009): 80–81.

[14] The prominent role that history would play at the trials was clear at *Akayesu*, as the prosecutor opened the case with a presentation on the history of Rwanda. ICTR–96–4, CONTRA001175, *Akayesu – Transcript of 09/1/1997*, 9 January 1997. See also Goldstone, 'Justice as a Tool for Peace-Making'.

peace and stability shifts the focus away from pure retribution, to notions of restoring the rule of law and justly establishing the truth, thereby preventing denials and revisionism.[15]

This emphasis on the didactic nature of the trials could be seen in the OTP's attempt to capture the diverse and widespread nature of the violence across Rwanda and so establish a 'just truth'. This was both in terms of the types of perpetrators that were responsible, but also the geographical reach of the violence.[16] The OTP's indictments, as such, targeted government ministers, *bourgmestres*, *préfets*, priests, business persons, journalists, singers, doctors, military personnel, gendarmes, local militiamen, *conseillers* and other local persons of significance.[17] Each of Rwanda's seven prefectures was covered and a broad spread of crimes in each case secured within the indictments. These indictments also captured the coordination between different types of actors, the movement of genocide – as minsters were sent back to their home regions to oversee the genocide or where bands of genocidaires moved between communes to kick start the violence – and the local dynamics of the violence. This reflected the OTP's view that there was 'one genocide' and that it was their duty to demonstrate this fact. When Louise Arbour took over as prosecutor in 1997, this drive to tell this genocide story led her to indict twenty-nine persons in a 'mega trial' that looked to mimic the Allies' approach at *Nuremberg*.[18] Whilst the indictment was rejected on procedural grounds, the attempt captured the importance for the OTP of trying to tell what they saw as the story of the genocide.

In pursuit of these broader historical accounts of violence, the prosecution also led charges that were not, strictly speaking, required to prove an accused's guilt. In Chapter 3 I noted how the prosecution

---

[15] Richard Goldstone, 'The Role of the United Nations in the Prosecution of International War Criminals,' *Washington University Journal of Law & Policy* 5 (2001): 120–21.

[16] Interview with Alfred Kwende, *Voices of the Rwanda Tribunal* (University of Washington, 2008): 5–6. It's perhaps of note here that Goldstone did not regard himself as having the right *legal* expertise for this position. He noted that on being asked to act as prosecutor: 'I regarded the invitation as being somewhat ridiculous. I've never prosecuted, I knew next to nothing about the former Yugoslavia, and I knew nothing about humanitarian law. On each of those grounds I was not the appropriate person.' Interview with Richard Goldstone, *Voices of the Rwanda Tribunal* (University of Washington, 2008): 3–4.

[17] Kingsley Moghalu, *Rwanda's Genocide: The Politics of Global Justice* (Basingstoke: Palgrave Macmillan, 2005), 84; *Prosecutor v. Jean Baptiste Gatete*, Case No. ICTR–00–61 (hereafter ICTR–00–61), TRA001643/1, *Gatete – Redacted Transcript of 20/10/2009*, 20 October 2009, 2.

[18] Interview with William Egbe, *Voices of the Rwanda Tribunal* (University of Washington, 2008): 8; Interview with Charles Adeogun-Phillips, *Voices of the Rwanda Tribunal* (University of Washington, 2008): 14–16.

pushed the temporal jurisdictions imposed by the statute to lead evidence of the *Media Trial* defendants' role in disseminating propaganda prior to the genocide. This particularly effected Hassan Ngeze, where adhering to the statute's temporal limits would have erased the role of his *Kangura* newspaper in preparing the ground for the genocide. There was more than enough evidence, however, of Ngeze's direct participation in the violence in 1994 as one of the leaders of the *Coalition pour la Défense de la République* (CDR) party to have held him to account.[19] Rather, at least part of the concern here appeared to be with capturing the full breadth of the accused's responsibility and role in the violence to present an accurate picture of what they had done.[20] This argument was also explicitly used when the prosecution pushed for concurrent sentences, which, whilst not elongating the accused's prison term, was said to more accurately capture the accused's criminality and their role in the violence.[21] Similarly, in *Karemera et al.*, the prosecution used the accused's senior position in the genocide to, much like with Arbour's attempt at a mega trial, construct a comprehensive account of the genocide.[22]

This broad strategy of truth, justice and reconciliation was also reflected in the manner witnesses were treated throughout the early trials. As was stated in Chapter 4, witnesses were often given space during the trials to expand on prior statements, judges seemed to work under a broad understanding of admissibility and to a certain extent, the law adapted to take into account the witnesses' experiences.[23] This concern of the impact of the trials on witnesses and the affected communities was also seen in *Akayesu*, as Robert Prosper, the lead prosecutor during *Akayesu*, travelled to Taba commune, where Akayesu had been *bourgmestre*, to personally deliver and explain the verdict.[24] Clearly, in these early trials the ICTR pushed beyond the reductionist vision of law that had underpinned *Nuremberg*.

---

[19] *Prosecutor v. Ferdinand Nahimana, Jean Bosco Barayagwiza and Hassan Ngeze*, Case No. ICTR–99–52, ICTR–99–52–1323/1, *Judgement and Sentence*, 3 December 2003, 83–117 and 257–85.

[20] Several interviewees noted how the early indictments contained a much wider range of charges, some of which were seen as being excessive (which was also viewed as being counterproductive to the legal goals of the case). OTP 5 (2015); and Interview with Member of ICTR OTP 2 (June 2015).

[21] See, for example, ICTR–96–4, CONTRA001233, *Akayesu – Transcript of 28/09/1998 – Sentencing Hearing*, 28 September 1998, 22.

[22] Interview with Member of ICTR OTP 4 (June 2015).

[23] See Chapter 4, 85–89.

[24] Victor Peskin, 'Courting Rwanda: The Promises and Pitfalls of the ICTR Outreach Programme', *Journal of International Criminal Justice* 3:4 (2005): 955.

This is not to say that this resulted, necessarily, in a tension between these 'extra-judicial' goals and the judicial focus of the case to secure verdicts; there was often an overlap between these goals. The decision to attempt the 'mega trial' was also driven by a (albeit misguided) belief that this would lead to the efficient execution of justice. The synergy between the legal and extra-judicial goals is perhaps best seen in the appeals chamber's decision in *Karemera et al.* to take judicial notice of the genocide.[25] This marked a symbolic moment in the tribunal's attempts to establish a verified account of the violence. But this also assisted in the legal determination of each subsequent case, as time and energy could be diverted away from establishing that genocide had occurred at a national level towards understanding the specifics of the case at hand.

Whilst not, then, suggesting an incompatibility between the legal and extra-judicial functions of the archive, this does at least suggest that a 'thicker' notion of justice was being pursued during these early trials than is often associated with international criminal justice. However, the records of the archive show that this approach to the trials did not last. The following sections explore this shift before explaining why this was the case.

RECONSTITUTING JUSTICE

Over time, however, trial practice shifted at the tribunal, which altered the content and purpose of the archive itself. In particular, this saw an increased emphasis on producing more streamlined and efficient trials.[26] This, first of all, meant that with time less emphasis was placed on telling the story of the genocide and more on simply establishing the guilt of the accused. In *Gatete*, one of the later trials, for instance, fourteen of nineteen specific allegations lodged against Gatete in the amended indictment were not pursed by the prosecution at the trial, including, and so unlike in the *Media Trial*, charges that related to Gatete's very substantial crimes committed pre-1994.[27]

---

[25] *Prosecutor v. Édouard Karemera, Matthieu Ngirumpatse and Joseph Nzirorera* (Government 1), Case No. ICTR–98–44 (hereafter ICTR–98–44), ICTR–98–44–2076/1, *[Government 1] – Karemera et al – Decision on Prosecution Motion for Judicial Notice*, 9 November 2005, 4–5; ICTR–98–44, ICTR–98–44–2411/1, *[Government 1] – Karemera et al – Decision on Prosecutor's Interlocutory Appeal of Decision on Judicial Notice*, 16 June 2006, 13–15.

[26] A number of interviewees also noted that the indictments shifted over time, from including a broad (and sometimes chaotic) spread of charges to being more tightly focused around a smaller number of charges and events. OTP 3 (2015); and OTP 5 (2015).

[27] ICTR–00–61, ICTR–00–61–0240/1, *Gatete – Judgement and Sentence*, 31 March 2011, 8–9; ICTR–00–61, ICTR–00–61–0166/1, *Gatete – the Pre-Defence Brief of Jean–Baptiste Gatete*, 29 January 2010, 8. ICTR–00–61–0025, *Gatete – Defence Preliminary Motions, Under Rule 72*

This was also reflected in changes to the prosecution's indictment and charging practice. Throughout the tenures of Carla Del Ponte and Hassan Jallow, the focus very much moved away from the use of broad indictments towards much more targeted accounts of the accused's criminality.[28] This can be seen especially in those indictments submitted or amended after the 2003 completion strategy was introduced – discussed more later. As a former member of the OTP noted, after this point the prosecution's strategy became more focused, and they stopped trying to construct 'fluffy histories' to focus more on trial efficiency.[29] A similar sentiment was also expressed by the *Karemera et al.* appeals bench in their 2005 decision, which saw them take judicial notice of the genocide. Here the judges noted:

> During its early history, it was valuable for the purpose of the historical record for Trial Chambers to gather evidence documenting the overall course of the genocide and to enter findings of fact on the basis of that evidence [...]. At this stage, the tribunal need not demand further documentation.[30]

The role of documentation had, it seemed, come to an end and now the focus was to turn increasingly just to the legal matters at hand.[31]

There was also a shift in how witnesses were treated, as over time they were used in an increasingly utilitarian manner. Compared with

---

of the Rules of Procedure and Evidence, 12 April 2003, 5; ICTR–00–61–0022, *Gatete – Prosecutor's Response to the Defense Preliminary Motion Challenging Defects in the Form of the Indictment Pursuant to Rule 72*, 9 May 2003, 5; ICTR–00–61–0029, Gatete, *Decision on Defence Preliminary Motion*, 29 March 2004, 3; ICTR–00–61, ICTR–00–61–0069, *Gatete – Defence Preliminary Motion Alleging Defects in the Form of the Amended Indictment*, 22 May 2009, 6; ICTR–00–61, ICTR–00–61–0073, *Gatete – Decision on Defence Motion Concerning Defects in the Amended Indictment*, 3 July 2009, 7; and ICTR–00–61, ICTR–00–61–0074/1, *Gatete – the Prosecutor's Submission Complying with the Decision on Defence Motion Concerning Defects in the Amended Indictment Dated 3 July 2009*, 7 July 2009. This was despite the prosecution having successfully rebutted the defence's attempts to exclude evidence pertaining to pre-1994 crimes ICTR–00–61, ICTR–00–61–0025, *Gatete – Defence Preliminary Motions, Under Rule 72 of the Rules of Procedure and Evidence*, 12 April 2003, 5–6; ICTR–00–61–010; ICTR–99–46–0072, 15; ICTR–00–61, ICTR–00–61–0022, *Gatete – Prosecutor's Response to the Defense Preliminary Motion Challenging Defects in the Form of the Indictment Pursuant to Rule 72*, 9 May 2003, 6; and ICTR–00–61–0029, 3.

[28] In a study of forty-four trials, Hannah Goozee found that the number of charges dropped over time. The trend line shows a decline in the number of charges from 8.6 charges per indictment in 1996 to just over 3.8 in 2005. Hannah Goozee, *ICTR Trial Data Report*, October 2020. Report on file with author.

[29] OTP 4 (2015).

[30] ICTR–98–44–2411/1, 14. See Rosemary Byrne, 'The New Public International Lawyer and the Hidden Art of International Criminal Trial Practice'. *Connecticut Journal of International Law* 243:25 (2010): 247.

[31] OTP 3 (2015).

Akayesu, in *Gatete* the witnesses were asked shorter and more targeted questions during the trial, and the prosecution, along with the judges and the defence, exerted more control over the proceedings.[32] Gone were the broader questions, featured during *Akayesu*, that probed the witnesses' backgrounds and their experiences in the lead up to the violence; instead, questions immediately directed the witness to the crimes charged against the accused in the indictment.[33] The prosecution even began to interject during *their own witnesses' testimony* to bring it back to order. During *Gatete*, even after what appears to be a relatively succinct answer, the prosecution reminded Witness BBJ to be as quick and succinct in their response as possible.

PROSECUTION: And do you know whether Jean-Baptiste Gatete knew you?

WITNESS BBJ: Yes, he knows me. He knows me very well.

PROSECUTION: Right. Now, back to April 1994, subsequent to the death of President Habyarimana on the 6th of April, did you ever see Gatete thereafter?

WITNESS: I saw Gatete in Nyagasambu that was in the month of May at 9 p.m. It was at night.

PROSECUTION: Witness, just try and be brief in your answers and if I need explanation I will ask follow up questions. And the question was: Whether or not you saw Gatete in the month of April subsequent to the death of President Habyarimana? And all I wanted was a yes or no.

WITNESS: Yes.

PROSECUTION: Now, the next question is: Do you recall how many times you saw Gatete in the month of April 1994 after the 6th of April?

WITNESS: I saw him six times.

PROSECUTION: Thank you, Witness.[34]

This approach was also reflected in the judges handling of witnesses. Whilst in *Akayesu* the judges tended to intervene in an inquisitive manner, even by *Cyangugu* they had become more interventionist.

---

[32] A particularly good example of this new style of questioning can be seen in the examination-in-chief of Witness BBJ during *Gatete*. TRA005459, 14–30.

[33] See the testimony of Witness NN as an example of this. ICTR–96–4, CONTRA001227, *Akayesu – Transcript of 3/11/1997*, 3 November 1997.

[34] TRA005459, *Gatete – Redacted Transcript of 05/11/2009*, 5 November 2009, 15. See also TRA005491/2, *Gatete – Redacted Transcript of 03/11/2009*, 3 November 2009, 81.

During Imanishimwe's re-examination of a witness the judges remonstrated:

> Mr President: I don't see where it takes us when you frame the question that way because he can't – he does not understand it, and I don't understand it either because I don't see why the question is put in that form [. . .].
>
> Don't bother to go into such detail..[35]

And later on:

> Mr President: I have a problem. You are simply reading – re–taking him through measurements that he gave in cross-examination. What is the purpose? Just to repeat what he said in cross-examination? Because that's all it is [. . .]. Where does this take us? It doesn't take us anywhere.[36]

Similarly, when Witness PCF seemed to be answering in a roundabout manner, the judges intervened and ordered:

> MR PRESIDENT: Just remind him that I'd indicated to him he should try and answer the questions in a direct manner and not give long, drawn out answers.
>
> WITNESS: Mr President, the way I'm answer [sic] the questions is the best way I know how to answer the questions that are being put to me. Thank you, Mr President.
>
> MR PRESIDENT: If he is asked when he got married, that's a straightforward answer. If he is married, he says when he got married; if he's not, he says so. He doesn't need to give any long, draw out answers. Just tell him that.[37]

This approach to witnesses was clearest during *Gatete* as questioning became even more combative. In fact, at some points the *Gatete* bench questioned the witnesses to the extent that it blurred the line between the judges on the one hand and the prosecution and defence on the other.[38]

---

[35] ICTR–99–46, TRA001621/2, *[Cyangugu] – Ntagerura et al – Redacted Transcript of 08/10/2002,* 8 October 2002, 4–5.

[36] TRA001621/2, 6.

[37] ICTR–99–46, TRA001795/1, *[Cyangugu] – Ntagerura et al – Redacted Transcript of 22/10/2002,* 22 October 2002, 24.

[38] For an example of this see ICTR–00–61, TRA005145/1, Gatete – *Redacted Transcript of 10/3/ 2010,* 10 March 2010, 5; and ICTR–00–61, CONTRA018748, Gatete, *Redacted Transcript of 11/3/2010,* 11 March 2010, 34.

JUDGE MUTHOGA: Yes. I'm asking you – look this side, Mr. Witness. I'm asking you to tell me, did you actually look out to see if Mr. Gatete was there or not, amongst those 50 of you?

THE WITNESS: As I was getting ready to strike him with a hammer, I had the time to look around me to see the people who were present or those who were not present. Gatete was not there.

JUDGE MUTHOGA: So Gatete is one of the people you expected to be there but was not there?

THE WITNESS: No. I wasn't expecting it. I am speaking in my capacity as a participant at that attack. And I am taking into account the other assailants who were with me. I am also speaking in my capacity as an eyewitness to these events who is willing to speak the truth. I am, therefore, repeating that I did not see Gatete at that scene.[39]

In an Interview reflecting on the ICTR's practice, Judge Muthoga, leading the questioning in the exchange mentioned earlier, even argued that the ICTR judges should have gone even further in curtailing witness testimony and noted that in his view future tribunals should use investigative judges found in the civil law jurisdictions to give the judges even greater powers to intervene.[40]

During Gatete, judicial interventions were particularly intrusive during the defence's case and this, unsurprisingly, led to a degree of friction between the defence and the judges. After the judges intervened once more, Gatete's defence counsel, Ms Poulain, argued:

---

[39] TRA005152/1, 76. A similarly odd approach taken by the judges during this witness's testimony was:

MADAM PRESIDENT: And with respect to that attack, you told us that there were a lot of people who attended; they came from all over; and that you could not remember all of their names because it happened a long time ago; right?

THE WITNESS: Yes. That is correct. I cannot remember all names, but I do remember some names.

MADAM PRESIDENT: And still you remember that Mr. Gatete ate – drank – drank beer in February 1993 when he visited the bar.

TRA005152/1, 74.

[40] What is particularly interesting about this is that Muthoga himself has a common-law background. Interview with Lee Muthoga, *Voices of the Rwanda Tribunal* (University of Washington, 2008), 20.

MS POULAIN:	And it is an open question which requires eventually a long answer. I'm very sorry, President, but it's *our* evidence.
MADAM PRESIDENT:	No. They are – not necessary – detailed answer. We don't need all these details. If he's a good administrator, say he's a good administrator, if he wants it to be said that he was a good leader and administrator and good – a good leader or authority in the commune. But he should not go on giving us each and everything.
MS POULAIN:	Well, I think it gives more weight to the evidence than a simple affirmation. I am sorry. (emphasis added)[41]

The judges also started to order the counsels to reduce the number of witnesses they were planning to call, so as to speed up the trials, when they thought that these were 'excessive' to the case at hand.[42] During *Cyangugu* the president of the court pleaded with the defence to reduce the witness lists:[43]

> Judge Ostrovsky is looking at the list in *which you are drowning us with witnesses, and we don't wish to be drowned*. So take us seriously about reducing this list substantially, substantially. (emphasis added)[44]

The judges, in some instances, even went as far as to suggest which of the witnesses should be dropped, predetermining what evidence was superfluous for the archive.[45]

This, unquestionably, impacted on the scope, speed and nature of the trials and is particular evident in the shift in the prosecution's approach to the trials. This is, I would argue, seen in the comparison between *Akayesu* and *Gatete* trials. In *Akayesu* (1998), then, the prosecution spread its charges over fifteen counts and called twenty-eight witnesses

---

[41] ICTR–00–61, TRA005147/1, *Gatete – Redacted Transcript of 09/03/2010*, 9 March 2010, 50.

[42] ICTR–99–46, TRA001998/1, *[Cyangugu] – Ntagerura et al – Redacted Transcript of 05/02/2003*, 5 February 2003, 44. See also ICTR–99–46, ICTR–99–46–0183, *[Cyangugu] – Bagambiki – Ntagerura et al – Compliance with Trial Chamber III Order of 23/08/2000* (Attached Shortened List of Witnesses), 18 September 2000; and ICTR–99–46–0488, *Proposed Reduction in the List of Defence Witnesses in the Cyangugu Case*, Case No. ICTR–99–46–T, 30 April 2002. Interview with Anonymous 2 (April 2016).

[43] ICTR–99–46, TRA000526/2, *[Cyangugu] – Ntagerura et al – Redacted Transcript of 12/03/2002*, 12 March 2002, 104–5.

[44] ICTR–99–46, TRA001601/2, *[Cyangugu] – Ntagerura et al – Redacted Transcript of 28/03/2002*, 28 March 2002, 7.

[45] ICTR–99–46, TRA001270/2, *[Cyangugu] – Ntagerura et al – Redacted Transcript of 14/05/2002*, 14 May 2002, 3–6.

over thirty-one trial days.[46] In *Gatete* (2010), a relatively similar defendant to Akayesu,[47] the prosecution called twenty-two witnesses over just twelve days to speak to seven counts.[48] The 2009 trial of Yussuf Munyakazi took a mere nineteen trial days, with the prosecution calling only eleven witnesses heard across seven trial days.[49] This focus on trial efficiency is also captured in a graphic used by President Byron to show the progress being made at the tribunal in his 2010 report to the Security Council:

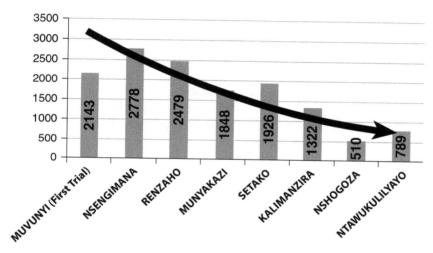

Figure 1 Table presented in ICTR Completion Strategy Report to the UNSC[50]

Combined, this demonstrates a shift in the notion of justice over the lifespan of the tribunal, from a broader more restorative vision of justice

[46] ICTR–96–4–0459/1, *Akayesu – Judgement*, 2 September 1998, para 24.
[47] If anything, Gatete, due to his role in central government, arguably was a more significant perpetrator than Akayesu.
[48] ICTR–00–61–0240/1, 1.
[49] ICTR-97-36A-T, *Prosecutor* v. *Yussaf Munyakazi – Judgement and Sentence*, 5 July 2010, 1. Overall, the trend line of trial data shows a fall from 211.68 trial days per trial at the tribunal's outset to 48.9 trial days at its end. Whilst the data here is slightly skewed by the trial of Nizeyimana (2011) (which was one of the longest single accused cases), overall there the average number of witnesses the prosecution called per defendant fell from 38 in 1997 to 14 in 2010. Interestingly, however, the average number of defence witnesses actually *rises* over the tribunal's history from 18.33 in 1997 to 26 in 2010. This suggests that the defence were not as in line with the efficiency drive as other actors at the tribunal. From this, whilst more data and research would be needed, it can be surmised that the defence kept average trial length higher than it might otherwise have been, which also indicates, given the overall quickening of the trials, that the prosecution's efficiency drive was even more pronounced. Goozee, ICTR Trial Data.
[50] UNSC, S/2010/574, UNSC, *Bi-Annual Completion Strategy Report for ICTR*, 5 November 2010, 9.

to a more strictly retributive model. The question is, why did the approach change?

THE POLITICS OF INTERNATIONAL CRIMINAL JUSTICE

This section offers two reasons behind this shift in practice and ultimately the understanding of justice that underpinned the archive. The first argues that over time substantive and procedural law became more settled, which meant that it became possible for the legal actors, and particularly the judges, to exert greater control over the proceedings. The second argues that this shift was the result of interventions by external actors, particularly the UNSC and the Rwandan government.

Establishing International Criminal Law

When the tribunal opened in 1996 with *Akayesu*, the legal actors had little to draw on in terms of substantive and procedural legal precedent. One trial attorney noted that

> [w]hen I was first here at the beginning of the tribunal in 1998, I, I, I found that the principles, the way of deciding, the way of doing trials was not yet settled. People did not know exactly how to conduct trials, well, in, in my perception of course.[51]

For guidance, the tribunal was almost completely dependent on the jurisprudence created at *Nuremberg* and *Tokyo*, the ICTY's rules of procedure and evidence (RPE), which formed the basis of the ICTR's RPE, and relevant precedent from municipal law. Many aspects of the tribunal's statute were described and explored for the first time within the early judgments.[52] As one former trial attorney noted: 'The law is being developed as we speak. We are the ones who are developing the law. We create the jurisprudence.'[53] This could be seen in judicial decisions discussed previously in this chapter, concerning rape as an act of genocide and the introduction of JCE. Perhaps the clearest example was the aforementioned reinterpretation of the role of the appeals as limited by Article 54 of the Statute.

This performativity could, of course, not be acknowledged by the judges, which resulted in some spurious arguments that tried to conceal

---

[51] Interview with Benoît Henry, *Voices of the Rwanda Tribunal* (University of Washington, 2008), 18.
[52] ICTR judge (2015).
[53] Interview with Adeogun-Phillips, 7.

the creativity with which the judges acted. In one case, the appeals chamber noted that

> to clarify that when [the appeals chambers] interprets certain provisions of the Statute or the Rules, it is merely identifying what the proper interpretation of that provision has always been, even though it was not previously expressed that way.[54]

With time, however, the law became more settled, as more and more jurisprudence was established.[55] It was possible to see the ripple effects of these decisions, as they provided a framework through which other acts of violence could be interpreted.[56] For instance, *Akayesu*'s finding that rape could constitute an act of genocide opened up the possibility that other trials could introduce sexual violence evidence into the record, in the knowledge that it now could be legally accepted as evidence of genocide.[57]

Two things were notable when comparing *Akayesu* and *Gatete* in this respect. First, *Akayesu*'s closing arguments and judgment paid greater attention to interpretations of law – interpretations that, as argued in Chapter 4, frequently relied on the witnesses' narratives to justify them – in comparison to *Gatete*, which contained little discussion of these matters.[58] This suggested that significant areas of law had become accepted as the legal interpretations of these crimes over this period.[59] Second, as suggested earlier, during *Gatete* and the tribunal's later trials, witnesses were questioned in a far more direct manner, as greater control was exerted over the proceedings by the prosecution, defence and the judges.[60] This, along with the much more compact nature of

---

[54] ICTR–99–46, ICTR–99–46–1735/2, *Cyangugu – Appeal Judgement*, 7 July 2006, 42.

[55] OTP 1 (2015); and Mégret, 'International Criminal Justice as a Juridical Field'; Jallow, p. 30. Eltringham similarly talks about the creation of an 'aura' around the trial practice, with rituals like citing precedent helping to produce a sense of authority.

[56] Interview with ICTR Investigator (June 2015).

[57] *Prosecutor* v. *André Ntagerura et al*, Case No. ICTR–99–46 (hereafter ICTR–99–46), TRA000434/2, [Cyangugu] – *Ntagerura et al – Redacted Transcript of 14/02/2001*, 14 February 2001, 13.

[58] Interview with Member of ICTR OTP 7 (June 2016).

[59] See ICTR–96–4, CONTRA001236, *Akayesu – Transcript of 23/3/1998*, 23 March 1998, 6–46; ICTR–96–4–0459/1, *Akayesu – Judgement*, 2 September 1998, 123–59. Indeed, it is notable that there is no discernible discrete reference to interpretations of the law in the *Gatete* closing. Similarly, whilst the *Akayesu* judgment had a separate section for 'The Law' running for thirty-six pages, there was no similar section in *Gatete* and 'what the law was' was dispensed withn in a relatively concise fashion by drawing heavily on previous key rulings. ICTR–00–61, TRA005592, *Gatete – Redacted Transcript of 08/11/2010*, 8 November 2010.

[60] A particularly good example of this new style of questioning can be seen in the examination-in-chief of Witness BBJ during *Gatete*. ICTR–00–61, TRA005459, *Gatete – Redacted Transcript of 05/11/2009*, 5 November 2009, 14–30.

Gatete, suggests that legal actors, by the end of the tribunal, had greater knowledge as to the rules of the court and so could proceed in a more targeted way.[61] This again meant that the witnesses' role changed as their testimony was more stringently controlled.

These ripple effects were similarly present as the tribunal fine-tuned its procedural law. These changed to provide the legal actors, but particularly judges, with greater influence over how the trials were conducted. A key shift in this respect was the judge's intervention over the prosecution's indictment policy in *Cyangugu*.

The prosecution encountered numerous problems with their indictment from the outset of *Cyangugu*, which was challenged in each of the defendants' preliminary motions.[62] The defendants argued that some of the prosecution's charges were incompatible with each other and that with others, most notably the conspiracy charges, the prosecution had failed to present sufficient material facts to establish a *prima facie* case against the accused.[63] Imanishimwe's defence stated that, from what they could work out, Imanishimwe was 'accused of living in Cyangugu',[64] and Ntagerura's defence went as far as to suggest that the indictment amounted to 'enormous ... diarrhoea'.[65]

Most of these motions were successful and the judges ordered the prosecution to amend the indictments to make both the charging and the statement of facts clearer.[66] The prosecution to a large extent complied with these orders.[67] This issue, however, reached a climax in the judgment. As the very first point addressed, the judges ruled that the prosecution's entire indictment was impermissibly vague, to the

---

[61] Here it was striking that, compared with *Akayesu*, the prosecution in *Gatete* wasted no time during their examinations and jumped straight to asking questions concerning the allegations in the indictment. For an example see *Ibid.*, 14.

[62] *Prosecutor v. Andre Ntagerura*, Case No. ICTR–96–10 (hereafter ICTR–96–10), ICTR–96–10A–0194, *Ntagerura – Preliminary Motion (Defects in the Indictment)*, 21 April 1997, 5–11; and ICTR–97–36, ICTR–97–36–00195, *Bagambiki – Audio Recording of 25/03/98 – AM*, 25 March 1998.

[63] ICTR–96–10A–0194, 8–9; and ICTR–97–36–0043, *Preliminary Motions*, 18 February 1998, 4.

[64] ICTR–97–36–00195, 25 March 1998.

[65] ICTR–99–46–01002, *Ntagerura – Audio Recording of 10/08/99 – AM*, 10 October 1999.

[66] ICTR–96–10, ICTR–96–10A–0208, *Ntagerura – Decision on the Preliminary Motion Filed by the Defence Based on Defects in the Form of the Indictment*, 28 November 1997, 6–7; ICTR–97–36, ICTR–97–36–0062, *Imanishimwe – Bagambiki – Munyakazi – Decision on the Defence Motion Regarding Defects in the Form of the Indictment*, 24 September 1998, 4; and ICTR–96–10, ICTR–96–10A–0224, *Ntagerura – Amended Indictment*, 29 January 1998.

[67] ICTR–99–46, TRA002066/1, *[Cyangugu] – Ntagerura et al – Redacted Transcript of 12/08/2003*, 12 August 2003, 8–11; ICTR–99–46, TRA000521/2, *[Cyangugu] – Ntagerura et al – Redacted Transcript of 05/03/2002 – Motion*, 5 March 2002, 86, 113–14, 140 and 148; and ICTR–99–46, TRA000552/2, *[Cyangugu] – Ntagerura et al – Redacted Transcript of 06/03/2002– Oral Hearing on the Motion of Imanishimwe for Acquittal on Conspiracy Count*, 6 March 2002.

extent that it was impossible to cure it through post-indictment disclosure.[68] This ruling carried with it a warning to the prosecution concerning their indictment policy: From then on, the chambers would have zero tolerance for an indictment strategy that relied on vague indictments which could be altered as a result of new evidence found through on-going investigations or the witnesses' in-court testimony.[69] Judge Dolenc took this argument even further, finding that the prosecution's conduct was so problematic that the whole of the indictment should have been thrown out and the case along with it.[70] As such, the judges made it clear that the prosecution's indictment policy had to change.

Several factors suggest that it was, to a certain extent, the prosecution's conscious decision to proceed under a vague indictment in *Cyangugu*.[71] First, whilst the prosecution clearly submitted the indictment in a hurry (as it was filed under Rule 40 *bis*, which provided for the late submission of an indictment),[72] the additional specificity contained within the indictment's supporting document that was *not* included in the main indictment showed that more detail could have been provided.[73] The prosecution also submitted an amended indictment in December 1999, in clear acknowledgement of the defects in the initial indictment, only to subsequently withdraw the

---

[68] ICTR–99–46–0599/1, *Trial Judgement – the Prosecutor v. André Ntagerura Emmanuel Bagambiki Samuel Imanishimwe*, 25 February 2004, 15–20; and ICTR–99–46–1735/2, 21, 25 and 41. This, then, supported the defence's position adopted in their closing briefs. ICTR–99–46, TRA002063/1, [Cyangugu] – *Ntagerura et al – Redacted Transcript of 13/08/2003*, 13 August 2003, 7–15; and TRA002066/1, 13–17.

[69] ICTR–99–46–0599/1, 18–20.

[70] Judge Schomburg made a similarly strong statement on appeal, arguing that the whole of the Ntagerura indictment should also have been thrown out. ICTR–99–46–1735/2, *Cyangugu – Appeal Judgement*, 7 July 2006, 131.

[71] Whilst not referring to *Cyangugu* directly, a senior trial attorney noted that this use of broad (or vague) indictments did underpin the OTP's approach to indictments throughout the early trials. OTP 2 (2015) and OTP 5 (2015).

[72] Rule 40 *bis* provides the prosecution with a time extension to file the indictment against the accused once they are in provisional detention.

[73] ICTR–96–10, ICTR–96–10–0212, *Ntagerura – Decision – Confirmation of the Indictment*, 10 August 1996; ICTR–99–46, TRA002960, [Cyangugu] – *Ntagerura et al – Redacted Transcript of 06/02/2006 – Appeals Hearing*, 6 February 2006, 73–74. A/54/634, *Financing the International Criminal Tribunal for the Prosecution of Persons Responsible for Genocide and Other Serious Violations of International Humanitarian Law Committed in the Territory of Rwanda and Rwandan Citizens Responsible for Genocide and Other Such Violations Committed in the Territory of Neighbouring States between 1 January and 31 December 1994: Report of the Expert Group to Conduct a Review of the Effective Operation and Functioning of the International Tribunal for the Former Yugoslavia and the International Criminal Tribunal for Rwanda*, 22 November 1999, 55–57; and ICTR–96–10, ICTR–96–10A–0014, *Ntagerura – Indictment – Supporting Material – Supporting Documentation*, 9 August 1996.

request.[74] Part of the decision not to amend the indictment (as will become more significant later) was an OTP policy that meant the prosecution should only alter an indictment where absolutely necessary to ensure that the trials proceeded apace.[75] However, at the very least the prosecution tested their luck and hoped that the judges would allow for the additional evidence that the prosecution knew they had to enter the courtroom via the witnesses' testimonies. It seems unlikely that they would have proceeded with the original indictment had they anticipated that the judges would react so adversely to the indictment in the judgment.

The judges' warning in *Cyangugu*, along with similar decisions rendered in *Semanza*, formed part of a broader shift in strategy that began in the late 1990s and saw the judges gain greater control over the way the trials proceeded to quicken their pace.[76] This was, moreover, largely successful, and as a result of these interventions, along with others discussed later in the chapter, the prosecution's indictments shifted towards the practice advocated by the *Cyangugu* judges.[77] Not only did they move towards using far more exacting and narrowly focused indictments, as discussed earlier, but they also introduced an indictment committee tasked with ensuring that the indictments were watertight, reflected current jurisprudence, and that the evidence to be led in court matched the charges in the indictment.[78]

---

[74] ICTR–96–10, ICTR–96–10A–0272, Ntagerura – *Prosecutor Request for Leave to File an Amended Indictment*, 2 December 1999, 4–5.

[75] OTP 3 (2015).

[76] ICTR–99–46, TRA002962, *[Cyangugu]* – Ntagerura et al – *Redacted Transcript of 07/02/2006 – Appeals Hearing*, 7 February 2006, 6–7. This message was, moreover, reinforced by the *Cyangugu* Appeals Chamber, which overturned the trial chambers finding that Imanishimwe was responsible for genocide because they found that, once again, the prosecution had failed to properly plead this allegation in the indictment. This meant that not one of the defendants from *Cyangugu* was found guilty of genocide. This also delivered an even clearer message to the prosecution about their indictment strategy: 'The Appeals Chamber wishes to express its concern regarding the Prosecution's approach in the present case. The Appeals Chamber recalls that the indictment is the primary accusatory instrument and must plead the Prosecution case with sufficient detail. Although the Appeals Chamber allows that defects in an indictment may be "remedied" under certain circumstances, it emphasizes that this should be limited to exceptional cases. In the present case, the Appeals Chamber is disturbed by the extent to which the Prosecution seeks to rely on this exception. Even if the Prosecution had succeeded in arguing that the defects in the indictments were remedied in each individual instance, the Appeals Chamber would still have to consider whether the overall effect of the numerous defects would not have rendered the trial unfair in itself.' ICTR–99–46, TRA003809/1, *[Cyangugu]* – Ntagerura et al – *Redacted Transcript of 07/07/ 2006 – Appeals Judgement*, 7 July 2006, 13 and 37.
Prosecutor v. Laurent Semanza, Case No. ICTR–97–20, ICTR–97–20–0779/1, *Judgement and Sentence*, 15 May 2003, 17; and Appeals Attorney 2 (2015).

[77] OTP 3 (2015).

[78] OTP 2 (2015).

An additional consequence of these changes was that there was a further concentration of power in the hands of the legal actors. This new stance moved away from the prosecution's initial indictment practice of, as one former trial attorney put it, 'modelling their prosecutions as they went ... ',[79] which allowed the witnesses to take a far greater role with how the indictments and trials were pursued. Rather, witnesses increasingly played a more restricted role. This was also reflected in the increasingly interventionist approach within the court, which worked to limit and interrupt the witnesses' testimonies, as the court's concern became far more oriented towards producing orderly and efficient trials.[80]

This shift in power towards the judges in particular also meant a (partial) migration towards a more civil law–orientated approach to the trials, evident also in the judges' revisions of the RPE.[81] This shift was even more starkly seen at the ICTY, where in 1998 the judges amended the RPE to include Rule in 73 *bis*, which effectively gave the judges the power to curtail the prosecution's cases both in terms of scope and

---

[79] *Ibid.*

[80] OTP 5 (2015); OTP 3 (2015); and Interview with Defence Counsel (February 2016); UNSC, S/2010/574, *Letter Dated 12 November 2010 from the President of the International Criminal Tribunal for Rwanda Addressed to the President of the Security Council: Report on the Completion Strategy of the International Criminal Tribunal for Rwanda (as of 1 November 2010),* 5 November 2010, 8. For an alternative account, albeit based on a much earlier set of trials see Rosemary Byrne, 'The New Public International Lawyer and the Hidden Art of International Criminal Trial Practice', *Connecticut Journal of International Law* 243:25 (2010): 248–303.

[81] ICTR judge (2015); A/54/315–S/1999/943, *Report of the International Criminal Tribunal for the Prosecution of Persons Responsible for Genocide and Other Serious Violations of International Humanitarian Law Committed in the Territory of Rwanda and Rwandan Citizens Responsible for Genocide and Other Such Violations Committed in the Territory of Neighbouring States between 1 January and 31 December 1994,* 7 September 1999, 5; ICTR–99–46, TRA000207/01, *[Cyangugu] – Ntagerura et al – Redacted Transcript of 18/09/2000,* 18 September 2000, 102; UNGA, A/58/140–S/2003/707, *Report of the International Criminal Tribunal for the Prosecution of Persons Responsible for Genocide and Other Serious Violations of International Humanitarian Law Committed in the Territory of Rwanda and Rwandan Citizens Responsible for Genocide and Other Such Violations Committed in the Territory of Neighbouring States between 1 January and 31 December 1994,* 11 July 2003, 3. Though not evidencing a shift to civil law, other changes to speed up trials include the decision in 1998 to merge both the judgment and sentence into one procedure, eradicating the sentencing hearing; reducing the time limits from 60 to 30 days with pre-trial motions; allowing the defence to use external language translations; allowing the confirming judge to sit on the trial; president being allowed to order the creation of directives to better regulate the trial; and, importantly, the power of the judges to impose sanctions for 'frivolous' motions. UNGA, A/53/429, *Report of the International Criminal Tribunal for the Prosecution of Persons Responsible for Genocide and Other Serious Violations of International Humanitarian Law Committed in the Territory of Rwanda and Rwandan Citizens Responsible for Genocide and Other Such Violations Committed in the Territory of Neighbouring States between 1 January and 31 December 1994,* 23 September 1998, 4. A/54/315–S/1999/943, 5; TRA000207/01, 102; A/58/140–S/2003/707, 3; S/2003/946, 12 and 14.

volume of witnesses. Tellingly, when I asked a former ICTR judge about why the tribunal had not introduced similar measures, I was told that this was because they had interpreted the ICTR's statute as already providing such authority, which had, moreover, been utilised in the search for efficiency.[82]

This shift in trial practice was also driven by a change in tribunal personnel. At the tribunal's 2014 'legacy conference', it was widely accepted that there was a step-change in the efficiency of the trials as a result of the appointment of Adam Dieng as registrar in 2001 and Hassan Jallow as prosecutor and Erik Møse as president in 2003.[83] Some of the key changes to trial practice that resulted included the creation of trial committees – with representatives from the trial chamber, prosecution and the registry – to ensure that the trials were on track. Informal use of status conferences, where issues between the defence and the prosecution could be settled without resorting to more time-consuming litigation, were also introduced.[84]

However, beyond the development and settling of law was a more significant factor that accounts for the shift in practice at the ICTR. This was the UNSC's imposition of the completion strategy. This will be examined in the following section as I consider the way in which these interventions resulted in the 'politicisation' of the archive. These issues are then explored further as I turn to the RPF's influence over the archive.

Politicising the Archive
The Search for Efficiency
There was a marked shift in the relationship of the ICTR and ICTY with other UN organs (particularly the UNSC) during the tribunals' first decade. As Chapter 2 set out, one of the initial draws of the tribunals was that they were seen as an 'economical' means of securing international peace and security, at least when compared to other

---

[82] Anonymous 2 (2015). For particularly clear evidence of how this effected proceedings at the ICTY see IT-9S-SI18-PT *Prosecutor v. Radovan Karadzic, Decision of the Application of Rule 73 BIS*, 8 October 2009.

[83] *ICTR Legacy Symposium – 20 Years of Challenging Impunity*, Arusha, 6–7 November 2014. Mégret also identifies a similar shift in personnel (and a correlative effect on trial practice) as there was a shift from actors with a background in international law, to those with a back ground in criminal law. Mégret, 'International Criminal Justice as a Juridical Field.'

[84] S/2003/946, *Letter Dated 3 October 2003 from the Secretary-General Addressed to the President of the Security Council: Completion Strategy of the International Criminal Tribunal for Rwanda*, 6 October 2003, 15; and S/PV.4999, 4999th Meeting, 29 June 2004, 12. Interview with Erik Møse, *Voices of the Rwanda Tribunal* (University of Washington), 5.

strategies, such as military intervention.[85] This goodwill towards the tribunals – and particularly the ICTR – was, however, relatively short-lived, as the tribunals proved to be costly, slow and inefficient – at least according to their critics.[86]

A series of other reputational issues, along with ingrained inter-departmental wrangling for control over the tribunal, led a number of UN organs (particularly the UNSC, UNGA and the Fifth Committee – the subsection of the UN charged with overseeing the finances of UN operations) to intervene and bring about change in the tribunal's practices.[87] Consequently, in the late 1990s and early 2000s, numerous reports into the tribunal's practices were published, the most substantial of which came as a result of the Fifth Committee's inter-ventions through the UN's Office of Internal Oversight Services (OIOS).[88] These reports were highly critical[89] and focused on how

---

[85] UNSC, S/PV.3377, 3377th Meeting, 16 May 1994, 19; and UNESC, E/1994/SR.8, *Provisional Summary Record of the 8th Meeting, 14/06/1994*, 4; and UNGA, A/C.5/48/SR.57, *Fifth Committee: Summary Record of the 57th Meeting: Financing of the United Nations Observer Mission Rwanda*, 29 March 1994, 2–3; UNSC, S/1995/134, *Report of the Secretary-General Pursuant to Paragraph 5 of Security Council Resolution 955 (1994)*, 13 February 1995, 4.

[86] Whilst this seemed to peak at the turn of the millennium, the concern expressed by member states over the progress being made by the tribunal goes back to as early as 1996. UNGA, A/51/PV.78, *51st Session, 78th Plenary Meeting*, 10 December 1996, 18; UNSC, *4429th Meeting*, S/PV.4429, 27/11/2001, 7; UNSC, S/PV.5453, *5453rd Meeting*, 7 June 2006, 23; UNSC, S/PV.5697, *5697th Meeting*, 18 June 2007, 22–23 and 28; and UNSC, S/PV.7192, *7192nd Meeting*, 5 June 2014. Byrne, 'The New Public Prosecutor', 263–65.

[87] Indeed, one interviewee informed me that during these early years the relationship between the Registry and the Chambers and OTP was particularly fraught as they each vied for control over the tribunal. Interview with Senior Legal Officer – ICTR Chambers (June 2016) and Appeals Judge (2016).

[88] UNGA, A/51/789, *Financing of the International Criminal Tribunal for the Prosecution of Persons Responsible for Genocide and Other Serious Violations of International Humanitarian Law Committed in the Territory of Rwanda and Rwandan Citizens Responsible for Genocide and Other Such Violations Committed in the Territory of Neighbouring States between 1 January and 31 December 1994: Report of the Secretary-General on the Activities of the Office of Internal Oversight Services*, 06/02/1997; and UNGA, A/C.5/57/L.35, *Financing of the International Criminal Tribunal for the Prosecution of Persons Responsible for Genocide and Other Serious Violations of International Humanitarian Law Committed in the Territory of Rwanda and Rwandan Citizens Responsible for Genocide and Other Such Violations Committed in the Territory of Neighbouring States between 1 January and 31 December 1994*, 4 December 2002; UNGA, A/RES/53/213, Resolution 53/213, 10 February 1999; UNGA, A/C.5/51/SR.39 *Fifth Committee: 51st Session: Summary Record of the 39th Meeting*, 11 December 1996; A/54/634; and UNGA, A/53/659, *Report of the Advisory Committee on Administrative and Budgetary Questions*, 11 November 1998, 10–11.

[89] UNGA, A/56/853, *Financing of the International Tribunal for the Prosecution of Persons Responsible for Serious Violations of International Humanitarian Law Committed in the Territory of the Former Yugoslavia since 1991: Financing of the International Criminal Tribunal for the Prosecution of Persons Responsible for Genocide and Other Serious Violations of International Humanitarian Law Committed in the Territory of Rwanda and Rwandan Citizens Responsible for Genocide and Other Such Violations Committed in the Territory of Neighbouring States between 1 January and 31 December 1994: Comprehensive Report on the Results of the Implementation of the*

the tribunal could be better managed, with a view to economising the tribunal's activities in terms of both time and resources.[90] This resulted in a significant change to the structure and functioning of the tribunal.[91]

What is important here, however, is that beyond administrative reform, these reports also made proposals about how the tribunal should change its approach to the trials themselves. For instance, these reports suggested that the judges needed to exert greater control over the trials to shorten the procedures and to make the trials more efficient.[92] The reports also called for an end to excessive lawyering and suggested that the OTP should cut down the scope of the charges being pursued, begin focusing solely on the more senior persons responsible for the violence in Rwanda (leaving lesser criminals to other jurisdictions), and that they should make greater use of plea agreements and judicial notice. There were also suggestions that specifically called for the tribunal to change its approach to witness testimony. These included calls for the judges to exert more control over how witnesses were examined, to ensure a reduction in the number of witnesses called, and for greater use to be made of Rule 92 *bis*, which allowed written statements to be submitted in substitute of in-court testimony.[93] One report produced in 1999 and co-written by Hassan Jallow before he became the ICTR's prosecutor stated:

> Some [witness answers] seem to be evoked by vague, multiple or com-
> pound questions and the relative infrequency of objections to them.
> There appears to be a disposition to tolerate this procedure, *particularly in
> the case of testimony by victims*, the thought being that allowing them to
> tell their stories in their own way has a salutary cathartic psychological

---

Recommendations of the Expert Group to Conduct a Review of the Effective Operation and Functioning of the International Tribunal for the Former Yugoslavia and the International Criminal Tribunal for Rwanda, 4 March 2002, 2 and 6.

[90] A/54/634, 9.

[91] For example UNGA, A/54/PV.48, *54th Session: 48th Plenary Meeting*, 8 November 1999, 15; A/ 54/634, 60, 74–78; A/51/7/Add.8, *Financing of the International Criminal Tribunal for the Prosecution of Persons Responsible for Genocide and Other Serious Violations of International Humanitarian Law Committed in the Territory of Rwanda and Rwandan Citizens Responsible for Genocide and Other such Violations Committed in the Territory of Neighbouring States between 1 January and 31 December 1994: Ninth Report of the Advisory Committee on Administrative and Budgetary Questions*, 29 May 1997, 15–16; and UNGA, A/53/PV.47, *53rd Session: 47th Plenary Meeting*, 28 October 1998, 5–12.

[92] A/54/634, 18–38; UNSC, S/2004/616, *The Rule of Law and Transitional Justice in Conflict and Post-Conflict Societies: Report of the Secretary-General*, 23 August 2004, 15; and S/PV.4429, 27 November 2001, 8. Byrne, 'The New Public Prosecutor', 265.

[93] S/2003/946, 11; and A/56/853, 4 and 10.

benefit. In addition, some judges may be *needlessly sensitive* to the potential for criticism if they intervene actively to exercise greater control over the proceedings. (emphasis added)[94]

These reports coincided with the period in the late 1990s and early 2000s when the judges' approach to the trials shifted as they gained greater control over the proceedings. At this point, as noted earlier, the judges, with greater energy, began to curb both the number of witnesses and the length of their testimony during trials.[95] Whilst some of the changes in practice, as noted previously, were also motivated by legal concerns, the language that underpinned these decisions demonstrated the significance of the UNSC's pressure.[96] This focused on the need to economise judicial time, in order to make the trials more judicially efficient, and also to make the trials *financially less costly*.[97] One of the judges' justifications for ordering the witness lists to be shortened in *Cyangugu* stated:[98]

> It's no point us having witnesses that are not advancing the issues very much. *Great expense* is involved in bringing these witnesses to the tribunal. Our budget has been seriously cut and so the *issue of economy* has to be taken into consideration as well. *We can't just bring witnesses here for the sake of bringing them. They have to be contributing materially to the issues that have to be considered.* (emphasis added)[99]

Similarly, a former judge noted,

> I think over the time we realised that we really need to be more assertive, to focus the proceedings. The parties might not have the same interest as

---

[94] A/54/634, 29.

[95] S/PV.4429, 27/11/2001, 8; and Anonymous 2 (2016).

[96] ICTR–99–46–0183, 18 September 2000; ICTR–99–46–0488, *Proposed Reduction in the List of Defence Witnesses in the Cyangugu Case*, Case No. ICTR–99–46–T, 30 April 2002; ICTR–99–46, TRA001998/1, *[Cyangugu] – Ntagerura et al – Redacted Transcript of 05/02/ 2003*, 5 February 2003, 44; and ICTR–99–46, TRA001601/2, *[Cyangugu] – Ntagerura et al – Redacted Transcript of 28/03/2002*, 28 March 2002, 7.

[97] ICTR–99–46, TRA000526/2, *[Cyangugu] – Ntagerura et al – Redacted Transcript of 12/03/2002*, 12 March 2002, 104–5. Indeed, the extent to which judicial time was prioritised was seen when one of the witnesses was brought to the courtroom without any shoes or socks on in order for the court session to start on time. ICTR–99–46, TRA001915/1, *[Cyangugu] – Ntagerura et al – Redacted Transcript of 24/03/2003*, 24 March 2003, 2.

[98] It was noted, moreover, that the push towards cutting down witness lists was in tension with the desire of the witnesses to have their moment in court. Interview with ICTR judge (2015). It was also noted that one of the reasons why the OTP choose the witnesses they did (and also did not diversify the pool of witnesses they drew upon as much as they might have) was because of a desire to keep costs low. OTP 3 (2015).

[99] TRA001601/2, 7.

we do, in moving the cases forwards .... It's a big challenge of international justice to curb the time, but also the costs.[100]

This 'efficiency drive' accelerated when, in 2002, an increasingly dissatisfied UNSC told the tribunal that, along with the ICTY, they needed to formulate a 'completion strategy' that would ensure that the tribunals would conclude their work as quickly as possible.[101] The strategy was finalised in 2003, and this dictated that the prosecution were to finish all investigations by 2004, with trials in the first instance concluded by 2008 and appeals by 2010.[102] As a former member of the OTP noted, the message was clear: '[L]ook, shut down, finish.'[103]

One of the first changes introduced in search of these goals was the creation of separate prosecutor posts for the ICTR and the ICTY. Hassan Jallow, who, as the statement mentioned earlier suggests, was already keen on making the OTP's approach more efficient, was appointed as prosecutor at the ICTR.[104] The prosecution subsequently created a new OTP policy that would streamline their prosecutions along the lines suggested in these reports, and as set out earlier.[105] As Jallow describes:

> [W]e decided that the indictments themselves had to be much more focused, much shorter, much leaner because the old indictments we had here were quite big, I mean very lengthy documents and we thought we should try and have what we call 'lean and mean' indictments rather than big ones. Try and focus on less crimes in respect of an accused, focus on the offenses with which, with which, for which we thought we had enough evidence and which could easily be established, rather than charging a dozen counts. If you had, if you could proceed on three counts you, you, you did that .... We thought we needed to reduce the number of witnesses as well because they were running into hundreds, close to 100 in some cases. Pick the best witnesses, proof them, prepare, I mean confirm them, make sure they, they are ready for court even before we filed our indictments, rather than the reverse which, which had seemed to be going on before.

---

[100] ICTR Judge (2015).

[101] A/C.5/57/L.35.

[102] S/RES/1503, *Resolution 1503*, 28 August 2003, 2.

[103] OTP 3 (2015).

[104] A/54/634, 9; and S/RES/1503, 2.

[105] Interview with Member of ICTR OTP 2 (June 2015); S/2003/946, 6 and 18; UNSC, S/PV.4999, 18–19. At this point in the OTP's history the number of estimated new indictees fell from 136 to 26. UNGA, A/57/PV.36, *57th Session: 36th Plenary Meeting*, 28 October 2002, 15; Interview with Egbe, 31.

Other significant changes that left a clear mark on the archive included the uptake of plea agreements – which meant severely cutting down the number of charges against the accused[106] – and refining the focus of indictments against only those deemed *most* responsible.[107] The effect on the archive of prosecuting only those 'most responsible' was clear, as this meant a reduction in the very number of persons to be tried at the ICTR, reducing the number from twenty-six to just sixteen.[108]

This is not to say that there was a complete abandonment of all of the extra-judicial goals. Under Jallow, for instance, there remained a commitment to capturing crimes spread throughout Rwanda to reflect the scope of the genocide.[109] Moreover, there was an argument that in establishing the broad brushstrokes of the genocide, and indeed securing judicial notice of the genocide, that the tribunal had achieved its role of documenting the genocide.[110] Yet such a view arguably marked a return to a more reductionist vision of what types of accounts courtrooms could tell, seen also in the more constrained scope of later trials.

The shift outlined saw the centring of efficient and economical justice as the poles against which 'success' was measured. A number of actors actively contested and condemned this approach. Peter Robinson, defence counsel in *Karemera et al.*, for example, submitted a request that called for President Byron (the presiding judge in the case) to be barred from deciding on a motion as he feared that his obligation to the completion strategy and efficiency would influence his decision to the detriment of the defendant's rights.[111] Judge Hunt, whilst participating in an interlocutory appeal in *Butare*, argued that the tribunal's focus on efficiency had overridden all other considerations, including the rights of

---

[106] A/56/853, 2 and 11; and A/54/634, 28–30; UNSC, S/2015/884, *Letter Dated 17 November 2015 from the President of the International Criminal Tribunal for Rwanda Addressed to the President of the Security Council: Report on the Completion of the Mandate of the International Criminal Tribunal for Rwanda as at 15 November 2015*, 17 November 2015, 15; Interview with Egbe, 9.

[107] Interview with Kwende, 7; Interview with Richard Karegyesa, *Voices of the Rwanda Tribunal* (University of Washington, 2008), 13.

[108] Daryl Mundis, 'The Judicial Effects of the "Completion Strategies" on the Ad Hoc International Criminal Tribunals', *The American Journal of International Law* 99:1 (2005): 145.

[109] Interview with Hassan Jallow, *Voices of the Rwanda Tribunal* (University of Washington, 2008), 20. Additionally, in the ICTR's final years, the head of the appeals, James Arguin, headed up a project, the 'Genocide Story Project', which looked to transform the tribunal's findings into a history of the genocide to help make the tribunal's work relevant to a wider audience. However, it is telling that, like the archivists' attempts to draw in more users discussed in Chapter 7, this work was a personal initiative rather than one at the heart of the ICTR's mandate.

[110] Anonymous 2 (2015); Interview with Member of the ICTR OTP 8 (June 2015); OTP 3 (2015).

[111] Defence Counsel (2016).

the defendant, which in that instance led him to submit a dissenting opinion.[112] Similarly, at the closing of the tribunal the New Zealand delegate to the UNSC noted, with regret, that '[a] budget-driven mentality seems to have distorted the conversation about the role and performance of the tribunals'.[113] These were, however, very much dissident voices, and by the end of the tribunal's existence, each of the ICTR's organs seemed committed to the pursuit of lean and efficient justice.

The RPF and the Archive

The previous section has shown that the early 2000s marked a key turning point for the archive's strategies as, overall, the search for a more expansive form of justice based on truth and reconciliation was replaced by a narrower understanding of the role of the trials. One other significant event also contributed to shift in the archive, and this was the RPF's interventions into the court's practice.

In 2002, the OTP, under the leadership of Carla Del Ponte, began making strides towards submitting indictments against leading members of the RPF. This, and not for the first time in the tribunal's history,[114] resulted in a considerable backlash from the RPF

---

[112] *Prosecutor v. Nyiramasuhuko et al*, Case No. ICTR-98–42, ICTR-98–42-A15bis, *Decision in the Matter of Proceedings under Rule 15bis(D) – Dissenting Opinion of Judge Hunt*, 24 September 2003; and S/PV.7574, 25.

[113] UNSC, S/PV.7574, 7574th Meeting, 9 December 2015, 26.

[114] Another example of this was the 'Barayagwiza affair'. In 1996, the Tribunal arrested Jean Bosco Barayagwiza in Cameroon for his contribution to the genocide as co-founder of the radio station RTLM and also a former head of the extremist CDR party. However, in November 1999 the appeals chamber ordered his release, having found that his rights had been irrevocably violated as a result of being detained for a year without being charged. Barayagwiza was a significant figure within the genocide's leadership, and the tribunal's decision was both legally and politically important, as this demonstrated that it would uphold the basic principles of the rule of law and the rights of the defendant *regardless* of the political significance of the accused. The decision caused outrage in Rwanda, as the RPF government argued that the tribunal was insulting the victims of the genocide by releasing a key defendant on a technicality. In protest the Rwandan government withdrew all support for the tribunal, which again brought the court to a standstill. Once more, this time under the pressure of Del Ponte, the tribunal reconsidered the prior ruling, and, as 'new evidence' was discovered, the case against Barayagwiza recommenced. James Stewart, 'NYU JILP Symposium: New Thoughts about Barayagwiza: Reactions to Policing International Prosecutors', *Opinion Juris*, 5 April 2014; Christopher Wren, 'UN Tribunal Wrong to Free Top Suspect, Rwanda Says', *New York Times*, 12 November 1999. Peskin, *International Justice*, 179; Moghalu, *Rwanda's Genocide*, 177. /2002/1375, *Letter Dated 16 December 2002 from the Secretary-General addressed to the President of the Security Council*, 19 December 2002, 2; UNGA, A/54/PV.48, *54th Session: 48th Plenary Meeting*, 8 November 1999, 24–27; UNGA, A/55/269, *Situation of Human Rights in Rwanda: Report of the Special Representative of the Commission on Human Rights on the Situation of Human Rights in Rwanda*, 4 August 2000, 36; and UNGA, A/57/PV.36, *57th Session: 36th Plenary Meeting*, 28 October 2002, 14.

government, as they severed all ties with the tribunal and barred witnesses from travelling to Arusha, effectively bringing the tribunal to a halt.[115]

This presented the ICTR with two options. The first was to continue with the prosecutions against the RPF and likely face a difficult period as Rwanda withheld witnesses. Whilst this would no doubt have been tricky to navigate, the ICTY had shown that using the appropriate diplomatic pressure could carve a way through this type of impasse. This would have also kept the hopes alive of the tribunal achieving its initial mandate of delivering impartial justice, as well as extra-judicial goals such as truth and reconciliation. The second option was to accept the Rwandan government's demands, shelve the indictments and settle for a less complete account of violence and a more limited, and distinctly one-sided, form of justice. The tribunal chose the latter and no member of the RPF has ever been prosecuted by the tribunal.[116]

The OTP's official line on why these charges never materialised is also instructive. Jallow, who also investigated RPF crimes only to decide not to prosecute, for instance, argued that the completion strategy meant that the focus of the ICTR should be on only prosecuting *those most responsible* for violations of international humanitarian law. As genocide was held as the crime of crimes, and the RPF's offences fell short of that definition, there was no grounds under the mandate to proceed to trial on any of these indictments.[117]

This episode, then, fed into the logic discussed previously, as the initial lofty goals of the court were, in the early 2000s, jettisoned for a focus on a narrower form of justice, as questions of efficiency took over. As with this example, the concern seemed to be simply to get the trials moving again as quickly as possible and accepting the more limited vision of justice that emerged with the competition strategy. As with the other decisions discussed in this chapter, this had additional consequences for the archive too. The first was that this has led to a profound and troubling silence in the records about the serious

---

[115] CERD/C/SR.1212, *International Convention on the Elimination of All Forms of Racial Discrimination, Summary of Record of the 1212th Meeting*, 26 March 1997, 3–4 and 7–8; and UNGA, A/C.3/52/SR.34, *Third Committee: Summary Record of the 34th Meeting*, 17 February 1998, 4–5.

[116] This also saw the end of Carla Del Ponte's time as prosecutor. Peskin, *International Justice*, 219–22.

[117] OTP 3 (2015); Interview with Member of ICTR OTP 4 (2015); and UNSC, S/RES/1503, *Resolution 1503*, 28 August 2003, 2. In defence of this decision, the OTP also point to the transferral of case files of four RPF military leaders to Rwanda for prosecution.

crimes committed by the RPF. Additionally, by erasing information pertaining to crimes largely committed against Hutus, this further solidified the link between Hutus and perpetratorhood and Tutsis and victimhood discussed in Chapter 3.

CONCLUSION

This chapter has demonstrated how the conception of justice that underpinned the archive shifted over time as various actors introduced different ideas about what it was the tribunal should try to achieve. This showed that relationships between different subject positions – such as witnesses and lawyers – were unstable and evolved over time, and responded to different contexts, highlighting the performative and dynamic nature of law. As time passed the construction of the archive increasingly became governed by principles of economic and efficient justice. This fractured the tribunal's initial claims that it could deliver a holistic vision of justice. This also suggests a shift in the type of community the archive imagined into existence. For this also meant that the centrality of the victim was removed from within the archive. These themes will be examined in the following chapter as I examine in more detail the question of what vision of community was projected from the archive.

CHAPTER SIX

IMAGINING COMMUNITY

In this chapter, the question of what type of international community was projected out from the archive is placed front and centre of the analysis. This, in part, pulls together findings from the previous chapters. But this also pushes that analysis further by considering the archive as a site where heterogeneous discourses underpinned by different imaginings of the international order intersected to influence the archive's rules. This looks to examine how these discourses impacted on the production of knowledge, the determination of guilt and the formation of a particular imagining of community.[1] This Chapter further highlights the importance of the archive's materialism for understanding archival politics. Ultimately, the chapter shows that the essentially liberal vision of community contained within the archive conceals a number of worrying, and often distinctly illiberal, undercurrents, particularly concerning colonialism, violence and gender.[2]

LIBERALISM AND THE ARCHIVE

In many respects, the creation of the ICTR in the mid-1990s captured the feeling of the age; this paradoxically reflected the rising concern with the spread of violent intra-state conflict and the hope of the possibility of a liberal world order after the end of the Cold War.[3]

---

[1] Michel Foucault, 'The Confession of the Flesh', in Gordon, *Power/ Knowledge*, 194–95.

[2] Some of the findings formed this chapter have been further discussed in Henry Redwood, 'Archiving (In)Justice: Building Archives and Imagining Community', *Millennium: Online First* (October 2020).

[3] Michael Cox, 'Power and the Liberal Order' in *After Liberalism?* eds. Rebekka Friedman, Kevork Oskanian and Ramon Pacheco Pardo (London: Palgrave Macmillan, 2013), 103–6;

Indeed, international courts like the ICTR are excellent examples of the types of liberal institutions that became increasingly prominent throughout the international system at this time, capturing both the normative-expressive[4] and rational-legal (or technocratic) functions that Michel Barnett and Martha Finnemore argue define liberal tools of governance.[5] Consequently, the ICTR's archive was anchored around a number of concepts that are linked to this normative liberal agenda: individualism, progress, equality and neutrality, and universalism.[6] Whilst it is already clear that the archive, as such, adhered to a *particular* world view as it tried to bring about a liberal world order, as the rest of this chapter demonstrates, an adherence to these principles concealed the formation of a distinctly more illiberal vision of community.[7]

RESPONSIBILITY, PROGRESS AND THE ARCHIVE

As Chapters 2 and 3 suggested, the archive was very much focused on the role of individuals in the Rwandan genocide. One of the tribunal's supposed strengths was its ability to determine individual responsibility in order to sort out the guilty from innocent. This, it was hoped, would contribute towards establishing peace and reconciliation in Rwanda. This focus on the individual also shaped the contents of the archive, as the need to find an individual responsible for a crime meant stressing that perpetrators were conscious and rational actors that had the ability to determine the course of events.[8] Within international humanitarian law the idea of rational actors is perhaps even more heightened when compared with municipal law as additional layers of intent are added. To establish a conviction for genocide, for instance, the prosecution had to prove that, in addition to the standard *mens rea*, the accused

---

Michel Barnett and Martha Finnemore. 'The Power of Liberal International Organizations', in *Power in Global Governance*, ed. Michael Barnett and Raymond Duvall (Cambridge: Cambridge University Press, 2005): 163–71.

[4] Michael Dillon and Julian Reid. 'Global governance, Liberal Peace, and Complex Emergency', *Alternatives* 25:1(2000): 117–19.

[5] Barnett and Finnemore, 'Power', 162–66; Vivienne Jabri, 'War, Government, Politics: A Critical Response to the Hegemony of the Liberal Peace', in *Palgrave Advances in Peacebuilding*, ed. Oliver Richmond (London: Palgrave Macmillan, 2010),47.

[6] Oliver P. Richmond, 'The Problem of Peace: Understanding the "Liberal Peace"', *Conflict, Security & Development*, 6:3 (2006): 291–15; Jabri, 'War, Government, Politics', 45–48.

[7] Roland Paris, 'Saving Liberal Peacebuilding', *Review of International Studies*, April 2010, 36:2 (2010): 337–65.

[8] Jabri, 'War, Government, Politics', 47.

intended that their act of violence contribute to the destruction of a particular group (in whole or in part).[9]

Interestingly, however, examining the archive's contents suggests that there was a shift in the rules which affected this focus on the individual. Indeed, as has been discussed, during the early years of the ICTR (and ICTY) there were changes in the jurisprudence to accommodate for the specific nature of crimes like genocide, including the collective nature of perpetration. This included the development of joint criminal enterprise (JCE) and command responsibility as modes of liability.[10]

As was noted in Chapter 3, command responsibility determined that a superior had the responsibility to 'prevent or punish' a crime committed by subordinates. The ICTR significantly added to this jurisprudence by expanding the applicability of command responsibility to private organisations (rather than just military or government structures as it had been previously limited to) and also inserting an expansive understanding of the roles and responsibilities of persons in the position of command. Initially, the *mens reas* was understood broadly, and so the prosecution merely had to establish that a superior *should have known* about their subordinates' crimes (either before or after the fact). This worked under a presumption of knowledge based on the accused's rank and responsibilities.[11] This would, theoretically at least, make it easier to hold superiors to account for crimes committed 'on their watch'.[12] A similar story can be told about the introduction of JCE. The prosecution, at both the ICTR and ICTY, developed an 'expanded' form of JCE, where a member of a JCE could be held to account for crimes committed by other JCE members as long as the occurrence of such as crime was a *foreseeable* consequence of the JCE.[13]

---

[9] This emphasis of the individual is not universally celebrated. As Mark Drumbl has argued, this focus on the individual is often seen as diminishing law's ability to understand the collective nature of crimes such as genocide. Mark Drumbl, 'Pluralising International Criminal Justice: From Nuremberg to the Hague: The Future of International Criminal Justice by Philippe Sands', *Michigan Law Review* 103:6 (2005): 1302–4. See also Tim Kelsall, *Culture under Cross-examination: International Justice and the Special Court for Sierra Leone* (Cambridge: Cambridge University Press, 2009), 8–16; and Michael Humphrey, 'International Intervention, Justice and National Reconciliation: The Role of the ICTY and ICTR in Bosnia and Rwanda', *Journal of Human Rights* 2:4 (2003), 498.

[10] See Chapter 4, 85–89.

[11] Allison Danner and Jenny Martinez, 'Guilty Associations: Joint Criminal Enterprise, Command Responsibility, and the Development of International Criminal Law', *California Law Review* 93:1 (2005): 124–30.

[12] Ibid., 148.

[13] Ibid., 132–37.

Whilst this suggested a shift towards more collective modes of liability, over time the archive refocused in on the individual. With regard to command responsibility, this saw a shift in the intent threshold so that to find a defendant guilty the prosecution had to establish the superior's *actual knowledge* of the crime.[14] This made it far harder to hold superiors to account. Similarly, with the extended form of JCE, there was a shift from emphasising the foreseeability of a crime, to the accused's explicit intent for the crime to occur, and/or that they had substantially contributed to its commission.[15] The effects of these shifts can be seen in the appeals judgment for '*Military 1*', against Colonel Théoneste Bagosora, Major Aloys Ntabakuze and Colonel Anatole Nsengiyumva, often seen as amongst the genocide's chief architects. In applying a more conservative reading of command responsibility, the appeals judgment overturned the trial chamber's ruling regarding the defendants' responsibility for crimes committed by their subordinates, resulting in a significant reduction in the accused's sentences.[16] This reduction was, as might be expected, not well received in Rwanda.

One explanation for this shift has already been discussed, which is that the initial, more expansive, reading of these modes of liability marked the intrusion of human rights–style methodologies into the judicial decision-making process.[17] As such, the shift to a more restricted understanding of responsibility simply represented the re-establishment of a more traditional approach to criminal justice. There is, however, an alternative explanation.

Judge Harhoff, a former appeals judge at the ad hoc tribunals, was dismissed after a leaked letter revealed his concern that the appeals chamber was increasingly restricting the applicability of command responsibility and JCE, as discussed earlier.[18] In the letter, Harhoff warned that leading world powers had pressured the appeals chamber to restrict the law due to a concern that the broader interpretations of

---

[14] *Ibid.*, 127; Beatrice Bonafé, 'Finding a Proper Role for Command Responsibility', *Journal of International Criminal Justice* 5:3 (2007): 606–7; Judge Harhoff, 'Leaked Letter', found: www.bt.dk /sites/default/files–dk/node–files/511/6/6511917–letter–english.pdf (last accessed 18 August 2019). For an interesting overview of the controversies and shifts in approaches to this jurisprudence see Jenny Martinez, 'Understanding Mens Rea in Command Responsibility: From Yamashita to Blaškić and Beyond', *Journal of International Criminal Justice* 5:3 (2007): 638–64.

[15] Harhoff, 'Leaked Letter'.

[16] *Prosecutor v. Théoneste Bagosora, Gratien Kabiligi, Anatole Nsengiyumva and Aloys Ntabakuze*, ICTR-98–41, *Appeal Judgement*, 14 December 2011.

[17] Danner, and Martinez, 'Guilty Associations', 103–20, 132–39 and 145–46.

[18] Harhoff, 'Leaked Letter'.

command responsibility and JCE would make it too easy to hold military commanders and heads of state to account for crimes committed by subordinates. This would in turn, they feared, overly restrict military operations, as commanders would become overly cautious so they did not fall foul of the law if their subordinates used excessive levels of violence.[19]

The tribunal has denied Harhoff's account. Yet other significant actors at the court have, nonetheless, offered support for the underpinning logic that IHL should not *overly* restrict military operations. President Meron (who was also the presiding judge in *Military 1*) has, for example, argued that the purpose of IHL is to 'diminish the evils of war, *as far as military requirements permit*' (emphasis added).[20]

The cause of this shift is less important, however, than what this means for the archive's rules and vision of community. For this shift re-centred the knowing individual at the heart of the archive. Indeed, with the change to 'actual knowledge' and the added emphasis on the defendant's intention, the tribunal's emphasis on the collective nature of the genocide diminished. With this a liberal notion of the individual and community, where each person takes responsibility for their own actions, was re-emphasised. This also, however, says something about the role of violence and responsibility within the community constituted by the archive. For instance, when thinking about the potential implications of this in terms of military and political governance, this shift in the jurisprudence *removed* some of the onus for those in positions of command to maintain strict oversight of subordinates and to prevent and punish their crimes.[21] It also lessened the likelihood of being prosecuted for becoming involved in a JCE. This, when combined with Meron's statement mentioned earlier, is suggestive that, whether conscious or otherwise, there was a shift in the application of the law which worked to reframe the archive's rules in a way that retained a greater space for violence to take place within the international community.[22]

[19] OTP 2 (2015); *Ibid.*, 149. Whilst Martinez and Danner placed greater emphasis on the return to a more traditional mode of criminal justice, it is worth acknowledging that they too suggest that external actors played a role. Danner, and Martinez, 'Guilty Associations', 96–102 and 189.

[20] Theodor Meron, 'The Humanization of Humanitarian Law', *American Journal of International Law* 94: 2 (2000): 243. See also p. 241. Interview with Member of ICTR OTP 9 (June 2015).

[21] Harhoff, 'Leaked Letter'.

[22] Bonafé, 'Finding a Proper Role for Command Responsibility', 604–12; Elizabeth Dauphinee, 'War Crimes and the Ruin of Law', *Millennium-Journal of International Studies* 37:1 (2008): 52; Jenny Edkins, *Trauma and the Memory of Politics* (Cambridge: Cambridge University Press, 2003), 5–15, 190–91 and 201.

This finding resonates with Elizabeth Dauphinee's argument that rather than seeking to *eradicate* violence from the international community, IHL works to delegitimise *certain* acts of violence and in the process legitimise others. Dauphinee argues that to a great extent war and IHL are dependent on each other: war needs IHL to separate off a domain of violence that is 'illegal', therefore legitimising other forms of violence; IHL needs some violence to be legitimate for it would have no function without drawing a line between illegitimate and legitimate acts.[23] As Louise Arbour, former ICTR prosecutor, argued:

> Another issue that is critical to the future of international justice is the recognition by the military of its *ownership* of international humanitarian law. International humanitarian law *is military law* .... International humanitarian law is the law that distinguishes a soldier in action from the common murderer. (emphasis added)[24]

As certain bodies are emphasised as victims of illegitimate violence, others are concealed and in the process war's need for violence and death to achieve its goals is put back into the shadows and it becomes possible both to view war again as simply politics by other means[25] – and not murder – and to detach war crimes from war, and the systems of power that enable it, in order to revive them.[26] Moreover, the use of terms like 'war crimes' not only acts to both simultaneously legitimise and de-legitimise certain forms of violence, but it also, with the technocratic legal response that is mobilised as a result, creates the sense that there is a solution to stop the 'excess' without altering the system altogether and that international courts are part of that solution.[27]

This is, then, also about how ideas of responsibility are structured (and ultimately restricted) within the archive and how this links to ideas of community. In this respect, another omission from the archive is

---

[23] Dauphinee, 'War Crimes and the Ruin of Law', 52.

[24] Louise Arbour, 'The Status of the International Criminal Tribunals for the Former Yugoslavia and Rwanda: Goals and Results', *Hofstra Law and Policy Symposium* 3 (1999): 44.

[25] *Ibid.*, 58–59.

[26] Edkins, *Trauma and the Memory of Politics*, 1–9; Michael Humphrey, 'From Victim to Victimhood: Truth Commissions and Trials as Rituals of Political Transition and Individual Healing', *The Australian Journal of Anthropology* 13: 2 (2003): 181; Austin Sarat and Thomas Kearns. 'A Journey through Forgetting: Toward a Jurisprudence of Violence', in *The Fate of Law*, eds. Austin Sarat and Thomas Kearns (Michigan: The University of Michigan, 1993), 210. 'The perpetrator's actions are seen to exclude him or her from human society in order to sustain to maintain the intersubjectivities ties between humans, and hence the possibility of humanity itself.' Kirsten Campbell, 'Victims and Perpetrators of International Crimes: The Problem of the "Legal Person"', *Journal of International Humanitarian Legal Studies* 2: 2 (2011), 339.

[27] Dauphinee, 'War Crimes', 62–63.

important: the responsibility of international actors during the genocide. One example of this was the contribution of the international arms trade, which by flooding Rwanda with cheap weapons significantly contributed to the violence.[28] Another important example is France's contribution to the genocide, by training, arming, and providing financial support to the genocidaires.[29] Again, part of the reason behind this omission is the tribunal's focus on individual responsibility. But importantly, as noted in Chapter 3, discussion of the international dimension of the violence was explicitly prohibited at the tribunal. During *Gatete* the judges took judicial notice of the *non*-international nature of the conflict, which unequivocally stated that there was no room for any records relating to the international nature of the genocide in the archive.[30] As will be recalled, one of the reasons for the decision was that the UNSC had only given the tribunal jurisdiction over crimes of a non-international nature in the statute, offering yet further evidence of how politics shaped law and the archive.[31] The result of this exclusion was that international structures and actors sank into the background within the archive.

This had a number of additional consequences. First, the archive's account of violence and responsibility became focused almost exclusively on Rwanda. This treated the genocide as a localised event and so portrayed Rwanda as an isolated site of barbarity. In contrast, and despite the prevalence of international actors assisting the genocide, the lack of records related to these aspects of the violence worked to separate the international, a site of peace, order and civilisation, from the violence committed in the local, and *absolve* the international community of its responsibility for the violence.[32] Not only this, the archive portrays the international, through enacting law and 'bringing justice' to Rwanda, as saviour.[33] This, as such, produced a dichotomy between the international and the local that mirrored Chinua Achebe's description of the West's portrayal of Africa as 'the other

[28] For an example of how important the supply of weapons was in the genocide see TRA005592, 13–14.

[29] See Chapter 2, *supra note 29.*

[30] *Prosecutor* v. *Jean Baptiste Gatete*, Case No. ICTR–00–61, ICTR–00–61–0086/1, *Gatete – Decision on Prosecution's Motion for Judicial Notice of Facts of Common Knowledge*, 21 August 2009.

[31] ICTR–99–46, TRA001278/2, *[Cyangugu] – Ntagerura et al – Redacted Transcript of 29/05/2002*, 29 May 2002, 129.

[32] For the link between archives and responsibility see John Dirks, 'Accountability, History, and Archives: Conflicting Priorities or Synthesized Strands?', *Archivia* 57 (2004): 29–49.

[33] Tim Kelsall, 'Politics, Anti-Politics, International Justice: Language and Power in the Special Court for Sierra Leone', *Review of International Studies* 32:4 (2006): 587–602. See also Edkins, *Trauma*, 1–19; Dauphinee, 'War Crimes'.

world, the antithesis of Europe and therefore of civilisation, a place where a man's vaunted intelligence and refinement are finally mocked by triumphant bestiality'.[34] It was exactly this dichotomy between civilisation and the Other that underpinned the sense of the *necessity* of colonial expansion as the barbarous Other was deemed incapable of ruling themselves. As such, within the archive this division between the international and the local reproduced a discourse and set of power relations which had been central to colonial domination.

As Chapter 2 demonstrated, this nomenclature of violence, and the division between the local and the international, also underpinned the international community's decision not to do more to prevent the genocide. This division also helped legitimise the creation of the ICTR as a site that could 'neutrally' administer justice due to the UN's impartiality throughout the conflict, concealing the imbedded nature of the 'international community' in the violence in the first place.[35]

Whilst there is a paradox here, in that this distinction between the local and international both prevented and legitimised intervention, cutting across these examples is the constitution of the local as an irrational and barbaric space, and that it is consistently those that claim to speak for the international community – often actors from the Global North with long colonial histories – rather than those experience the violence – often actors from the Global South – that decide the terms upon which, and indeed when, intervention takes place.[36]

As such, when combined with particular discursive imaginings about the international order, the liberal undercurrents of the arch-ive, especially its focus on individuals, had a number of unintended consequences for how the international community was imagined within the archive. As this has shown, this includes both creating a space within which 'military necessity' trumps protecting potential

---

[34] Chinua Achebe, 'An Image of Africa', *Massachusetts Review* 18:4 (1977), 784. As discussed in Chapter 2, this way of understanding the violence also dominated the Western media's coverage of the genocide. See Chapter 2, *supra note*, 17. Indeed, this was the narrative framework that underpinned the ICTR's only prosecution of a non-Rwandan, George Ruggiu, a former radio presenter for RTLM. ICTR-97–32-I, *Prosecutor v. George Ruggiu, Judgement and Sentence*, 1 June 2000, paras 61–72.

[35] A number of former ICTR employees also noted that the ICTY was considered to be a superior institution to the ICTR and dealt with more interesting matters of law. This, also, I believe represents a degree of Othering as once more the violence committed on the borders of Europe is treated more seriously than that on the African continent. Interview with Appeals Judge (June 2015); Interview with Member of ICTR OTP 9 (June 2015).

[36] Jessica Whyte, "Always on Top"? The "Responsibility to Protect" and the Persistence of Colonialism', in *The Postcolonial World*, eds. Jyotsna Singh and David Kim (London: Routledge, 2016), 310–11; Jabri, 'War, Government, Politics', 47–49.

victims and where an understanding of the causes of violence as centred around the individual and the local obscured the wider structures and processes that underpin violence within the international community. This, I would argue, raises questions about the idea that developing international criminal justice *necessarily* signals progress in terms of establishing international peace and security. As this has also shown, the archive divided the international domain into the international, a site of peace and order, and the local, a site of barbarity, introducing what can be interpreted as a colonial rationality into the heart of the archive.

EQUALITY AND NEUTRALITY: GENDER, VIOLENCE AND THE ARCHIVE

The principles of equality and neutrality were also important features of the archive's liberal and enlightenment world view. From this perspective, deciding a case is about the rational assessment of evidence and the technical application of the law. Such a vision of law has already been roundly critiqued throughout this book. This section, however, delves deeper into this claim, as I examine the gendered nature of the archive, which had a significant bearing on both how cases were decided and what vision of community was projected. The following examines this in two ways: the first shows how gender helped construct the archive's objects and the second examines how gender affected how evidence was collected and processed for the archive.

Imagining Actors

Gender played a role in defining the archive's understanding of both perpetrators and victims. As discussed in Chapter 3, within the archive victims were often constituted as passive and innocent, which ensured that they were seen as non-combatants and therefore illegitimate targets of violence. However, a close examination of the records shows that these objects were also gendered, as victims became strongly associated with feminine identities, such as women, children and the elderly.[37] During *Cyangugu* Judge Ostrovsky asked a witness:

---

[37] Prosecutor v. Jean-Paul Akayesu, Case No. ICTR–96–4 (hereafter ICTR–96–4, CONTRA001184, *Akayesu – Transcript of 16/1/1997*, 16 January 1997, 37. See also ICTR–96–4, CONTRA001179, *Akayesu – Transcript of 21/1/1997*, 21 January 1997, 57; CONTRA001195, 108 and 117; ICTR–96–4, CONTRA001208, *Akayesu – Transcript of 18/11/1997*, 18 November 1997, 115; ICTR–96–4, CONTRA001183, *Akayesu – Transcript of 15/1/1997*, 15 January 1997, 139; UNSC, S/1994/1157/Add.1, *Situation of Human Rights in Rwanda: Third Report on the Situation of Human*

And please, tell me. You attended several cabinet meetings, starting from 16th April. During those cabinet meetings, was there ever a discussion of extermination of *women, elderly persons, children; that is, civilian population.* And you referred to the term 'the Tutsi of within'. *That would include the civilian population; i.e., women, children and elderly persons.* (emphasis added)[38]

Within this logic, feminine subjects were automatically seen as civilians and therefore illegitimate targets of violence. This also, however, worked to reproduce the myth that 'women and children' are inherently passive subjects of international politics.

This understanding of the gendered nature of victimhood has now been thoroughly critiqued by feminist scholars,[39] and this association between feminine subjects and victimhood obfuscates the more complex role that women play in conflict.[40] This includes the direct participation of women in the violence, which, as the Special Rapporteur on Violence against Women noted, was a particular feature of the Rwandan genocide. Whilst overstating the novelty of this, the report concluded:

The genocide in Rwanda was sadly characterized by a new phenomenon which has not been observed in any armed conflict in history, namely the massive involvement of women as perpetrators of the violence. Survivors testify that not only did women take part in the general violence and fighting during the conflict, but were also actively involved in committing violence against other women, including acts of sexual violence.[41]

Rights in Rwanda Submitted by Mr. René Degni-Ségui, Special Rapporteur of the Commission on Human Rights, Under Paragraph 20 of Resolution S–3/1 of 25 May 1994, 14 November 1994, 11; ICTR–96–4, CONTRA001222, *Akayesu – Transcript of 23/10/1997,* 23 October 1997, 30 and 34; ICTR–99–46, TRA000527/2, *[Cyangugu] – Ntagerura et al – Redacted Transcript of 13/03/2002,* 13 March 2002, 75; and *Prosecutor* v. *Jean Baptiste Gatete,* Case No. ICTR–00–61 (hereafter, ICTR–00–61), TRA005145/1, *Gatete – Redacted Transcript of 10/3/2010,* 10 March 2010, 64. 'It requires as well a deeper understanding and respect for the rights of minorities and respect for the needs of the more *vulnerable groups of society, especially women and children* (emphasis added).' A/47/277–S/24111, *An Agenda for Peace: Preventative Diplomacy, Peacemaking and Peace-Keeping: Report of the Secretary-General Pursuant to the Statement Adopted by the Summit Meeting of the Security Council on 21 January 1992,* 17 June 1992, 23.

[38] *Prosecutor* v. *André Ntagerura, Emmanuel Bagambiki and Samuel Imanishimwe,* Case No. ICTR–99–46 (hereafter ICTR–99–46), TRA001277/2, *[Cyangugu] – Ntagerura et al – Redacted Transcript of 28/05/2002,* 28 May 2002, 80.

[39] Caron E. Gentry and Laura Sjoberg, *Mothers, Monsters, Whores: Women's Violence in Global Politics* (Chicago: Zed Books, 2007); Cynthia Enloe, *Bananas, Beaches, and Bases: Making Feminist Sense of International Politics* (London: Pandora, 1989).

[40] Sara Brown, 'Female Perpetrators of the Rwandan Genocide', *International Feminist Journal of Politics* 16:3 (2014): 448–69; Lisa Sharlach, 'Gender and Genocide in Rwanda: Women as Agents and Objects', *Journal of Genocide Research* 1:3 (1999): 387–99.

[41] The report also notes that '[i]n the 19 central prisons in Rwanda, 2,687 prisoners out of a total of 77,349 (or 3.7 per cent) are women'. E/CN.4/1998/54/Add.1, 24.

Despite this, the archive overlooked the role that women played in the violence, and it is, on the whole, only men that were allowed to act as perpetrators. Only one woman was indicted by the tribunal for their role in the genocide (Pauline Nyamirashoko, in *Butare*), but this is very much the exception that proves the rule. This silence as to the role that women played in the violence permeated through all trial records considered here, as not one witness from the three cases examined in depth presented evidence of women as anything but victims. This silence, then, fed back to reaffirm the gendered understanding of victimhood and perpetratorhood.

There are broader implications for this association between feminine subjects, victimhood and passivity. As the work of Kieran McEvoy and Kirsten McConachie shows, the idea of the passive victim can be seen as part, at least, of the reason why victims remain excluded from transitional justice processes.[42] If victims are simply passive figures, it is unsurprising that transitional justice mechanisms continue to focus on the perpetrators, who, as the active participants in the conflict, need to be dealt with to secure peace. If gender is added to this analysis, then this also helps to explain why women are so often sidelined in transitional justice processes.[43]

Building the Archive

Catherine MacKinnon, Martha Walsh, Kirsten Campbell and Binaifer Nowrojee, amongst others, have led the way examining how gender and patriarchy affect the practice of international law.[44] Each has shown that gender-based crimes are under-investigated and -prosecuted and that even when these types of crimes make it to trial they are subjected to higher standards of proof.[45] These patterns were clearly evident at the ICTR. This is, moreover, despite the fact that the ICTR remains

[42] Kieran McEvoy and Kirsten McConnachie, 'Victims and Transitional Justice: Voice, Agency and Blame', *Social and Legal Studies* 22:4(2013): 489–513.

[43] Laura Shepherd and Caitlin Hamilton, 'Gender and Peacebuilding', in *Handbook on Gender and War*, eds. Simona Sharoni, Julia Welland, Linda Steiner, and Jennifer Pedersen (Cheltenham: Edward Elgar Publishing, 2016), 467–83; Maria O'Reilly, 'Gender and Peacebuilding', *Routledge Handbook of Peacebuilding*, eds. in Roger MacGinty (London: Routledge, 2013): 72–83.

[44] Martha Walsh, 'Gendering International Justice: Progress and Pitfalls at International Criminal Tribunals', in *Gender Peace: Women's Struggle for Post-War Justice and Reconciliation*, ed. Donna Pankhurst (Abingdon: Routledge, 2009), 31–65; Kirsten Campbell, 'Testimonial Modes: Witnessing, Evidence and Testimony before the International Criminal Tribunal for the Former Yugoslavia', in *The Future of Testimony*, ed. Antony Rowland *et al.* (London: Routledge, 2014), 83–113; and Catherine MacKinnon, 'The ICTR's Legacy on Sexual Violence', *New England Journal of International and Comparative Law* 14:1 (2007), 211–21.

[45] Walsh, 'Gendering International Justice', 33–34; Campbell, 'Testimonial Modes', 92–95; MacKinnon, 'Sexual Violence', 214–15; and Catherine MacKinnon, 'Crimes of War, Crimes of Peace', *UCLA Women's Law Journal* 4 (1993): 59–87.

seen as having been at the forefront of the development of gender-sensitive jurisprudence – a narrative that the tribunal itself has carefully cultivated.[46]

By the time the ICTR's investigations into the genocide began, it was already clear that sexual violence had formed an integral part of the genocide. According to Richard Goldstone (the first prosecutor) and Patricia Sellers (who was in charge of addressing gender-related issues at the ICTR, both institutionally and in terms of investigations) prosecuting sexual violence crimes was, consequently, a priority for the OTP from the tribunal's outset.[47] As the following demonstrates, this supposed prioritisation, however, failed to translate into practice.[48] And in this respect, problems began with the initial investigations. One former employee at the tribunal during the early years suggested that a male-dominated atmosphere clouded the tribunal's investigations and stopped gender-based crimes emerging as a priority.[49] Lisa Pruitt, who was sent to Rwanda to investigate the possibility of adding sexual violence charges to *Akayesu*, similarly noted that the investigators she met gave the impression that '[w]ell, we can't be concerned about some women who got raped. We can't divert resources to investigate those crimes. We had a genocide down here.'[50]

As this suggests a hierarchy of victimhood was imbedded within the archive from the off, which entrenched the notion that gender-based violence was less significant when compared to other crimes, such as genocide (and despite the fact that rape could be classified as genocide). Whilst this did partially improve with the creation of the sexual violence investigation unit in 1998 (discussed in Chapter 3),[51] throughout the

---

[46] The finding in *Akayesu* that rape could be considered an act of genocide is often cited here. OTP ICTR, 'Prosecution of Sexual Violence: Best Practices Manual for the Investigation and Prosecution of Sexual Violence Crimes in Post-conflict Regions: Lessons Learned from the Office of the Prosecutor for the International Criminal Tribunal for Rwanda', (2014) found: www.unmict.org (last accessed 1 August 2017).

[47] Interview with Richard Goldstone, *Voices of the Rwanda Tribunal* (University of Washington, 2008); Interview with Patricia Sellers, *Voices of the Rwanda Tribunal* (University of Washington, 2008).

[48] Moreover, as Catherine Franke notes, gender-based violence was (and remains) problematically and narrowly conceived of as sexual violence alone to the detriment of other crimes that also specifically target women. Katherine Franke, 'Gendered Subjects of Transitional Justice', *Journal of Gender and Law* 15:3 (2006), 818–20.

[49] Interview with ICTR Appeal Judge (June 2016); see also Interview with Sellers, 20.

[50] Jina Moore, 'This Is the Story a UN Court Didn't Want Three Rape Survivors to Tell', *Buzzfeed*. Found: www.buzzfeed.com/jinamoore/this-is-the-story-a-un-court-didnt-want-three-rape-survivors ?utm_term=.efwZxxYY8#.jawdwwrrm (last accessed 16 January 2017); Interview with Richard Karegyesa, *Voices of the Rwanda Tribunal* (University of Washington, 2008), 10.

[51] UNGA, A/53/429, *Report of the International Criminal Tribunal for the Prosecution of Persons Responsible for Genocide and Other Serious Violations of International Humanitarian Law Committed*

tribunal's history gender-based violence remained insufficiently investigated. Even where evidence was collected, it was poorly incorporated into the prosecution's case strategy, which had significant consequences for the archive and its imaginings of community.

The effects of this could clearly be seen in *Cyangugu*. The initial indictment did not contain any specific reference to sexual violence charges.[52] The first suggestion that the prosecution intended to present evidence relating to sexual violence crimes came on 2 December 1999 when the prosecution submitted an amended indictment that specifically contained sexual violence charges.[53] However, this was then withdrawn two months later, and with this the specific references to sexual violence were seemingly removed from the case.[54] The situation became murkier still as both the prosecution's pre-trial brief and opening statement in *Cyangugu* noted the intention to prosecute the accused for sexual violence crimes, specifically linked to the charge against Bagambiki and Imanishimwe relating to their participation in the abduction and killing of refugees from the Karamapaka stadium.[55] The matter came to a head when Witness LBH started testifying to the occurrence of sexual violence at Karamapaka stadium but was stopped as the defence objected that they had not been made aware of the prosecution's intention to press charges on this matter, noting the absence of any reference to sexual violence in the indictment. The prosecution's argument that the pre-trial brief, opening statement, *and the amended indictment* (even though it was withdrawn) had put the defendants on notice was ultimately rejected by the judges, and the prosecution were subsequently prohibited from presenting evidence

---

in the Territory of Rwanda and Rwandan Citizens Responsible for Genocide and Other Such Violations Committed in the Territory of Neighbouring States between 1 January and 31 December 1994, 23 September 1998, 9–10; UNESC, E/CN.4/1998/54/Add.1, *Further Promotion and Encouragement of Human Rights and Fundamental Freedoms, Including the Question of the Programme and Methods of Work of the Commission Alternative Approaches and Ways and Means within the United Nations System for Improving the Effective Enjoyment of Human Rights and Fundamental Freedoms Report of the Special Rapporteur on Violence Against Women, Its Causes and Consequences, Ms. Radhika Coomaraswamy Addendum Report of the Mission to Rwanda on the Issues of Violence against Women in Situations of Armed Conflict*, 4 February 1998, 12–13.

[52] ICTR–96–10, ICTR–96–10A–0224, Ntagerura – *Amended Indictment*, 29 January 1998; and *Prosecutor v. Emmanuel Bagambiki et al.*, Case No. ICTR–97–36 (hereafter ICTR–97–36), ICTR–97–36–0071, Bagambiki – Imanishimwe – *Indictment – Redacted*, 9 October 1997, 7.

[53] ICTR–96–10A–0224, 4–5.

[54] ICTR–99–46, ICTR–99–46–0046, [Cyangugu] – Bagambiki – Ntagerura et al – *Notice of the Prosecutor to Withdraw All Pending Motion*, 14 February 2000.

[55] ICTR–99–46, ICTR–99–46–0072, [Cyangugu] – Bagambiki – Ntagerura et al – *The Prosecutor's Preliminary Pre–Trial Brief*, 24 May 2000, 13–14; and ICTR–99–46, TRA000542/1, [Cyangugu] – Ntagerura et al – *Redacted Transcript of 18/09/2001*, 18 September 2001, 53.

concerning sexual violence.[56] Following this, an *amicus curie* was submitted by the Coalition for Women's Human Rights in Conflict Situation, which called for the prosecution to amend their indictment so as to include sexual violence charges (as they had also successfully done in *Akayesu*), but this was rejected by both the judges and the prosecution and as such sexual violence remained absent from the prosecution's account of violence in *Cyangugu*.[57]

Part of the reason that the prosecution did not follow through with the amended indictment was because of the OTP's policy to avoid amending indictments unless absolutely necessary so as not to slow down the trials.[58] This decision should be understood within the context, as discussed in Chapter 5, of the considerable pressure being applied by the UNSC at the turn of the millennium for trials to speed up. However, in this instance it should have been clear that the prosecution was going to struggle to pursue sexual violence charges under the explicit accusation that Bagambiki and Imanishimwe had abducted and killed refugees from Karamapaka stadium. At best this shows the prosecution chancing their luck. However, when considered alongside the prosecution's broader treatment of sexual violence, this suggests a concerning lack of focus on gender-based violence.

The archive contains numerous traces of where the treatment of sexual violence evidence goes beyond indifference and shows an overt hostility to this type of potential record.[59] For example, during *Cyangugu*, a reference to sexual violence was *erased* from the archive on the request of the defence in light of the aforementioned decision to exclude evidence of sexual violence from the trial. This erasure is signified in Figure 2 by '[DELETED TEXT]'.

---

[56] TRA000434/2, 13–16 and 103–5; and ICTR–99–46, TRA000437/2, [Cyangugu] – Ntagerura *et al – Redacted Transcript of 20/02/2001*, 20 February 2001, 1–2.

[57] ICTR–99–46, ICTR–99–46–0270, [Cyangugu] – Imanishimwe – *Response of the Defence for Samuel Imanishimwe to Amicus Curiae Application Filed by the NGO Coalition for Women's Human Rights in Conflict Situation*, 27 April 2001; and ICTR–99–46, ICTR–99–46–0287, [Cyangugu] – Bagambiki – Ntagerura et al – *Decision on the Application to File an Amicus Curiae Brief According to Rule 74 of the Rules of Procedure and Evidence Filed on Behalf of the NGO Coalition for Women's Human Rights in Conflict Situations*, 24 May 2001.

[58] OTP 3 (2015).

[59] The poor success rate was also admitted by Prosecutor Jallow. Interview with Hassan Jallow, *Voices of the Rwanda Tribunal* (University of Washington, 2008), 23. The statistics contained in the prosecution's own 'best practice' guide to prosecuting sexual violence are telling in this respect. Of the thirty-seven defendants that had been accused of rape at the time the report was published, only seven were found guilty and upheld on appeal. Of the rest, sixteen defendants were acquitted at the trial of first instance, three on appeal and four saw the charges removed as part of their plea agreements. See ICTR Office of the Prosecution – Annex B: Statistics from the ICTR's Rape and Sexual Violence Cases (January 2014).

1   Q.   So, Witness LBH, what you are telling us is

2   that this building which belonged to a white

3   person, whose first name was Marcel, was

4   used by only one gendarme; is that correct?

5   A.   There were also a few Interahamwe who lived

6   in that house, the Interahamwe who I

7   mentioned whom came to select people. There

8   were also girls who were brought into that

9   building by gendarmes. The gendarmes would

10   select them from among the refugees from the

11   camp [DELETED TEXT].

12   MR. HENRY:

13   Mr. President, I'm going to expressly

14   request that this part of the testimony be

15   withdrawn, because you have already rendered

16   a decision on this type of evidence. And I

17   think in conformity with your decision, you

18   should not admit this type of evidence

19   adduced by the witness and which goes beyond

20   a question which I put to the witness; that

21   is, evidence related to rape.

22   MS. MAKWAIA:

23   Mr. President, the Prosecutor moves the

24   Court only to delete "rape", but the rest of

25   the evidence is relevant -- Interahamwe and

SHANNON L FLEMING - OFFICIAL COURT REPORTER
ICTR - TRIAL CHAMBER III
25

Figure 2 Extract from ICTR Record, TRA000436/2, 25[60]

[60] ICTR–99–46, TRA000436/2, [Cyangugu] – Ntagerura et al – Redacted Transcript of 19/02/2001, 19 February 2001, 25.

The significance of the erasure cannot be overstated. I am not aware of any other instance where a phrase is ex post facto *erased* from the archive. Sometimes when sensitive information was accidently included (that might, for example, lead to the identification of a protected witness) parts of the records might be put under seal and so concealed from the public. But in every other instance where evidence that exceeded the parameter of an indictment was uttered and successfully objected to, the judges argued they would simply ignore this evidence during deliberations.[61] Here, however, it seemed necessary to erase all *material* traces of this utterance so as not to taint the judges' future deliberations and, ultimately, the archive.

Two other instances demonstrate this concerning approach to sexual violence evidence.[62] The first comes from the *Rukundo* appeals.[63] In the *Rukundo* judgment, Rukundo, a military chaplain in FAR, was found guilty of genocide, in part, for sexually assaulting Witness CCH. The chamber found that at Kabgayi Parish:

> Rukundo forced sexual contact with [Witness CCH] by opening the zipper of his trousers, trying to remove her skirt, forcefully lying on top of her and caressing and rubbing himself against her until he ejaculated and lost his erection.[64]

The chamber also found that the assault had been coercive and caused serious mental harm and that Rukundo possessed the necessarily special intent because he had specifically targeted Witness CCH as a Tutsi. Here the judges relied on Rukundo's utterance to Witness CCH that he could not save her because she was related to *Inyenzi* (which literally

---

[61] *Prosecutor v. Jean Baptiste Gatete*, Case No. ICTR–00–61 (hereafter *Gatete*), ICTR–00–61–0133, *Gatete – Decision on Defence Motion on Admissibility of Allegations Outside the Temporal Jurisdiction of the Tribunal*, 03/11/2009; and *Gatete, Decision on Defence Motion for Exclusion of Evidence and Delineation of the Defence Case*, 26 March 2010.

[62] MacKinnon, 'Sexual Violence', 214–15. OTP ICTR, 'Prosecution of Sexual Violence', Appendix B, found: https://unictr.irmct.org/sites/unictr.org/files/publications/ICTR-Prosecuti on-of-Sexual-Violence.pdf (last accessed 30 October 2019). This also came up in a number of my interviews. Interview with Member of ICTR OTP 5 (June 2015); OTP 2 (2015); and OTP 3 (2015).

[63] Several decisions at trial level evidence this, including those made during *Kajelijeli* and *Nizeyimana*. Ibid., 214–15. Judge Ramaroson's dissenting decision in *Kajelijeli* captured their dissatisfaction with the majority's decision. 'In conclusion, and in the light of the foregoing, there is *substantial, specific and corroborative* evidence to sustain the allegation that Kajelijeli ... is responsible for the rapes perpetrated on women' (emphasis added). *Prosecutor v. Juvénal Kajelijeli*, Case No. ICTR–98–44, ICTR–98–44A–0320/1, *Judgment and Sentence*, 1 December 2003, 14. OTP 3 (2015); OTP 4 (2015).

[64] *Prosecutor v. Emmanuel Rukundo*, Case No. ICTR–01–70, ICTR–01–70–0393, *Judgement and Sentence*, 27 February 2009, 115.

translates as 'cockroach' and was a term strongly associated with the Tutsis during the genocide – see Chapter 4).[65]

The appeals chamber, however, found that the trial chamber had been wrong to find Rukundo guilty of genocide for this act:

> [T]he Appeals Chamber [...] finds that *no reasonable trier of fact* could find that the only reasonable inference available from the evidence was that Rukundo possessed genocidal intent in relation to the sexual assault of Witness CCH. (emphasis added)[66]

With this, the appeals chamber accepted the defence's argument that the assault was 'unplanned and spontaneous' and not the result of Rukundo's genocidal intent.[67] Bearing in mind the extremely high threshold that must be attained for an appeals chamber to overturn a trial chamber's decision (they must determine that *no reasonable* trier could have found this to be the true), it requires a significant leap of faith to believe that this would have been overturned if it had been *any other act of violence*.[68] Because Rukundo had only been charged with genocide for his assault of Witness CCH – *which the court accepted as fact* – he was acquitted of all criminal wrongdoing in relation to this crime.

Part of this decision can be explained by the gendered understanding of violence and evidence. Because Witness CCH was *sexually* assaulted it seemed impossible for the court to see that she could have also been targeted because of her ethnicity. Rather the attack was solely motivated by some seemingly natural desire that possessed Rukundo. In this regard, the court's rejection of the probative value of Rukundo's utterance that Witness CCH was an 'Inyenzi' was telling. Part of this decision, however, also comes back to the legal framework of the tribunal, and the tribunal's understanding of genocide and crimes against humanity, which contained no provisions for the court to consider that a victim could be targeted specifically because of their gender. This ultimately led to a decentring of women as the primary target of these crimes and supports MacKinnon's suggestion that when it comes to the law '[w]hat happens to women is either too particular to

---

[65] *Ibid.*, 117–18 and 172.

[66] *Prosecutor* v. *Emmanuel Rukundo*, Case No. ICTR–01–70, ICTR–01–70–0400/1, *Appeals Judgement*, 20 October 2010, 76.

[67] *Ibid.*, 76.

[68] MacKinnon, 'Sexual Violence', 215.

be universal or too universal to be particular, meaning either too human to be female or too female to be human'.[69]

Second, within the archive it is possible to see a worrying trend with how gender jurisprudence developed, which mirrored the trajectory of JCE and command responsibility jurisprudence. For instance, whilst *Akayesu* ruled, in an important decision, that the issue of consent was irrelevant for crimes that fell within the court's jurisdiction (because of the coercive nature of the surrounding environment), the *Gacumbitsi* appeals judgment (2006) found that a victim's lack of consent and *the perpetrator's knowledge* that this consent was absent *were* legally relevant and had to be established by the prosecution.[70] With this, the significant – and arguably more gender-sensitive – rulings of the early years were replaced with more conservative interpretations of the law. This meant, moreover, that the standard of proof for crimes of sexual violence became higher and the balance of power shifted from the victim to the defendant.[71]

This has shown how gendered and legal discourses intercepted within the archive to determine the legal outcome of the trials. As this clearly demonstrates, courts are not hermetically sealed-off spaces, but ones that are influenced by, and reproduce, particular social imaginings.[72] This was shown here both in how gendered discourse influenced how the archive identified 'victims' and processed and assessed evidence and in some cases even resulted in the erasure of evidence – rendering the material archive distinct from what had been discursively uttered in court. If the archive's function was to determine what violence is (il)legitimate and which subjects are considered worthy of protection within the community, then the absence of records relating to gender-based violence suggests that the archive reproduces a patriarchal understanding of community, where gender-based violence was considered as a secondary concern.

---

[69] MacKinnon, 'Crimes of War', 60.

[70] Patricia Sellers, 'The Prosecution of Sexual Violence in Conflict: The Importance of Human Rights as Means of Interpretation,' found: www.ohchr.org/Documents/Issues/Women/WRGS/Paper_Prosecution_of_Sexual_Violence.pdf (last accessed 1 June 2017), 23–23. More generally, after some initial success in securing convictions for sexual violence crimes, the prosecution's success rate fell off dramatically. Interview with Sellers, 34.

[71] For another example see Redwood, 'Archiving (In)Justice', 20–21.

[72] See Chapter 1, *supra note*. 51.

UNIVERSALISM: VOICE, COLONIALISM AND THE ARCHIVE

International courts are rooted in claims to universalism. Such is the power of this claim that even states that do not recognise the authority or legitimacy of international courts can fall within their jurisdiction – as was the case with Rwanda and the ICTR in the end. The universal reach of international criminal law was emphasised further at the ICTR through the prosecution of the leaders of the genocide, including the former head of state, showing no one was above the law. As Chapter 1 argued, however, this claim to universality masks the selectivity with which international criminal justice is practised, with prosecutions focused, almost without exception, on the Global South, and on African subjects more specifically. This has, then, led scholars to accuse international courts of acting as neo-colonial forms of interventions.

These claims to the coloniality of international law, however, go beyond who is the target of these prosecutions. Indeed, this goes to the heart of the Western-centric enlightenment logic that drives international criminal justice, discussed in Chapter 1, which means that these courts, critics argue, operate epistemologically (as well as often physically) at a distance from the Global South communities directly affected by these prosecutions.[73] In subsuming the subaltern voice within a Western-centric approach to knowledge production these sites can be seen to reproduce a colonial rationality.[74]

Yet such a clear-cut denunciation of international criminal justice needs to be considered alongside the argument developed in Chapter 4 that Rwandan witnesses played a role in determining the archive's rules. As was shown, not only did the witnesses shape the content of the archive, but also the ICTR looked to consider the specificity of Rwandese culture in its decision making.[75] This type of dynamic opens

---

[73] Paul Gready, 'Reconceptualising Transitional Justice: Embedded and Distanced Justice', *Conflict, Security and Development* 5:1(2005): 3–21. See Tim Kelsall, *Culture under Cross-examination: International Justice and the Special Court for Sierra Leone.* Cambridge: Cambridge University Press, 2009; Phil Clark, *Distant Justice: The Impact of the International Criminal Court on African Politics* (Cambridge: Cambridge University Press, 2018), 305.

[74] Vivienne Jabri, 'Colonial Rationalities, Postcolonial Subjectivities, and the International', in *Against International Relations Norm*, ed. Charlotte Epsteins (Basingstoke: Routledge, 2017): 38–56; Gayatri Spivak, 'The Rani of Sirmur: An Essay in Reading the Archives', *History and Theory* 24:3 (1985): 271.

[75] As Meera Sabaratnam argues scholars should be cautious of redrawing a clear demarcation between the international and local – where the latter is either reified or rendered abject and passive. Meera Sabaratnam, 'Avatars of Eurocentrism in the Critique of the Liberal Peace', *Security Dialogue* 44:3 (2013): 264.

up the possibility that these courts are representative of a post-colonial international order, as in addressing the post-colonial subject as a legitimate actor, the rules and norms of the international community are altered.[76]

When the archive's rules are considered, however, it becomes apparent that the ICTR's sensitivities to the witnesses' experiences were both short-lived and relatively superficial. Rather, an epistemological gap between the court and the witnesses remained.[77] A witness from *Cyangugu* noted:

> My experience of this tribunal, in both Rwanda and Arusha, comes down to one point: the judges do not understand the genocide that engulfed Rwanda in 1994. I know this for a fact. It would have been better if the judges had spent sufficient time in Rwanda, and among the Rwandese, before they began their work. This would have given them a better understanding of what actually happened, and how events unfolded.[78]

This sense that those deciding the cases could not fully understand the evidence was, in some respects, very literally the case. For instance, legal actors – with the exception of Rwandan staff – were solely reliant on French and English translations of the witness's testimonies (which were nearly always given in Kinyarwanda). The centrality of translation in this process was representative of the international nature of the court and also of a particular world order where French and English remain the working languages of diplomacy.[79] But significantly, as with all translations, much was lost through these real-time translations, particularly when translating from what is an incredibly rich and pictorial language such as Kinyarwanda. One translator noted, in this respect,

---

[76] Jabri, 'Peacebuilding', 10–11.

[77] This is not to overstate the uniqueness of international criminal justice in this respect. A number of former ICTR lawyers noted that they had seen a similar gulf in those that administered, and were subject to, law in municipal courts. One noted: 'If you're so far removed from, from reality and from society, it is difficult for you not to, to understand what obtains in reality.' Interview with Charles Adeogun-Phillips, *Voices of the Rwanda Tribunal* (University of Washington, 2008), 18.

[78] African Rights and Redress. *Survivors and Post-genocide Justice in Rwanda: Their Experiences, Perspectives and Hopes* (November 2008), 58.

[79] It is, moreover, notable that for the ICTR's first decade, outside of interpreters no Rwandese staff were employed because of the fear that this might negatively impact on the court's neutrality. Interview with Karegyesa (2008), 6.

There's a Kinyarwanda booth there that translates from Kinyarwanda into Fren-, into English and I pick it up, you know, into French. In the process some, there's a loss, there's a loss, especially when the witness speaks fast and the emotion, et cetera, okay. Those are from the professional point of view some details that, that are frustrating, really frustrating.[80]

Arguably, as such, the tribunal's decisions, and indeed the archive that has formed the basis of this very book, were never based on wholly complete accounts of the witnesses' experiences, nor were they based on what might be considered a culturally situated understanding of the genocide. This is in no means a criticism of the important work of the translators, but there is inescapably a loss in meaning that results from all translations, no matter how good. This is an inevitable outcome of any international procedure which relies on personnel who are unable, linguistically, culturally or anthropologically, to fully understand the community under investigation.

More generally, despite attempts to 'accommodate' the specifics of Rwandan culture, the gap between the tribunal's approach to knowledge production and the witnesses remained[81] – a sentiment echoed by Rwandese staff at the tribunal interviewed.[82] A Rwandese ICTR prosecutor noted, with some anger, for instance, what he saw as the inappropriate questioning of witnesses' knowledge without due sensitivity to the witnesses' traumatic experience and lack of familiarity with criminal trials.[83] In *Akayesu*, for instance, Witness N became frustrated by questions about the veracity of her knowledge regarding the death of her family. Yet, rather than adapting court practice to accommodate the witness, it was the witness that was requested to alter her way of testifying, and the judges ordered that she 'speak without hatred, without any emotion [as] it seems that she is getting a bit carried away'.[84] Moreover, whilst the tribunal made attempts to adapt to the witnesses approach to testifying, for instance by acknowledging the value of hearsay evidence to Rwandans, rather than giving this greater probative weight, courtroom practice adapted to ask more specific questions as to the source of witnesses testimony so as to be able to

[80] Interview with François Bembatoum, *Voices of the Rwanda Tribunal* (University of Washington, 2008), 7. See also Eltringham, *Genocide Never Sleeps*, 131.
[81] Ruzindana (2015); Interview with Appeals Judge (2016). Redress. *Survivors*, 55–72.
[82] Interview with Member of ICTR OTP 6 (June 2015).
[83] Interview with Member of ICTR OTP 7 (June 2015).
[84] CONTRA001183, 131.

distinguish between the 'more substantive' sight witnessing and the 'less credible' hearsay.[85] What Stoler refers to as the 'hierarchy of credibility' very much remained rooted with the legal actors' understanding of the social world and in the enlightenment logics of criminal law.[86] As Eltringham argues, in this approach culture was problematically both essentialised and rendered as a 'difficulty' to be overcome.[87]

A manual that was circulated to witnesses prior to participating in the trials further evidences this power imbalance.[88] This reminded witness of the importance of witnesses telling the 'truth' (including stressing the penalty for those that lied to the tribunal), how they should deliver their testimony (to speak slowly, and to only speak of what they really *knew* – including distinguishing between what they saw and heard), and their need to respect the status and duties of tribunal staff when questioned.[89] This underlined the importance that witnesses adhered to the logics of the criminal trial process and made clear the power relations at play between the different actors in the production of the archive and the witnesses' subservience to those rules.[90]

This power imbalance becomes even more problematic when the tribunal's approach to witnesses more generally is considered. Of particular importance here was the *danger* that testifying brought for some witnesses, as a number of ICTR witnesses were threatened or even killed as a result of being linked to the tribunal.[91] During *Akayesu* alone twenty potential witnesses linked to the case were, according to one report, killed due to their association with the tribunal.[92]

---

[85] Interview with Reviser – ICTR Registry (June 2015); CONTRA001189, 172–76; Interview with Erik Møse (2008), *Voices of the Rwanda Tribunal* (University of Washington), 9.

[86] Ann Stoler, *Along the Archival Grain: Epistemic Anxiety and Colonial Common Sense* (Princeton: Princeton University Press, 2010), 96.

[87] Eltringham, *Genocide Never Sleeps*, 127–46.

[88] ICTR, 'Testifying Before the International Criminal Tribunal for Rwanda', 06FB002 (Arusha: 2005).

[89] *Ibid.*, 8–21.

[90] The manual was also directed at convincing witnesses to testify, noting that '[r]efusing to testify amounts to showing disregard for the law and for your country. Examine your conscience ... to find the answer. Ask yourself this: What good would it really do to have the events of Rwanda happen again? No one but you has the answer to the restoration of trust among the Rwandan people.' ICTR, 'Testifying before the International Criminal Tribunal for Rwanda', 10.

[91] A/54/PV.48, *54th Session: 48th Plenary Meeting*, 8 November 1999, 63. See also Nicola Palmer and Phil Clark, 'Testifying to Genocide: Victim and Witness Protection in Rwanda', *Redress* (2012), found: http://protectionline.org/files/2012/11/121029ProtectionReport.pdf (last accessed 17 July 2017). Some of these murders were also linked to the defence counsel's employing of former genocidaires. Redress, *Survivors and Post-genocide Justice in Rwanda*, 59–63.

[92] Andrew Trotter, 'Witness Intimidation in International Trials: Balancing the Need for Protection against the Rights of the Accused', *George Washington International Law Review* 44

Worryingly, the tribunal officially claimed (and continues to claim) that no witness was ever killed due to being associated with the tribunal, something that was celebrated in the keynote speech delivered at the ICTR's legacy conference dinner in 2014.[93] Tellingly, as Richard Goldstone noted:

> During my time as Chief Prosecutor of the [ICTR and ICTY], I used [to] tell people in my office that the first dead witness will likely be the last witness. When people fear for their lives or safety, you cannot expect them to come forward willingly and give evidence.[94]

As was examined in Chapter 5, in many respects this power imbalance grew worse as the tribunal progressed and the archive became underpinned with an emphasis on efficient and lean justice.[95] In 1998 the OIOS even *blocked* the registrar from further exploring possible ways that the tribunal could help victims through the Voluntary Trust Fund (VTF) (a separate budget to the tribunal's main budget, which was financed by voluntary state contributions),[96] and in 2000 the judges actively decided *not* to expand the tribunal's mandate to include victim compensation.[97]

(2012): 133; and Immigration and Refugee Board of Canada. 'Rwanda: Whether People Who Give Testimony at the Trials and Hearings of Those Accused of Genocide and Crimes against Humanity Are Being Harassed, Intimidated and Threatened', found: www.refworld.org/docid/3ae6ac5950.html (last accessed 1 February 2015). E/CN.4/1998/54/Add.1, *Further Promotion and Encouragement of Human Rights and Fundamental Freedoms, Including the Question of the Programme and Methods of Work of the Commission Alternative Approaches and Ways and Means within the United Nations System for Improving the Effective Enjoyment of Human Rights and Fundamental Freedoms Report of the Special Rapporteur on Violence against Women, Its Causes and Consequences, Ms. Radhika Coomaraswamy Addendum Report of the Mission to Rwanda on the Issues of Violence against Women in Situations of Armed Conflict*, 4 February 1998, 9.

[93] Appeals Judge (2016).

[94] Human Rights Brief, 'Moving Forward: A Reflection on Current Issues Facing International Criminal Justice with Richard Goldstone', *Human Rights Brief* 21:2 (2014): 32.

[95] Another example of these gulf in expectations came during *Cyangugu*, where a witness was denied the opportunity to present a letter to the registry concerning the horrific state of their detention in Rwanda, because this was not seen as a matter that fell within the tribunal's 'competence'. ICTR–99–46, TRA001916/1, *[Cyangugu] – Ntagerura et al – Redacted Transcript of 25/03/2003*, 25 March 2003, 2–3.

[96] The tribunal was actively prohibited from using the main budget to fund outreach programmes. Interview with Member of ICTR OTP 8 (June 2015).

[97] UNGA, A/52/784, *Financing of the International Criminal Tribunal for the Prosecution of Persons Responsible for Genocide and Other Serious Violations of International Humanitarian Law Committed in the Territory of Rwanda and Rwandan Citizens Responsible for Genocide and Other Such Violations Committed in the Territory of Neighbouring States between 1 January and 31 December 1994: Report of the Secretary-General on the Activities of the Office of Internal Oversight Services*, 6 February 1998, 14; UNSC, S/2000/11989, *Letter from President Pillay to the President of the United Nations Security Council*, 15 December 2000, 1 and 5; and UNSC, S/PV.4229, *4229th Meeting*, 21 November 2000, 6; and Anonymous 2 (2016). A former senior

This failure to adequately address victim's needs was also reflected in the tribunal's other 'outreach' and 'legacy' policies. The terms 'outreach' and 'legacy' were only really introduced into the tribunal's vernacular around the turn of the millennium, again as criticism mounted, this time over the tribunal's lack of relevance for Rwandans.[98] These programmes included establishing information centres in Rwanda to inform the population about the tribunal's work.[99] Other similar educational policies followed, such as internships at the tribunal for Rwandan students studying law and the production of radio broadcasts in Kinyarwanda about the activities of the tribunal.[100] Importantly, however, these were directed at informing rather than engaging with the Rwandan population and seemed more like sensitisation campaigns than anything else.[101] As Vivienne Jabri has argued this type of unidirectional pastoral oversight is an important technique of colonial governance.[102] Indeed, this once more mirrors

figure within the OTP also noted that in this respect the Tribunal was a 'victim' of the statute they were given. Anonymous 2 (2016).

[98] A/52/784, 14–15; A/55/512, 49; S/PV.4229, 2 and 7–8; A/54/315–S/1999/943, 23; and A/54/PV.48, 8, 11 and 17. A prosecution attorney noted that '[w]e had an outreach program here but it was like an afterthought' (Egbe, p. 24).

[99] UNGA, A/56/853, *Financing of the International Tribunal for the Prosecution of Persons Responsible for Serious Violations of International Humanitarian Law Committed in the Territory of the Former Yugoslavia since 1991: Financing of the International Criminal Tribunal for the Prosecution of Persons Responsible for Genocide and Other Serious Violations of International Humanitarian Law Committed in the Territory of Rwanda and Rwandan Citizens Responsible for Genocide and Other Such Violations Committed in the Territory of Neighbouring States between 1 January and 31 December 1994: Comprehensive Report on the Results of the Implementation of the Recommendations of the Expert Group to Conduct a Review of the Effective Operation and Functioning of the International Tribunal for the Former Yugoslavia and the International Criminal Tribunal for Rwanda*, 4 March 2002, 12.

[100] UNGA, A/59/183–S/2004/601, *Report of the International Criminal Tribunal for the Prosecution of Persons Responsible for Genocide and Other Serious Violations of International Humanitarian Law Committed in the Territory of Rwanda and Rwandan Citizens Responsible for Genocide and Other Such Violations Committed in the Territory of Neighbouring States between 1 January and 31 December 1994*, 27 July 2004, 15; and UNGA, A/60/229–S/2005/534, *Report of the International Criminal Tribunal for the Prosecution of Persons Responsible for Genocide and Other Serious Violations of International Humanitarian Law Committed in the Territory of Rwanda and Rwandan Citizens Responsible for Genocide and Other Such Violations Committed in the Territory of Neighbouring States between 1 January and 31 December 1994*, 15 August 2005, 1 and 3. Perhaps particularly problematic was the tribunal's participation in genocide awareness raising in the 'solidarity camps', where people suspected of harbouring 'genocide ideology' were sent for 're-education'. UNSC, S/2013/310, *Letter Dated 23 May 2013 from the President of the International Criminal Tribunal for Rwanda Addressed to the President of the Security Council: Report on the Completion Strategy of the International Criminal Tribunal for Rwanda (as at 10 May 2013)*, 23 May 2013, 14.

[101] A/56/853, 12. Over time, however, the focus moved ever further from the 'local', as the legacy and outreach work became more about ideas of 'best practice' and the tribunal's *institutional memory* than anything else. OTP 8 (2015).

[102] Jabri, 'Colonial Rationalities', 109.

the logics discussed earlier where the international, the site of civilisa-tion, intervenes to guide the local to a more peaceful and civilised future. The lack of relevance of these measures for the Rwandan population was clearly seen, however, as the information centres were closed down after they were handed over to the Rwandan government as the ICTR drew to an end.

Each of these examples demonstrates two things. The first is just how far the tribunal had moved away from the initial hopes and aspirations for what international criminal justice could achieve, which saw the archive as a site of historical exploration, reconciliation and post-conflict state-building. The second is that a significant power imbal-ance operated at the heart of the archive which in forwarding the perspectives and interests of the tribunal, and the 'international com-munity' more generally, undermined the significance of the experiences and interests of those that had endured the violence in 1994 – exactly the constituency of actors that the court was created to help.

This observation is not meant to eradicate the sense of agency of the witnesses, and the subaltern, within this process, as was demonstrated in both Chapters 4 and 5, nor reify the divide between the 'inter-national' and the 'local'. As Jabri has argued, these are hybrid concepts that continuously constitute each other.[103] Yet what this does continue to point to is the uneven distribution of power and voice within these relations and the re-subordination of the post-colonial subject within the international order. The very way that 'culture' was rendered as something to be 'overcome' – that is, simultaneously both essentialised and problematised – is important for understanding the power dynam-ics built into the archive.[104] There was, as such, a 'colonial rationality' flowing throughout the archive.

CONCLUSION

This chapter has examined how different discourses and power rela-tions undercut the archive's rules, which altered the conditions through which guilt was established but also shaped the record of violence in distinctive ways and constructed a particular understanding

---

[103] Vivienne Jabri, 'Disarming Norms: Postcolonial Agency and the Constitution of the International', *International Theory* 6:2 (2014): 372–83. See also Hannah Partis-Jennings, 'The (In)Security of Gender in Afghanistan's Peacebuilding Project: Hybridity and Affect', *International Feminist Journal of Politics* 19:4 (2017): 411–25.

[104] Eltringham, *Genocide Never Sleeps*, 121–27; Sabaratnam, 'Avatars of Eurocentrism', 272.

of the international community. Whilst an essentially liberal vision of community was projected out from the archive, a closer inspection of the archive's rules reveals an altogether more concerning picture. First, the archive's focus on individuals, when aligned with other imaginings of the international order, led to the erasure of the role of international actors in the genocide. This in turn contributed towards the construction of a binary between the international and the local, which continues to play an important role in the governance of the international community. This also worked to preserve a space where violence was permitted as a legitimate aspect of the international community.

The chapter also showed how gendered discourses undercut the archive's claims to neutrality and impartiality. Rather, gender both framed the archive's understanding of perpetrators and victims and shaped how the court processed evidence. This meant that sexual violence testimony was scrutinised more closely and was more likely to be rejected, and so was less likely to find a place within the archive.[105] This, as such, forwarded a patriarchal understanding of community. In showing the significance of the absence and erasure of this type of evidence within the archive, this also demonstrated the importance of the archive's materiality. Finally, the chapter also revealed how, despite some gestures towards accommodating the specificity of the Rwandan witnesses' experiences, the archive sidelined alternative ways of knowing as it re-entrenched a liberal and enlightenment world view. As Phil Clark has suggested in relation to the ICC, this evidences international criminal justice's inability to incorporate ways of knowing that sit in contrast to a liberal vision of community.[106] As was shown, moreover, this power imbalance only became worse with time as after the completion strategy the tribunal focused on questions of efficiency. This, then, inserted a colonial rationality into the archive.

As will be discussed more in the Conclusion, this is not necessarily to wholesale condemn the value of international courts. Nor is it to argue that it is necessarily inevitable that liberal institutions such as the ICTR propagate this vision of community. However, what this does, at least, show is that underneath these liberal claims lies a more concerning image of the type of community constituted within the archive.

---

[105] This mirrors findings about how sexual violence type of testimony is treated in municipal courts. John Conley and William O'Barr, *Just Words: Law, Language, and Power* (Chicago: The University of Chicago Press: Second Edition, 2005), 32–39.

[106] Clark, *Distant Justice*, 306. See also Eltringham, *Genocide Never Sleeps*, 123.

CHAPTER SEVEN

THE RESIDUAL MECHANISM AND THE ARCHIVE

Almost exactly twenty-two years after the UNSC brought the ICTR into existence, on 16 November 2016 the Residual Mechanisms for the International Criminal Tribunals (MICT) opened its doors in Arusha, marking a new chapter in the tribunal's history. The MICT was conceived of as part of the completion strategy, taking over the residual functions of both the ICTR and ICTY after they closed down.[1] This marked a greater integration of the two tribunals, as under the MICT both would share a prosecutor and registrar. However, it was deemed necessary to maintain two separate MICT branches, one in the Hague (taking over from the ICTY) and one in Arusha (taking over from the ICTR). Given the inadequacy and enormous size of former ICTR offices at the AICC, it was decided that a new complex should be built on the outskirts of Arusha, on a site known as Lakilaki. Whilst the estimated cost of the complex was initially set at $7 million, in the end the total cost for the new site was $8.7 million – much to the dismay to those that thought too much had already been spent on the tribunal.[2]

At the opening of the site, representatives from the tribunal and the UN proclaimed that this marked an important moment in the fight for global justice and restated many of the claims made at the start of the

---

[1] It was decided that the MICT should be created after it became clear that the ICTs were not going to meet their expected completion strategy closure targets. UNSC, S/PV.6041, *6041st Meeting*, 12 December 2008, 13.

[2] Mechanism for the International Criminal Tribunals (MICT), 'Construction of the Arusha Facility', found: www.irmct.org/specials/arusha-facility/index.html (last accessed 1 September 2019).

ICTR about its multifaceted purpose. Miguel de Serpa Soares, the United Nations Under-Secretary-General for Legal Affairs, declared that

> [t]he Mechanism and the inauguration of these premises reinforce our shared resolve that those whose deeds defy the conscience of humankind will not go unpunished, and that the rule of law will prevail for everyone, everywhere.[3]

The President of the MICT, Theodore Meron, stated that the

> [m]echanism is a reflection of a purpose that we all share – to provide support to vulnerable victims and witnesses of some of the worst atrocities the world has ever seen, to preserve and make accessible a vital record of our collective history, to meet the demands of justice and the rule of law, and to ensure accountability for the crimes committed during the 1994 genocide in Rwanda, crimes that devastated hundreds of thousands of families – crimes that strike at us all.

> . . . .

> With the Mechanism rooted firmly [in Africa], in mandate, culture, and context, it is not too much to say that this is an African court, and that in carrying out the vital mandate that it has been given, the Mechanism will serve, first and foremost, the people of this region of the world.[4]

Twenty-two years on and the message was still the same: The tribunal was a site of truth and justice, and where victims could find support in their search for peace. Moreover, it was clear that the MICT was seen as serving both the interests of the international community as a whole (working to prevent crimes that defy the conscience of humankind) and Africa, gesturing also, then, towards (though interestingly not specifically naming) the tribunal's relationship with Rwanda.

At the heart of the MICT sits the new archival building, and indeed, as discussed later, a key reason behind the decision to build a new complex was the need to create a facility that could store the records in perpetuity. This penultimate chapter looks at what this archival complex can tell us about the politics of the archive, its legacy and what imaginings of community emerged from it. In the first part, it does so primarily through a reading of the materiality of the archive, looking for

---

[3] MICT, 'Mechanism for International Criminal Tribunals Opens Its New Premises of the Arusha Branch', found: www.irmct.org/en/news/mechanism-international-criminal-tribunals-opens-its -new-premises-arusha-branch (last accessed 1 September 2019).
[4] MICT, 'Remarks of Judge Theodor Meron', 3.

how this can offer insights into what the new archive's purpose was and whom it was for. The chapter then examines how the archive is currently being used to explore the extent to which the politics and power relations of the archive are being reproduced as its records are drawn on by external users.

BUILDING AN ARCHIVE

There is a tension between the statements made at the inauguration of the MICT, which suggested that the tribunal's strategic function had remained unchanged since its creation, and Chapter 5's findings. In Chapter 5, I showed that over time, and particularly after the introduction of the completion strategy, there was a shift in the rules that underpinned the archive as a more restrictive understanding of justice took hold.[5] This section examines this tension as it considers the materiality of the new archive.

Whilst discussed throughout, the book centres the archive's materiality at this point for two reasons. First, when I was examining the transcripts from the MICT's opening I was struck by just how many times the physical structure and location of the MICT's new complex were mentioned, whether this was the architecture, the building materials used, or the symbolic importance of the site itself. Second, as was stated in Chapter 1, the archive is very much a *material* space and so turning to the materiality of the archive offers a way into understanding the archive's rules and purpose. This is especially useful in this instance where there has been, overall, a considerable slowing down of production of new records for the archive since the MICT was opened. As will be argued, examining the materiality of the archive reveals that underneath the grand rhetoric of the MICT's opening lay a more limited vision of justice.

At the opening, alongside the statements about the multifaceted function and purpose the MICT, President Meron also noted that

> [m]inimalist in nature and devised to maximize flexibility when ad hoc work so requires, these facilities embody the United Nations Security Council's vision that the Mechanism be *lean and efficient*, open and transparent, and – in all that it does – a reflection of best practices. (emphasis added)[6]

---

[5] See Chapter 5, 108–12.
[6] MICT, 'Remarks of Judge Theodor Meron', 2.

This concern with the efficiency of the building was emphasised in the concept note that framed the design of the building.[7] The design of the building, then, gives an insight into the vision underlying the MICT, as the very materiality of the new complex and archive was to encapsulate the same mantra of 'lean and efficient' justice that came to underpin the ICTR's function by its end. Whilst Meron presented this as working in harmony with the tribunal's claims about its broader value, as a site of justice, truth and reconciliation, looking at the MICT's statute further suggests that a narrow understanding of the MICT's purpose and function underpinned the operation of the MICT and its archive.

The MICT's statute shows that many of the powers and responsibility that had underpinned the functioning of the ICTR were removed, substantially weakened or reallocated to different actors at the tribunal. The statute meant that the OTP, for instance, was no longer permitted to submit indictments against new suspects and was restricted in *who* could be prosecuted, as the mandate specifically stated they were only allowed to target 'the most senior leaders suspected of being most responsible for the crimes'.[8] This marked a significant shift in the initial mandate, where there was no specification regarding seniority, leaving the prosecution with space to pursue a broad indictment strategy. As will be recalled, this meant the prosecution could capture the variety of types of actors that made the genocide possible. Moreover, the MICT's statute also gave the judges the right to refer cases to a different jurisdiction if they felt this would be in the interests of the tribunal, even without the OTP's consent.[9] This, as such, marked an even greater shift in power to the judges as it seemed as though the judges had the right to determine prosecutorial strategy in terms of who was ultimately brought to trial. If anything, then, the MICT marked an even more heightened version of the lean and efficient justice that had come to underpin the ICTR's archive.

The materiality of the new archive building is also important when understanding the function and purpose of the MICT. In fact, the conditions of the new archive were initially deemed to be unsuitable for storing records, and so the archive was kept in the AICC to begin with. Whilst these initial problems were dealt with, and now most of

---

[7] UNGA, A/69/734, *Financing of the International Residual Mechanism for Criminal Tribunals: Construction of a New Facility for the International Residual Mechanism for Criminal Tribunals, Arusha Branch*, 19 January 2015, 4.

[8] UNSC, S/RES/1966, *Resolution 1966*, 22 December 2010, 6.

[9] S/RES/1966, 8.

the records have been moved to the new site, there remain a number of issues with the storage facilities. This, at the time of my visit in 2019, included an inability to control the temperature and humidity levels inside the archive, which meant that the paper records (the majority of the records) could not be kept in the new archive indefinitely due to the risk of degradation. Whilst these issues seem to be relatively easy to solve, that this problem ever came about is telling about the politics of the archive.[10] Indeed, it seems that this issue was at least partially caused by a reduction in the budget allocated for the new archive. It remains unclear exactly who was responsible for the alteration in the archive's design and budget, but this again suggests that budget and efficiency had come at the cost of some of the tribunal's broader goals, as the very record of the court was potentially put at risk.

There are traces of this issue elsewhere in the new MICT complex. Almost immediately after the MICT was opened, building work began to construct temporary cabins for the defence counsels as it was realised that there was insufficient space within the new lean and efficient main building. It seems that this issue potentially affects other organs of the tribunal too, with insufficient working space for the chambers once a full complement of judges (and their support teams) take up residence for trial. In October 2019, the initial appearances took place in one of the MICT's first proceedings, *Prosecutor v. Turinabo et al.* (MICT-18–116), a contempt of court case initially featuring five defendants.[11] Whilst the new court space just about accommodated the five accused with their lead counsel, the new courtroom looked very much at capacity. It will be interesting to see how the space copes with the trial when it begins its hearings. This again underlines that, as the New Zealand representative to the UNSC lamented at the ICTR's closure, a 'budget-driven mentality' had taken over, which had a potentially detrimental impact on the tribunal's attempts to realise its mandate, even when conceived of in more limited terms.

One more observation can be made here about the materiality of the MICT complex. As suggested earlier, the court was very much seen as representative of the harmonious relationship between the UN, tribunal and 'Africa', going as far to describe this as an 'African Court'.[12]

---

[10] Interview with MICT Archivists (August 2019).
[11] This later saw the addition of the prosecution's contempt proceedings against Ngirabatware, bringing the total number of defendants to six.
[12] MICT, 'Remarks of Judge Theodor Meron', 2. See also MICT, 'Official Opening Ceremony of the New Premises of the MICT Arusha Branch, Serge Brammertz, Chief Prosecutor, UN Mechanism for International Criminal Tribunals, 25 November 2016', found: www.irmct.or

This idea was symbolically imbedded at the heart of MICT complex with the planting of 'an iconic tree, an emblem throughout many parts of Africa of wisdom and of justice'.[13] Yet, against this presentation of harmony and unity sits a more uncomfortable reading of this symbolic gesture, which is the continued friction between the practice of international criminal justice and Africa,[14] and between the MICT/ICTR and Rwanda specifically.[15] This friction is, perhaps, most seriously demonstrated by the very decision that the archive was to remain in Arusha after the closing down of the ICTR.

Indeed, as the ICTR was winding down, two different claims were made as to who owned the archive, where it should be located and ultimately what it was for. The Rwandan government argued that the archives had been produced largely by Rwandan witnesses and supposedly for Rwanda. As such, it contained *their* history, *their* memories, and so belonged in Rwanda, where it could help the country to come to terms with the genocide.[16] The UN, however, saw the archive differently. Whilst it acknowledged that there was a *secondary* value in the archive as a source of history and memory, its *primary* value was that it contained the institutional memory of the tribunal and so was valuable from a legal and bureaucratic perspective. Consequently, it was argued that the archive needed to stay in Arusha, Tanzania, where it could assist the MICT.[17]

The UN won this battle and it was decided that the archive would remain in Arusha. Moreover, this outcome also cemented the decision to build a new facility for the MICT, as the tribunal's previous home in

---

g/sites/default/files/statements-and-speeches/161125-prosecutor-speech-opening-ceremony-o f-arusha-premises-en.pdfm (last accessed 4 September 2019); and MICT, 'Opening of the New Premises of the Mechanism for International Criminal Tribunals *Arusha, United Republic of Tanzania, 25 November 2016*, "Together We built" by Mr. John Hocking', found: www.irmct .org/sites/default/files/statements-and-speeches/161125-registrar-speech-opening-ceremony-of- arusha-premises-en.pdf (last accessed 30 October 2019).

[13] MICT, 'Remarks of Judge Theodor Meron', 2.

[14] See Phil Clark, *Distant Justice: The Impact of the International Criminal Court on African Politics* (Cambridge: Cambridge University Press, 2018).

[15] For overview of this relationship see Victor Peskin, 'Courting Rwanda: The Promises and Pitfalls of the ICTR Outreach Programme', *Journal of International Criminal Justice* 3:4 (2005), 950–61; and Kingsley Moghalu, *Rwanda's Genocide: The Politics of Global Justice* (Basingstoke: Palgrave Macmillan, 2005).

[16] UNSC, S/PV.5453, *5453rd Meeting*, 7 June 2006, 32; UNSC, S/PV.5697, *5697th Meeting*, 18 June 2007, 33; UNSC, S/PV.6228, *6228th Meeting*, 3 December 2009, 33.

[17] UNSC, S/2009/258, *Report of the Secretary-General on the Administrative and Budgetary Aspects of the Options for Possible Locations for the Archives of the ICTY and ICTR and the Seat of the Residual Mechanism(s) for the Tribunals*, 21 May /2009, 14.

the AICC was considered an unsuitable facility, not least because of the inadequacy of the archive there.

The decision brought to the fore a number of contradictions about the tribunal's purpose. As discussed, at the outset of the ICTR, it appeared that the tribunal could be all things to all people. Up to having decide on the location of the court, the tribunal had, rhetorically at least, been able to keep all of these different potentialities in play simultaneously. The attempt to find a permanent home for the physical archive, however, fractured what it was claimed the tribunal and archive could achieve and reaffirmed the gap between the Rwandan government's and the UN's vision of justice.

The decision about the archive's final location also reveals further evidence of the problematic relationship between the international and local. Indeed, another reason behind the UN's reluctance to transfer the archive to Rwanda was a suspicion that the Rwandan government would destroy parts of the archive, including those that contained information relating to RPF crimes.[18] The validity of these fears is perhaps less important than the way that this continues to reify the sense of the international as saviour and local as barbaric. It should also be remembered that under the UN's stewardship, parts of the archive were left to rot in containers and that even the new state-of-the-art archive has had a number of teething problems due to the 'budget-driven mentality' at the tribunal.

Underneath the discursive attempts to claim the MICT as a site where a holistic form of justice could be achieved, and where multiple communities could have their interests represented, lies a different account of the role and function of the archive. What is further important here is that, again, the very materiality of the archive points to a fracturing of the discourse's claims concerning the purpose of the tribunal and its archive. These questions about the purpose, and indeed effect, of the archive will be explored in the following section as I examine how the records of the archive have used beyond the tribunal.

THE ARCHIVE AS A *LIEUX DE MEMOIRE*

Especially after the introduction of the completion strategy, the archive became a key part of the tribunal's understanding of its legacy. At the

---

[18] Interview with Former ICTR Archivist (June 2015).

closing of the tribunal, it was noted that '[a]s one of our longest-lasting, most permanent legacy projects, the archives will help to ensure that the international community remains conscious of the battle against impunity that the ICTR has fought for so many years'.[19] This sentiment is reinforced on the archive's website:

> The records related to the investigations and prosecutions provide insight into the motivations and causes that led to these atrocities, thereby having the potential to educate and inform in the interest of preventing the occurrence of future violations of international humanitarian law.[20]

As such, the archive is, in many respects, a continuation of the tribunal's work, seeking to prevent future acts of violence and maintain international peace and security.[21] And yet, how is the archive used beyond those involved in the running of the tribunal, and to what extent does this use align with this vision?

My visit to the new archive in August 2019 was revealing in this respect. The new MICT complex at Lakilaki sits on top of a remote hill on the outskirts of Arusha, a kilometre off the main road, and some thirty-minute drive from the centre of the town. It is certainly both a difficult-to-access and a beautiful location, with Mount Meru looming in the background. Despite having arranged my visit with the archive section prior to arrival, on my first day there was some confusion at the security gates as to why I was there. My explanation about my research on, and in, the archive did not seem to help clear up the confusion as the security guards could not seem to understand what I would want from the archive, and especially why I would be coming back for the next six days. Upon finally entering the building it became slightly clearer as to why my presence might have elicited this type of response, as it emerged that even though the archive had been open for three years, I was amongst the first researchers to have come out to the new facility.

This sparked a whole set of questions as to what and who the archive was for. The fact that the value of the archive's record was seen in its ability to help develop an understanding of humanity's 'collective history' and protect future generations from the scourge of genocide seemed to sit awkwardly with the isolated and largely unused facility.

[19] S/PV.6678, 8.
[20] MICT, 'Archives', found: www.irmct.org/en/archives (last accessed 18 October 2019).
[21] MICT Archives (2019).

These thoughts took me back to an interview with a former ICTR archivist, when I asked similar questions about what the purpose of the archive was given how difficult it was to access, and that for a variety of reasons whole sections of it were completely inaccessible to the public. They responded that it was to maintain an accurate record of what had taken place at the tribunal for the future, and within this response there seemed to be a faith in the inherent value of the very act of preservation.[22] As a non-archivist it struck me as peculiar to be so concerned with preservation but without thinking about *who* it was being preserved for. Yet this response seemed to align with current fate of the archive: as a state-of-the-art facility that can preserve the record in perpetuity but seemingly without the users to engage with the physical record that has been amassed.

This description of the MICT's archive ultimately brought me back to Pierre Nora's concept of a *lieux de memoire*. Contrary to popular misconception, *lieux de memoire* does not simply mean a 'site of memory', where memory is recorded 'in stone'. Rather, for Nora, *lieux de memoire* signifies the complex relationship between remembering and forgetting.[23] Nora explores how the rise in the construction of memorials and other public monuments in eighteenth- and nineteenth-century Europe coincided with the disintegration of the communities and traditions that had, until then, underpinned the memory of community.[24] These monuments, then, were as much signs of the anxiety of forgetting, as the community that retained the memory was erased, as they were markers of memory. Interestingly, moreover, Nora explicitly points to the rise of the national archives in the nineteenth century as an example of this process of remembering and forgetting, as these again marked an anxiety that it was no longer possible to remember the history and identity of a community without recording and storing it.[25] There is, moreover, a certain futility in this process. Drawing on a distinctly Halbawchsian understanding of collective memory, Nora argues that it is the community that enables memory, as a dynamic and organic process, to be kept alive; once that community is gone, all that is left in the monument is an imitation (a *lieux de memoire*) of a now largely forgotten past.[26]

---

[22] ICTR Archivist (2015).

[23] Pierre Nora, 'Between Memory and History: Les Lieux de Mémoire', *Representations* 26 (1989): 7–24.

[24] Ibid., 9.

[25] Ibid., 12–14. As Chapter 1 suggested, archives form an important part of the nationalist state building project. See Chapter 1, 'Archives as Governance'.

[26] Maurice Halbwachs, *On Collective Memory* (Chicago: University of Chicago Press, 1992).

This relationship between remembering and forgetting is very much present within the MICT/ICTR's archive, as the urgency and frequency with which statements about the need to remember the 'collective history' sits against the current reality of the archive – what felt like an almost forgotten building sitting on a remote hill on the outskirts of Arusha. This is also, then, perhaps suggestive of the fragility of the 'international community' whose 'collective history' is being stored in the archive.

In addition to the physical archive, however, there is the online digital archive. Given the remoteness of the physical archive this, in many respects, is a more important repository when thinking about how the public engage with the archive. Indeed, in 2019 alone, approximately 15,000 unique users engaged with the online archive and downloaded a total of 44,000 documents.[27] Much like the new facilities at the MICT, the online archive has also had a serious, and impressive, makeover in recent years. In 2015 a new online interface, the Judicial Records and Archives Database (JRAD), replaced the former TRIM online catalogue.[28] As anyone who struggled with TRIM will attest, this was incredibly cumbersome and contained only a patchy collection of the ICTR's vast judicial records. JRAD has certainly addressed many of these issues. Nearing complete files can now be remotely accessed for the majority of the tribunal's cases. Moreover, its usability has been significantly enhanced by a more advanced search function that allows users to search *across* different case files. As such, whilst the former interface encouraged users to search through the records in a very legalistic way – as it restricted searches to a particular case file, and then organised these records by different types of legal records (transcripts, motions, etc.) – this new interface renders the archive of greater value to a variety of different types of user. For instance, this makes the archive of considerably more use for historians, as it is now possible to search for a particular massacre site and pull out all references made about that site across all trials.

The archive section has also increasingly given more thought about how to expand its user base. Though, importantly, this work is not considered part of the archive's official mandate – and so is the result of the archive team's dedication to the archive – this has included producing a number of online exhibitions that highlight the historical value

[27] MICT Archivists (2019).
[28] MICT, Judicial Records Archive Database (JRAD), found: https://jrad.unmict.org/ (last accessed 24 October 2019).

of these records and draw attention to the diverse range of records held within the archive. Such exhibitions include 'Worth a Thousand Words',[29] which highlights the predominance of visual evidence within the archive, such as drawings and videos, and 'Children of Conflict', which details how children were affected by the conflict.[30]

As part of this drive to attract new users, the archive section has also started to collect data to better understand who is using the archive and for what purpose. Two types of data are currently accessible in this respect. The first is information about users of the online archive.[31] This remains relatively broad brush – only recording when the database was accessed and the country from which it was accessed. However, whilst any conclusions from this must remain speculative given the limited amount of data, at least one trend emerges from this data. This is that the majority of users of the online archive come from the Global North. Whilst Rwanda (503 users) is the seventh most frequent user, which is significant, the top five (representing 52 per cent of the overall total) are the Netherlands (3,083), USA (2,913), UK (784), France (616) and Canada (559). When taken as a whole, users from the Global North make up two-thirds of the online users. Whilst the caveats remain, this imbalance of users is nonetheless suggestive again of *who* these courts are for.

The issue of translation from Chapter 6 also reappears here. When thinking about who this archive is for, it is telling that, by and large, it is the English and French versions of the court proceedings that are available online. For instance, whilst a search for English documents attached to *Akayesu* returned 230 documents, an equivalent search for Kinyarwanda documents returned only two records. Whilst both French and English are relatively widely spoken in Rwanda, the dearth of documents in Kinyarwanda is further suggestive of whom the archive is for.

The archive section has also started to collect information concerning specific access requests that have been made.[32] These offer a little more detail – recording the purpose of the request, the country of the applicant and also their profession – and are also specific to requests made about the MICT/ICTR's archive. The results here are also

---

[29] MICT, 'Worth a Thousand Words', found: www.irmct.org/specials/1000words/index.html (last accessed 18 October 2019).
[30] MICT, 'Children of Conflict', found: www.irmct.org/specials/1000words/index.html (last accessed 18 October 2019). Interview with MICT Archivists (August 2019).
[31] Analytics, 'JRAD All Web Site Data', 1 August 2018 –31 July 2019, 1808–907. Record on file with author.
[32] 'Direct Requests April – July 2019'. Record on file with author.

informative, if not, again, limited. Between March and August 2019, thirty-seven requests were made to the archive team. First, the patterns in terms of where these users are from is the same as with online access as a whole, and twenty-three (nearly two-thirds) of the requests come from the Global North. Second, of these users, the vast majority (81 per cent) were either 'Academics' or 'Independent Researchers', with two requests from lawyers, one from MICT staff, and the rest 'unknown'. It is hard to determine exactly what these users then did with these records, although the professions of the users give some indication. Perhaps unsurprisingly, this is suggestive of the fact that the archive is at present predominantly used as a tool of academic research. Whilst the data offers no more specifics on the fields that these researchers are situated in, a survey of literature that draws on ICTR records suggests that the archive remains predominantly used by legal and political science scholars (as has been the case here).[33] Indeed unlike the wave of historical scholarship that drew on Holocaust trial records,[34] there is yet to be the similar acknowledgment of the value of ICTR's archive as a historical record of the violence in Rwanda,[35] rather than a record of the legal and institutional history of the tribunal.[36] How these records are used, then, seems to match the UN's determination, as discussed earlier, that the records are of primarily legal and bureaucratic value.[37]

---

[33] A useful reference for ICTR-related literature is MICT, 'International Criminal Tribunal for Rwanda (ICTR) Special Bibliography', found: www.un-ilibrary.org/international-law-and-justice /bibliography-on-ictr-icty-and-irmct-2018_59527281-en-fr (last accessed 31 October 2019). For a rare example of a text that uses (although still not extensively) the ICTR records in order to produce a historical account of the genocide, see Linda Melvern, *Conspiracy to Murder: The Rwandan Genocide* (London: Verso, 2006). Another example comes (perhaps unsurprisingly) from a former ICTR expert witness, André Guichaoua. André Guichaoua, *From War to Genocide: Criminal Politics in Rwanda, 1990–1994*, (Madison: University of Wisconsin Press, 2015).

[34] For examples see Raul Hilberg, *The Destruction of the European Jews*, VOL I–III (London: Yale University Press, 1961); Christopher Browning, *Ordinary Men: Reserve Police Battalion 101 and the Final Solution in Poland* (London: Penguin Books, 2001).

[35] As the previous chapters argued, however, any future use of the archive should be aware of the power relations that underpinned the archive. Without this awareness, any research drawing on these records would be in danger of reproducing the problematic vision of community as outlined in Chapter 6.

[36] It is worth noting, however, that the wave of scholarship that drew on the Holocaust Trial records was not immediate either. Hilberg's *The Destruction of the European Jews*, one of the most significant historical accounts of the Holocaust, and which substantially relied on the Nuremberg record, was first published in 1961. Raul Hilberg, *The Destruction of the European Jews*, VOL I–III (London: Yale University Press, 1961).

[37] UNSC, S/2009/258, *Report of the Secretary-General on the Administrative and Budgetary Aspects of the Options for Possible Locations for the Archives of the ICTY and ICTR and the Seat of the Residual Mechanism(s) for the Tribunals*, 21 May 2009, 14.

CONCLUSION

The MICT marked a new chapter in the tribunal's history. Yet, to a great extent, the logics and drive that underpinned the archive by the end of the ICTR were replicated in the MICT. If anything, the MICT represented an even more extreme vision of the lean and efficient understanding of justice than had underpinned the ICTR. Moreover, as has been explored in this chapter there is an important material dimension to the archive, as the very materiality of the new MICT complex and archive came to reflect this new vision of justice. The power relations that underpinned the ICTR also appeared to continue at the MICT. The new facility and specifically the new archive represent a re-entrenchment of the subordination of Rwanda's interests to those of the UN and the tribunal, as the rejection of Rwanda's demands over the archive suggests.

However, this offers only a partial glimpse into the way that the archive is put to use and the effects that this has in terms of reproducing the archive's rules. Much more work is needed to trace the political consequences of the archive's afterlife in this respect. As Derrida reminds us, to an extent the archive is written anew each time its records are withdrawn and put to use, as the user brings their own world view, and prejudices, to bear on the documents.[38] Whilst, in the next chapter, and building on this, it appears that there is a danger that at the ICC the archival logics discussed throughout this book have been reproduced, it is also the case that the archive's logics can be challenged.[39] This has been demonstrated in this book's analysis; in this respect, I argue, that excavating the archive's rules and vision of community is one way of potentially contesting the archival drive.

The artwork of Vladimir Miladinović, who provided the artwork for the front cover of this book (see Figure 3), is another example of this type of contestation, and, I would argue, demonstrates how the archive can be further contested.

---

[38] Jacques Derrida, 'Archive Fever: A Freudian Impression', *Diacritics* 25:2 (1995): 9–63.

[39] This idea of challenging and resisting the archival drive also resonates with the ideas of the counter-archive and the anti-colonial archive, which have been explored in two recent edited volumes. Stewart Motha and Honni van Rijswijk (eds.), *Law, Memory and Violence: Uncovering the Counter Archive* (London: Routledge, 2016). Shiera el-Malik and Isaac Kamola (eds.) *Politics of African Anticolonial Archive* (London: Rowman & Littlefield International, 2017). See also Michelle Caswell, 'Defining Human Rights Archives: Introduction to the Special Double Issue on Archives and Human Rights', *Archival Science* 14 (2014): 207–13; Verne Harris, 'Antonyms of Our Remembering', *Archival Science* 14:3–4 (2014): 215–29.

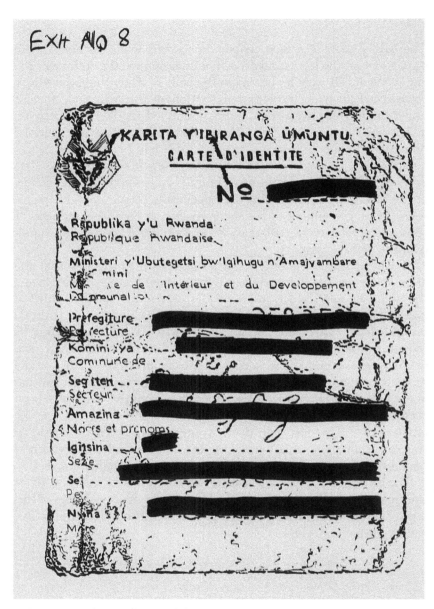

Figure 3 ID Card by Vladimir Miladinović

Miladinović's work carefully traces the boundaries of archival knowledge by producing ink wash drawings of forgotten records or forgotten instances of violence from the 1990s wars in the Western Balkans, often drawing on the ICTY's archive. In doing so the logics of the archive that produced these records are examined as Miladinović literally draws back in these narratives, and through this process the distribution of the sensible, which led to the erasure of the violence from the societal consciousness, is also revealed.[40] Engaging with these archives from an aesthetic perspective also injects an emphasis on the role of imagination, as the viewer is also asked to actively work to understand the image and archive. The front cover of this book, then, contains a redacted version of a Rwandan ID card from the archive, which encourages the viewer to reflect not only on the role that certain understandings of identity played in the genocide, but also on what *isn't* recorded in the archive and what is erased from the archive. It further encourages us to '*read in*' what is behind the black marks of the redactions. With this, Miladinović's work rejects the legal archive's attempts at closure and the sanitation of violence and truth, and instead, this signals a call for an imaginative encounter with the rules of the archive and the possibility of community. What this also suggests, I would argue, is that to a great extent the real legacy of the archive, its afterlife, is yet to be determined, and there is space for the archive's users to determine and reimage what type of community is to be realised.

---

[40] Jacques Rancière, *The Politics of Aesthetics* (London: Bloomsbury Publishing, 2013).

CONCLUSION: *THE ICTR'S ARCHIVE*

This book has provided the first sustained analysis of the archives produced by international courts. Having established the link between archives and community and how the archive can be analysed, I then offered a detailed account of the politics of knowledge production at the ICTR and showed what understanding of the international community emerged from within the archive's records. This fine-grained analysis of the way in which records were produced revealed how the archive's strategies, concepts, enunciative modalities and objects, and the *inter-relation* between these, along with the very materiality of the archive, resulted in a particular articulation of justice and community. In doing so, it has reinforced the value of the archive as an empirical site, and theoretical mode of encounter, for both legal and international relations scholars.

One of the most important findings, in this respect, was that, as a result of the dynamic and changing relationship between the different types of statements within the archive, the very conception of justice that underpinned the archive shifted over time. Whilst at the tribunal's outset a broader vision of (albeit weak) restorative justice was mobilised, after the intervention of the UNSC and the implementation of the completion strategy a more limited form of retributive justice came to dominate the archive, as the tribunal became fixated on ideas of efficiency and economy. This fundamentally altered the very materiality of the archive, as the types of records produced became more legalistic, and to an extent 'thinner', and also reformulated the power relations at the heart of the archive. This saw the legal actors, and particularly the judges, gain control of the production of records as witnesses were used in an increasingly utilitarian way. These dynamics became yet more heightened at the MICT. In drawing on an archaeological methodology, the book has consequently highlighted the contingent, dynamic and political nature of knowledge production and the practice of law within international courts.

This concern with the political nature of law was also at the heart of the book's overarching question of what vision of the international community emerged from within the archive. As Chapter 6 examined in detail, as both a legal institution and one founded at the height of the liberal internationalism of the post–Cold War era, the archive unsurprisingly forwarded a liberal vision of community. Yet this also demonstrated that underneath the ideals of progress, individual responsibility, neutrality and equality, and universalism lay a different, and altogether more illiberal, story. This suggested that the archive carved out a worrying division within the international community between the international and the local, and that, over time, a greater space for the perpetration of violence in international affairs was constructed, and the subaltern subsumed within the Western enlightenment logic of the archive. This also showed how a patriarchal vision of community was reproduced as gendered discourses affected how evidence was produced and assessed. As was argued in Chapter 6, this was of more than semantic importance, but these particular imaginings have consequences for how the international community is governed, which voices are given space to be heard, and also which subjects are afforded protection from harm.

These findings resonate with the long-running critique of liberal responses to war, and particularly so-called liberal peace.[1] In many respects, the mechanisms associated with liberal peace, like international courts, appear trapped in reproducing the logics and power relations that led to the very emergence of liberalism and enlightenment, and so, for instance, remain bound up with patriarchal and racist visions of society.[2] From this perspective the findings of this book will,

---

[1] E.g. Oliver Richmond, 'The Problem of Peace: Understanding the "Liberal Peace"', *Conflict, Security & Development* 6:3 (2006): 291–314; Oliver Richmond and Roger Mac Ginty, 'Where now for the Critique of the Liberal Peace?', *Cooperation and Conflict* 50:2 (2015): 171–89; Maria O'Reilly, 'Muscular Interventionism, International Feminist Journal of Politics', 14:4 (2012): 529–48; Hannah Partis-Jennings, 'The (In)Security of Gender in Afghanistan's Peacebuilding Project: Hybridity and Affect', *International Feminist Journal of Politics* 19:4 (2017): 411–25.

[2] This is also about the way in which these interventions reproduce the *logics* of colonialism. Vivienne Jabri, 'Peacebuilding, the Local and the International: a Colonial or a Postcolonial

perhaps, come as little surprise. The question is, however, whether or not current practices of these liberal international institutions, such as international courts, can be disentangled from these conditions of emergence. Whilst such an enquiry would warrant a whole other volume, a number of observations can be made here specifically about the potential and limits of international criminal justice to meaningfully respond to these critiques.

RESPONDING TO THE LIBERAL CRITIQUE

In many respects, the issues highlighted earlier about the practice of the ICTR do seem intractably linked to the application of criminal law as a form of liberal governance. One such issue, in terms of law's inability to reform, is its refusal to meaningfully engage in a self-reflective critique of its own practice. As the work of Martha Minow has shown in relation to US courts, any push for judges to recognise racial bias, for instance, has been met with a rebuke that to acknowledge this would be to *inevitably deliver politicised and biased justice*.[3] Law relies on its claims to impartiality, and for understandable reason. If courts cannot apply the law in a neutral fashion then the legitimacy of using it as a means to curtail an individual's freedom comes into question. The same applies for law's need to see perpetrators as conscious and rational actors, which appears to be another obstacle in the way of law addressing some of the critiques levelled at it, particularly around its inability to understand the collective nature of crimes like genocide. Whilst international criminal law has tried to 'soften' some of the more damaging aspects of its universalising claims, through principles such as complementarity, this has so far failed to really unsettle the power dynamics of international law as a practice imposed by the powerful onto the marginalised within the international community.[4] There is, moreover,

Rationality?', *Peacebuilding* 1:1 (2013): 3–16; Vivienne Jabri, 'War, Government, Politics: A Critical Response to the Hegemony of the Liberal Peace', In *Palgrave Advances in Peacebuilding*, ed. Oliver Richmond (London: Palgrave Macmillan, 2010): 41–57; Dianne Otto, 'Subalternity and International Law: the Problems of Global Community and the Incommensurability of Difference', *Social & Legal Studies* 5:3 (1996): 339–440; Aníbal Quijano, 'Coloniality and Modernity/Rationality', *Cultural Studies* 21:2–3 (2007): 168–78; Walter D. Mignolo, 'Introduction', *Cultural Studies* 21:2–3 (2007): 62 Meera Sabaratnam, 'Avatars of Eurocentrism in the Critique of the Liberal Peace', *Security Dialogue* 44:3 (2013): 259–78.

[3] Martha Minow 'Foreword: Justice Engendered', *Harvard Law Review* 101:10 (1987): 14.

[4] Phil Clark, *Distant Justice: The Impact of the International Criminal Court on African Politics* (Cambridge: Cambridge University Press, 2018).

a more fundamental limit to which international criminal law can ever really loosen its universal claims. The very legitimacy of international criminal law is predicated on the idea that certain crimes are so egregious that they are violations of the laws of humankind and that, as such, the normal limits of the international order, such as the sacrosanct nature of sovereignty, are reformulated to allow, and even demand, for the deliverance of justice, often at the hand of international actors.

Yet, at the same time, as was seen particularly in Chapters 4 and 5, international criminal law is a dynamic and ever-evolving entity. This book has shown, moreover, that even if only for a brief moment, an arguably more sensitive and expansive vision of justice did emerge at the ICTR. This was, of course, not without issues – not least that the state subjected to the ICTR's jurisdiction, Rwanda, rejected the tribunal's legitimacy. These chapters showed, however, at least some potential to tackle some of the problems that have been central to critique of international courts and liberal responses to war more broadly, such as the consideration of the experiences of those that endured and survived the genocide, the potential to address gender-based violence and to provide a more collective vision of justice that worked to try to protect the rights of victims, whilst continuing to recognise the rights of the accused.

It is true that this potential was short-lived. But it is (albeit it with the benefit of hindsight) also easy to see how this could have been otherwise. Better provisions for victims throughout, clearer and more genuine engagement with the affected community, a real commitment to gender-based violence, and the pursuit of jurisprudence that protects victims *not* the sovereign's right to use force were all within the grasp of the tribunal. Similarly, it would have made for a significant statement if any of the international actors that aided and abetted the violence in Rwanda were held to account, as was, technically, possible under the provisions of the tribunal's statute. Addressing these issues would have required a greater level of reflexivity from the tribunal's practitioners to challenge the consequences of their own world views – such as around gender-based violence or their approach to 'Rwandan culture'. This would also have required greater political will from the UN and its member states. For instance, the inability to meet the needs of the victims was the product of a clearly political decision by the UN that this wasn't worth the time or money. The UN's obsession with efficiency was also at the heart of the tribunal's shift to a more reductionist vision of justice. There were some real and legitimate concerns with aspects of the tribunal's operations in the early years which warranted a change in tack. But there was not the need to lose sight so fundamentally of the community that was affected by the violence.

There is a danger that this argument might reinforce the sense of the unquestioned legitimacy of the practice of international courts by suggesting that minor adjustments can make things right. This could also, then, potentially reproduce some of the power relations and discourses that the book has critiqued, such as the division of the international community into the international as saviour and the local as barbarous other.[5] Throughout, such a division has been both criticised and revealed as a (powerful) illusion.[6] Furthermore, to draw attention to the performative and dynamic nature of the regime and argue it could be otherwise is not to suggest that the effects of this current imagining are not serious and enduring. Indeed, what is perhaps particularly worrying is that similar power relations and visions of community have continued at the ICC, as a very narrow understanding of justice, fixated with the efficiency of the trial process, has taken hold, and the needs and rights of communities affected by war are ignored. This is, moreover, *despite* the statute being specifically designed around a form of quasi-restorative justice by, for instance, integrating the needs of the victims and those directly affected by the violence into the court's practice.[7] Moreover, the ICC seems to have remained incapable of adequately dealing with gender-based violence, as was seen in *Lubanga*, and the relationship between the ICC and the Global South is, in many respects, worse than ever.[8]

This is not, then, to sweep these issues aside or claim that any meaningful change would be easy. Yet, when the arguments of this book are taken as a whole, it does suggest that whilst these problems are

---

[5] Sabaratnam, 'Avatar', 270.

[6] Vivienne Jabri, 'Disarming Norms: Postcolonial Agency and the Constitution of the International', *International Theory* 6:2 (2014): 372–83.

[7] Rosemary Byrne has also similarly argued that the ICC's regime is based on ideas of 'efficiency'. Rosemary Byrne, 'The New Public International Lawyer and the Hidden Art of International Criminal Trial Practice', *Connecticut Journal of International Law* 243:25 (2010): 245. Such measures include allowing victims, under the Rules of Procedure and Evidence 85 and 86, to represent their interests at trial, and there is also now a direct mechanism in place for victims to apply for reparations. ICC, 'Rules of Procedure and Evidence', found: www.icc-cpi.int/resource-library/Documents/RulesProcedureEvidenceEng.pdf#page=32 (last accessed 31 October 2019).

[8] Marianna Pena and Gaelle Carayon, 'Is the ICC Making the Most of Victim Participation?', *The Journal of Transitional Justice* 7 (2013): 526 and 529–30; Claire Garbett, 'The Truth and the Trial: Victim Participation, Restorative Justice, and the International Criminal Court', *Contemporary Justice Review* 16: 2 (2013): 205–6. Clark, *Distant Justice*, 302–4.

deeply engrained, they are, perhaps not inevitably so. I would also argue that at least some of these issues could be dealt with, or at least more squarely and openly discussed, if the question at the heart of this book, 'what type of community?', was asked of the ICTR, ICC or any post-conflict intervention.

As this book has shown, this question encourages a consideration of the wider systems of power that govern community, and the position and role of individual interventions and sites of governance within this. This also, as a result, pushes back against the idea that building peace, and the mobilisation of mechanisms such as international courts, is simply a technocratic exercise or an inevitable 'good' – a view which, I would argue, still dominates. The question 'what type of community' removes the sense that what community is constituted is an inevitability, and so re-politicises this question in a way that, as I argued at the end of Chapter 7, opens it up for contestation, debate and the possibility for new understandings of community to emerge. Once such a question is asked, perhaps internationally dominated interventions like the ICTR and ICC may lose some of their appeal and play a more diminished role in the governance of community. But what seems clear is that without this fundamental question, which remains so often ignored, the chances of meaningfully addressing the legacies of atrocity or building a just notion of community diminish, no matter what form of intervention is used.

BIBLIOGRAPHY

PRIMARY RESEARCH

Interviews

Interview with Anonymous (June 2015).
Interview with Anonymous 2 (April 2016).
Interview with Appeals Judge (June 2016).
Interview with Defence Counsel – ICTR and ICTY (February 2016).
Interview with Former ICTR Archivist (June 2015).
Interview with ICTR Judge (June 2017).
Interview with Member of ICTR OTP 2 (June 2015).
Interview with Member of ICTR OTP 3 (June 2015).
Interview with Member of ICTR OTP 4 (June 2015).
Interview with Member of ICTR OTP 5 (June 2015).
Interview with Member of ICTR OTP 6 (June 2015).
Interview with Member of ICTR OTP 7 (June 2015).
Interview with Member of ICTR OTP 8 (June 2015).
Interview with Member of ICTR OTP 9 (June 2015)
Interview with Member of the ICTR Victim and Witness Support Section (June 2015).
Interview with MICT Archivists (August 2019)
Interview with Senior Information and Evidence Section Officer – ICTR Office of the Prosecutor (June 2015).
Interview with ICTR Investigator (June 2015).
Interview with Senior Legal Officer – ICTR Chambers (June 2016).
Interview with Reviser – ICTR Registry (June 2015).

Trial Documents[1]

Akayesu (Case No: ICTR–96–4)

ICTR–96–4, Akayesu, Audio Recording: Interview of Jean Paul Akayesu in Zambia, 10 April 1996, Tape I.

---

[1] Organisational note: these transcript references are organised by trial, in the subheadings, and then by specific document code, as CONTRA00001 in the first record. The latter are then used for the shortened footnotes.

184

Prosecutor v. *Jean-Paul Akayesu*, Case No. ICTR–96–4, ICTR–96–4–0028, *Akayesu* – *Inter-Office Memo Transmitting a Brief in Response to a Preliminary Motion*, 4 September 1996.

Prosecutor v. *Jean-Paul Akayesu*, Case No. ICTR–96–4, ICTR–96–4–0160, *Akayesu* – *Decision on the Preliminary Motions Presented by the Prosecution and the Defence*, 17 February 1997.

Prosecutor v. *Jean-Paul Akayesu*, Case No. ICTR–96–4, ICTR–96–4–0183, *Akayesu* – *Amicus Brief Respecting Amendment of the Indictment and Supplementation of the Evidence to Ensure the Prosecution of Rape and Other Sexual Violence within the Competence of the Tribunal*, 28 May 1997.

Prosecutor v. *Jean-Paul Akayesu*, Case No. ICTR–96–4, ICTR–96–4–0459/1, *Akayesu* – *Judgement*, 2 September 1998.

Prosecutor v. *Jean-Paul Akayesu*, Case No. ICTR–96–4, ICTR–96–4–0531, *Akayesu* – *Decision on the Preliminary Motion Submitted by the Prosecutor for Protective Measures for the Witnesses*, 27 September 1996.

Prosecutor v. *Jean-Paul Akayesu*, Case No. ICTR–96–4, ICTR–96–4–0555, *Akayesu* – *Leave to Amend the Indictment*, 17 June 1997.

Prosecutor v. *Jean-Paul Akayesu*, Case No. ICTR–96–4, ICTR–96–4–0868/1, *Akayesu* – *Appeal Judgement*, 1 June 2001.

Prosecutor v. *Jean-Paul Akayesu*, Case No. ICTR–96–4, ICTR–96–4–0003, *Akayesu* – *Indictment*, 13 February 1996.

Prosecutor v. *Jean-Paul Akayesu*, Case No. ICTR–96–4, CONTRA000049, *Akayesu* – *Transcript of 1/11/2000* – *Appeals Hearing*, 1 November 2000.

Prosecutor v. *Jean-Paul Akayesu*, Case No. ICTR–96–4, CONTRA000050, *Akayesu* – *Transcript of 2/11/2000* – *Appeals Hearing*, 2 November 2000.

Prosecutor v. *Jean-Paul Akayesu*, Case No. ICTR–96–4, CONTRA001175, *Akayesu* – *Transcript of 09/1/1997*, 9 January 1997.

Prosecutor v. *Jean-Paul Akayesu*, Case No. ICTR–96–4, CONTRA001176, *Akayesu* – *Transcript of 10/1/1997*, 10 January 1997.

Prosecutor v. *Jean-Paul Akayesu*, Case No. ICTR–96–4, CONTRA001178, *Akayesu* – *Transcript of 14/1/1997*, 14 January 1997.

Prosecutor v. *Jean-Paul Akayesu*, Case No. ICTR–96–4, CONTRA001179, *Akayesu* – *Transcript of 21/1/1997*, 21 January 1997.

Prosecutor v. *Jean-Paul Akayesu*, Case No. ICTR–96–4, CONTRA001180, *Akayesu* – *Transcript of 22/1/1997*, 22 January 1997.

Prosecutor v. *Jean-Paul Akayesu*, Case No. ICTR–96–4, CONTRA001181, *Akayesu* – *Transcript of 23/1/1997*, 23 January 1997.

Prosecutor v. *Jean-Paul Akayesu*, Case No. ICTR–96–4, CONTRA001183, *Akayesu* – *Transcript of 15/1/1997*, 15 January 1997.

Prosecutor v. *Jean-Paul Akayesu*, Case No. ICTR–96–4, CONTRA001184, *Akayesu* – *Transcript of 16/1/1997*, 16 January 1997.

Prosecutor v. *Jean-Paul Akayesu*, Case No. ICTR–96–4, CONTRA001182, *Akayesu* – *Transcript of 24/1/1997*, 24 January 1997.

Prosecutor v. *Jean-Paul Akayesu*, Case No. ICTR–96–4, CONTRA001186, *Akayesu – Transcript of 27/1/1997*, 27 January 1997.

Prosecutor v. *Jean-Paul Akayesu*, Case No. ICTR–96–4, CONTRA001187, *Akayesu – Transcript of 28/1/1997*, 28 January 1997.

Prosecutor v. *Jean-Paul Akayesu*, Case No. ICTR–96–4, CONTRA001189, *Akayesu – Transcript of 30/1/1997*, 30 January 1997.

Prosecutor v. *Jean-Paul Akayesu*, Case No. ICTR–96–4, CONTRA001190, *Akayesu – Transcript of 4/2/1997*, 4 January 1997.

Prosecutor v. *Jean-Paul Akayesu*, Case No. ICTR–96–4, CONTRA001191, *Akayesu – Transcript of 13/2/1997*, 13 February 1997.

Prosecutor v. *Jean-Paul Akayesu*, Case No. ICTR–96–4, CONTRA001192, *Akayesu – Transcript of 14/2/1997*, 14 February 1997.

Prosecutor v. *Jean-Paul Akayesu*, Case No. ICTR–96–4, CONTRA001193, *Akayesu – Transcript of 18/2/1997*, 18 February 1997.

Prosecutor v. *Jean-Paul Akayesu*, Case No. ICTR–96–4, CONTRA001195, *Akayesu – Transcript of 6/3/1997*, 6 March 1997.

Prosecutor v. *Jean-Paul Akayesu*, Case No. ICTR–96–4, CONTRA001197, *Akayesu – Transcript of 5/2/1997*, 5 February 1997.

Prosecutor v. *Jean-Paul Akayesu*, Case No. ICTR–96–4, CONTRA001198, *Akayesu – Transcript of 6/2/1997*, 6 February 1997.

Prosecutor v. *Jean-Paul Akayesu*, Case No. ICTR–96–4, CONTRA001199, *Akayesu – Transcript of 11/2/1997*, 11 February 1997.

Prosecutor v. *Jean-Paul Akayesu*, Case No. ICTR–96–4, CONTRA001200, *Akayesu – Transcript of 12/2/1997*, 12 February 1997.

Prosecutor v. *Jean-Paul Akayesu*, Case No. ICTR–96–4, CONTRA001205, *Akayesu – Transcript of 4/11/1997*, 04 November 1997.

Prosecutor v. *Jean-Paul Akayesu*, Case No. ICTR–96–4, CONTRA001207, *Akayesu – Transcript of 17/11/1997*, 17 November 1997.

Prosecutor v. *Jean-Paul Akayesu*, Case No. ICTR–96–4, CONTRA001208, *Akayesu – Transcript of 18/11/1997*, 18 November 1997.

Prosecutor v. *Jean-Paul Akayesu*, Case No. ICTR–96–4, CONTRA001209, *Akayesu – Transcript of 22/5/1997*, 22 May 1997.

Prosecutor v. *Jean-Paul Akayesu*, Case No. ICTR–96–4, CONTRA001210, *Akayesu – Transcript of 23/5/1997*, 23 May 1997.

Prosecutor v. *Jean-Paul Akayesu*, Case No. ICTR–96–4, CONTRA001211, *Akayesu – Transcript of 24/5/1997*, 24 May 1997.

Prosecutor v. *Jean-Paul Akayesu*, Case No. ICTR–96–4, CONTRA001212, *Akayesu – Transcript of 17/6/1997 – Motion*, 17 June 1997.

Prosecutor v. *Jean-Paul Akayesu*, Case No. ICTR–96–4, CONTRA001214, *Akayesu – Transcript of 19/11/1997*, 19 November 1997.

Prosecutor v. *Jean-Paul Akayesu*, Case No. ICTR–96–4, CONTRA001217, *Akayesu – Transcript of 9/2/1998*, 9 February 1998.

Prosecutor v. *Jean-Paul Akayesu*, Case No. ICTR–96–4, CONTRA001222, *Akayesu* – *Transcript of 23/10/1997*, 23 October 1997.

Prosecutor v. *Jean-Paul Akayesu*, Case No. ICTR–96–4, CONTRA001224, *Akayesu* – *Transcript of 27/10/1997*, 27 October 1997.

Prosecutor v. *Jean-Paul Akayesu*, Case No. ICTR–96–4, CONTRA001227, *Akayesu* – *Transcript of 3/11/1997*, 3 November 1997.

Prosecutor v. *Jean-Paul Akayesu*, Case No. ICTR–96–4, CONTRA001231, *Akayesu* – *Transcript of 12/3/1998*, 12 March 1998.

Prosecutor v. *Jean-Paul Akayesu*, Case No. ICTR–96–4, CONTRA001233, *Akayesu* – *Transcript of 28/09/1998* – *Sentencing Hearing*, 28 September 1998.

Prosecutor v. *Jean-Paul Akayesu*, Case No. ICTR–96–4, CONTRA001235, *Akayesu* – *Transcript of 19/03/1998*, 19 March 1998.

Prosecutor v. *Jean-Paul Akayesu*, Case No. ICTR–96–4, CONTRA001236, *Akayesu* – *Transcript of 23/3/1998*, 23 March 1998.

Prosecutor v. *Jean-Paul Akayesu*, Case No. ICTR–96–4, CONTRA001238, *Akayesu* – *Transcript of 26/03/1998*, 26 March 1998.

Cyangugu (Case Nos.: ICTR–96–10, ICTR–97–36 and ICTR–99–46)

Prosecutor v. André Ntagerura, Case No. ICTR–96–10

Prosecutor v. *André Ntagerura*, Case No. ICTR–96–10, ICTR–96–10–0212, *Ntagerura* – *Decision* – *Confirmation of the Indictment*, 10 August 1996.

Prosecutor v. *André Ntagerura*, Case No. ICTR–96–10, ICTR–96–10A–0006, *Ntagerura* – *Request for Extension of Detention*, 18 June 1996.

Prosecutor v. *André Ntagerura*, Case No. ICTR–96–10, ICTR–96–10A–0014, *Ntagerura* – *Indictment* – *Supporting Material* – *Supporting Documentation*, 9 August 1996.

Prosecutor v. *André Ntagerura*, Case No. ICTR–96–10, ICTR–96–10A–00347, *Ntagerura* – *Audio Recording of 19/03/99* – *AM*, 19 March 1999.

Prosecutor v. *André Ntagerura*, Case No. ICTR–96–10, ICTR–96–10A–0072, *Ntagerura* – *Brief in Response to the Preliminary Motions*, 29 July 1997.

Prosecutor v. *André Ntagerura*, Case No. ICTR–96–10, ICTR–96–10A–0194, ICTR–96–10, *Ntagerura* – *Preliminary Motion (Defects in the Indictment)*, 21 April 1997.

Prosecutor v. *André Ntagerura*, Case No. ICTR–96–10, ICTR–96–10A–0208, *Ntagerura* – *Decision on the Preliminary Motion Filed by the Defence Based on Defects in the Form of the Indictment*, 28 November 1997.

Prosecutor v. *André Ntagerura*, Case No. ICTR–96–10, ICTR–96–10A–0224, *Ntagerura* – *Amended Indictment*, 29 January 1998.

Prosecutor v. André Ntagerura, Case No. ICTR–96–10, ICTR–96–10A–0272, *Ntagerura – Prosecutor Request for Leave to File an Amended Indictment*, 2 December 1999.

Prosecutor v. Emmanuel Bagambiki, Samuel Imanishimwe and Yussuf Munyakazi, ICTR–97–36

Prosecutor v. Emmanuel Bagambiki, Samuel Imanishimwe and Yussuf Munyakazi, Case No. ICTR–97–36, ICTR–97–36–00189, *Bagambiki – Audio Recording of 08/09/97 – AM*, 8 September 1997.

Prosecutor v. Emmanuel Bagambiki, Samuel Imanishimwe and Yussuf Munyakazi, Case No. ICTR–97–36, ICTR–97–36–00195, *Bagambiki – Audio Recording of 25/03/98 – AM*, 25 March 1998.

Prosecutor v. Emmanuel Bagambiki, Samuel Imanishimwe and Yussuf Munyakazi, Case No. ICTR–97–36, ICTR–97–36–0039/1, *Imanishimwe Preliminary Motions*, 28 January 1998.

Prosecutor v. Emmanuel Bagambiki, Samuel Imanishimwe and Yussuf Munyakazi, Case No. ICTR–97–36, ICTR–97–36–0043, *Preliminary Motions*, 18 February 1998.

Prosecutor v. Emmanuel Bagambiki, Samuel Imanishimwe and Yussuf Munyakazi, Case No. ICTR–97–36, ICTR–97–36–0048, *The Prosecutor's Brief in Reply to the Defence Preliminary Motions on Behalf of Samuel Imanishimwe*, 24 March 1998.

Prosecutor v. Emmanuel Bagambiki, Samuel Imanishimwe and Yussuf Munyakazi, Case No. ICTR–97–36, ICTR–97–36–0062, *Imanishimwe – Bagambiki – Munyakazi – Decision on the Defence Motion Regarding Defects in the Form of the Indictment*, 24 September 1998.

Prosecutor v. Emmanuel Bagambiki, Samuel Imanishimwe and Yussuf Munyakazi, Case No. ICTR–97–36, ICTR–97–36–0071, *Bagambiki – Imanishimwe – Indictment – Redacted*, 9 October 1997.

Prosecutor v. André Ntagerura, Emmanuel Bagambiki and Samuel Imanishimwe, Case No. ICT–99–46

Prosecutor v. André Ntagerura, Emmanuel Bagambiki and Samuel Imanishimwe, Case No. ICTR–99–46, ICTR–99–46–0001, *Prosecutor's Motion for Joinder of the Accused (Ntagerura, ICTR–96–10A–T0, Bagambiki ICTR–97–36–T, Imanishimwe ICTR–97–36–I, and Munyakazi ICTR–97–36–I)*, 2 April 1999.

Prosecutor v. André Ntagerura, Emmanuel Bagambiki and Samuel Imanishimwe, Case No. ICTR–99–46, ICTR–99–46–0018, *[Cyangugu] – Bagambiki – Ntagerura et al – Decision on the Prosecutor's Motion for Joinder*, 11 October 1999.

Prosecutor v. André Ntagerura, Emmanuel Bagambiki and Samuel Imanishimwe, Case No. ICTR–99–46, ICTR–99–46–0046, *[Cyangugu] – Bagambiki –*

Ntagerura et al – Notice of the Prosecutor to Withdraw All Pending Motion, 14 February 2000.

Prosecutor v. André Ntagerura, Emmanuel Bagambiki and Samuel Imanishimwe, Case No. ICTR–99–46, ICTR–99–46–0072, *[Cyangugu] – Bagambiki – Ntagerura et al – The Prosecutor's Preliminary Pre-Trial Brief*, 24 May 2000.

Prosecutor v. André Ntagerura, Emmanuel Bagambiki and Samuel Imanishimwe, Case No. ICTR–99–46, ICTR–99–46–01002, *Ntagerura – Audio Recording of 10/08/99 – AM*, 10 October 1999.

Prosecutor v. André Ntagerura, Emmanuel Bagambiki and Samuel Imanishimwe, Case No. ICTR–99–46, ICTR–99–46–0130, *[Cyangugu] – Bagambiki – Ntagerura et al – The Prosecutor's Pre-Trial Brief*, 3 July 2000.

Prosecutor v. André Ntagerura, Emmanuel Bagambiki and Samuel Imanishimwe, Case No. ICTR–99–46, ICTR–99–46–0183, *[Cyangugu] – Bagambiki – Ntagerura et al – Compliance with Trial Chamber III Order of 23/08/2000 (Attached Shortened List of Witnesses)*, 18 September 2000.

Prosecutor v. André Ntagerura, Emmanuel Bagambiki and Samuel Imanishimwe, Case No. ICTR–99–46, ICTR–99–46–0183, *Compliance with Trial Chamber III Order of 23 August, 2000*, 18 September 2000.

Prosecutor v. André Ntagerura, Emmanuel Bagambiki and Samuel Imanishimwe, Case No. ICTR–99–46, ICTR–99–46–0270, *[Cyangugu] – Imanishimwe – Response of the Defence for Samuel Imanishimwe to Amicus Curiae Application Filed by the NGO Coalition for Women's Human Rights in Conflict Situation*, 27 April 2001.

Prosecutor v. André Ntagerura, Emmanuel Bagambiki and Samuel Imanishimwe, Case No. ICTR–99–46, ICTR–99–46–0287, *[Cyangugu] – Bagambiki – Ntagerura et al – Decision on the Application to File an Amicus Curiae Brief According to Rule 74 of the Rules of Procedure and Evidence Filed on Behalf of the NGO Coalition for Women's Human Rights in Conflict Situations*, 24 May 2001.

Prosecutor v. André Ntagerura, Emmanuel Bagambiki and Samuel Imanishimwe, Case No. ICTR–99–46, ICTR–99–46–0488, *Proposed Reduction in the List of Defence Witnesses in the Cyangugu Case, Case No. ICTR–99–46–T*, 30 April 2002.

Prosecutor v. André Ntagerura, Emmanuel Bagambiki and Samuel Imanishimwe, Case No. ICTR–99–46, ICTR–99–46–0599/1, *Trial Judgement – the Prosecutor V. André Ntagerura Emmanuel Bagambiki Samuel Imanishimwe*, 25 February 2004.

Prosecutor v. André Ntagerura, Emmanuel Bagambiki and Samuel Imanishimwe, Case No. ICTR–99–46, ICTR-99-46-0609/1, *[Cyangugu] – Prosecutor's Notice of Appeal*, 25 March 2004;

Prosecutor v. André Ntagerura, Emmanuel Bagambiki and Samuel Imanishimwe, Case No. ICTR–99–46, ICTR-99-46-1735/2, *Cyangugu – Appeal Judgement*, 7 July 2006.

Prosecutor v. André Ntagerura, Emmanuel Bagambiki and Samuel Imanishimwe, Case No. ICTR–99–46, CONTRA002340, *[Cyangugu] – Ntagerura et al – Redacted Transcript of 13/02/2001,* 13 February 2001.

Prosecutor v. André Ntagerura, Emmanuel Bagambiki and Samuel Imanishimwe, Case No. ICTR–99–46, TRA000122/01, *[Cyangugu] – Ntagerura et al – Redacted Transcript of 09/10/2000,* 9 February 2000.

Prosecutor v. André Ntagerura, Emmanuel Bagambiki and Samuel Imanishimwe, Case No. ICTR–99–46, TRA000124/01, *[Cyangugu] – Ntagerura et al – Redacted Transcript of 10/10/2000,* 10 October 2000.

Prosecutor v. André Ntagerura, Emmanuel Bagambiki and Samuel Imanishimwe, Case No. ICTR–99–46, TRA000126/02, *[Cyangugu] – Ntagerura et al – Redacted Transcript of 23/10/2000,* 23 October 2000.

Prosecutor v. André Ntagerura, Emmanuel Bagambiki and Samuel Imanishimwe, Case No. ICTR–99–46, TRA000131/1, *[Cyangugu] – Ntagerura et al – Redacted Transcript of 21/11/2000,* 21 November 2000.

Prosecutor v. André Ntagerura, Emmanuel Bagambiki and Samuel Imanishimwe, Case No. ICTR–99–46, TRA000207/01, *[Cyangugu] – Ntagerura et al – Redacted Transcript of 18/09/2000,* 18 September 2000.

Prosecutor v. André Ntagerura, Emmanuel Bagambiki and Samuel Imanishimwe, Case No. ICTR–99–46, TRA000209, *[Cyangugu] – Ntagerura et al – Redacted Transcript of 20/09/2000,* 20 September 2000.

Prosecutor v. André Ntagerura, Emmanuel Bagambiki and Samuel Imanishimwe, Case No. ICTR–99–46, TRA000217/1, *[Cyangugu] – Ntagerura et al – Redacted Transcript of 24/10/2000,* 24 October 2000.

Prosecutor v. André Ntagerura, Emmanuel Bagambiki and Samuel Imanishimwe, Case No. ICTR–99–46, TRA000218/1, *[Cyangugu] – Ntagerura et al – Redacted Transcript of 25/10/2000,* 25 October 2000.

Prosecutor v. André Ntagerura, Emmanuel Bagambiki and Samuel Imanishimwe, Case No. ICTR–99–46, TRA000251/2, *[Cyangugu] – Ntagerura et al – Redacted Transcript of 18/01/2001,* 18 January 2001.

Prosecutor v. André Ntagerura, Emmanuel Bagambiki and Samuel Imanishimwe, Case No. ICTR–99–46, TRA000254/2, *[Cyangugu] – Ntagerura et al – Redacted Transcript of 24/01/2001,* 24 January 2001.

Prosecutor v. André Ntagerura, Emmanuel Bagambiki and Samuel Imanishimwe, Case No. ICTR–99–46, TRA000258/2, *[Cyangugu] – Ntagerura et al – Redacted Transcript of 31/01/2001,* 31 January 2001.

Prosecutor v. André Ntagerura, Emmanuel Bagambiki and Samuel Imanishimwe, Case No. ICTR–99–46, TRA000324/2, *[Cyangugu] – Ntagerura et al – Redacted Transcript of 04/03/2002 – Motion,* 4 March 2002.

Prosecutor v. André Ntagerura, Emmanuel Bagambiki and Samuel Imanishimwe, Case No. ICTR–99–46, TRA000404/1, *[Cyangugu] – Ntagerura et al – Redacted Transcript of 11/09/2001,* 11 September 2001.

Prosecutor v. *André Ntagerura, Emmanuel Bagambiki and Samuel Imanishimwe,* Case No. ICTR–99–46, TRA000409/2, *[Cyangugu]* – *Ntagerura et al* – *Redacted Transcript of 07/05/2001,* 7 May 2001.

Prosecutor v. *André Ntagerura, Emmanuel Bagambiki and Samuel Imanishimwe,* Case No. ICTR–99–46, TRA000433/2, *[Cyangugu]* – *Ntagerura et al* – *Redacted Transcript of 14/02/2001* – Decision, 14 February 2001.

Prosecutor v. *André Ntagerura, Emmanuel Bagambiki and Samuel Imanishimwe,* Case No. ICTR–99–46, TRA000434/2, *[Cyangugu]* – *Ntagerura et al* – *Redacted Transcript of 14/02/2001,* 14 February 2001.

Prosecutor v. *André Ntagerura, Emmanuel Bagambiki and Samuel Imanishimwe,* Case No. ICTR–99–46, TRA000436/2, *[Cyangugu]* – *Ntagerura et al* – *Redacted Transcript of 19/02/2001,* 19 February 2001.

Prosecutor v. *André Ntagerura, Emmanuel Bagambiki and Samuel Imanishimwe,* Case No. ICTR–99–46, TRA000437/2, *[Cyangugu]* – *Ntagerura et al* – *Redacted Transcript of 20/02/2001,* 20 February 2001.

Prosecutor v. *André Ntagerura, Emmanuel Bagambiki and Samuel Imanishimwe,* Case No. ICTR–99–46, TRA000438/1, *[Cyangugu]* – *Ntagerura et al* – *Redacted Transcript of 21/02/2001,* 21 February 2001.

Prosecutor v. *André Ntagerura, Emmanuel Bagambiki and Samuel Imanishimwe,* Case No. ICTR–99–46, TRA000441/1, *[Cyangugu]* – *Ntagerura et al* – *Redacted Transcript of 28/02/2001,* 28 February 2001.

Prosecutor v. *André Ntagerura, Emmanuel Bagambiki and Samuel Imanishimwe,* Case No. ICTR–99–46, TRA000443/1, *[Cyangugu]* – *Ntagerura et al* – *Redacted Transcript of 02/05/2001,* 2 May 2001.

Prosecutor v. *André Ntagerura, Emmanuel Bagambiki and Samuel Imanishimwe,* Case No. ICTR–99–46, TRA000444/2, *[Cyangugu]* – *Ntagerura et al* – *Redacted Transcript of 03/05/2001,* 3 May 2001.

Prosecutor v. *André Ntagerura, Emmanuel Bagambiki and Samuel Imanishimwe,* Case No. ICTR–99–46, TRA000446/2, *[Cyangugu]* – *Ntagerura et al* – *Redacted Transcript of 09/05/2001,* 9 May 2001.

Prosecutor v. *André Ntagerura, Emmanuel Bagambiki and Samuel Imanishimwe,* Case No. ICTR–99–46, TRA000521/2, *[Cyangugu]* – *Ntagerura et al* – *Redacted Transcript of 05/03/2002* – Motion, 5 March 2002.

Prosecutor v. *André Ntagerura, Emmanuel Bagambiki and Samuel Imanishimwe,* Case No. ICTR–99–46, TRA000525/1, *[Cyangugu]* – *Ntagerura et al* – *Redacted Transcript of 19/03/2002,* 19 March 2002.

Prosecutor v. *André Ntagerura, Emmanuel Bagambiki and Samuel Imanishimwe,* Case No. ICTR–99–46, TRA000526/2, *[Cyangugu]* – *Ntagerura et al* – *Redacted Transcript of 12/03/2002,* 12 March 2002.

Prosecutor v. *André Ntagerura, Emmanuel Bagambiki and Samuel Imanishimwe,* Case No. ICTR–99–46, TRA000527/2, *[Cyangugu]* – *Ntagerura et al* – *Redacted Transcript of 13/03/2002,* 13 March 2002.

Prosecutor v. *André Ntagerura, Emmanuel Bagambiki and Samuel Imanishimwe,* Case No. ICTR–99–46, TRA000528/2, *[Cyangugu]* – *Ntagerura et al* – *Redacted Transcript of 11/03/2002,* 11 March 2002.

Prosecutor v. *André Ntagerura, Emmanuel Bagambiki and Samuel Imanishimwe,* Case No. ICTR–99–46, TRA000533/1, *[Cyangugu]* – *Ntagerura et al* – *Redacted Transcript of 14/05/2001,* 14 May 2001.

Prosecutor v. *André Ntagerura, Emmanuel Bagambiki and Samuel Imanishimwe,* Case No. ICTR–99–46, TRA000542/1, *[Cyangugu]* – *Ntagerura et al* – *Redacted Transcript of 18/09/2001,* 18 September 2001.

Prosecutor v. *André Ntagerura, Emmanuel Bagambiki and Samuel Imanishimwe,* Case No. ICTR–99–46, TRA000543/01, *[Cyangugu]* – *Ntagerura et al* – *Redacted Transcript of 19/09/2001,* 19 September 2001.

Prosecutor v. *André Ntagerura, Emmanuel Bagambiki and Samuel Imanishimwe,* Case No. ICTR–99–46, TRA000546/2, *[Cyangugu]* – *Ntagerura et al* – *Redacted Transcript of 20/09/2001,* 20 September 2001.

Prosecutor v. *André Ntagerura, Emmanuel Bagambiki and Samuel Imanishimwe,* Case No. ICTR–99–46, TRA000552/2, *[Cyangugu]* – *Ntagerura et al* – *Redacted Transcript of 06/03/2002,* 6 March 2002.

Prosecutor v. *André Ntagerura, Emmanuel Bagambiki and Samuel Imanishimwe,* Case No. ICTR–99–46, TRA000552/2, *[Cyangugu]* – *Ntagerura et al* – *Redacted Transcript of 06/03/2002*– *Oral Hearing on the Motion of Imanishimwe for Acquittal on Conspiracy Count,* 6 March 2002.

Prosecutor v. *André Ntagerura, Emmanuel Bagambiki and Samuel Imanishimwe,* Case No. ICTR–99–46, TRA000750/01, *[Cyangugu]* – *Ntagerura et al* – *Redacted Transcript of 06/06/2001,* 6 June 2001.

Prosecutor v. *André Ntagerura, Emmanuel Bagambiki and Samuel Imanishimwe,* Case No. ICTR–99–46, TRA001270/2, *[Cyangugu]* – *Ntagerura et al* – *Redacted Transcript of 14/05/2002,* 14 May 2002.

Prosecutor v. *André Ntagerura, Emmanuel Bagambiki and Samuel Imanishimwe,* Case No. ICTR–99–46, TRA001277/2, *[Cyangugu]* – *Ntagerura et al* – *Redacted Transcript of 28/05/2002,* 28 May 2002.

Prosecutor v. *André Ntagerura, Emmanuel Bagambiki and Samuel Imanishimwe,* Case No. ICTR–99–46, TRA001278/2, *[Cyangugu]* – *Ntagerura et al* – *Redacted Transcript of 29/05/2002,* 29 May 2002.

Prosecutor v. *André Ntagerura, Emmanuel Bagambiki and Samuel Imanishimwe,* Case No. ICTR–99–46, TRA001286/2, *[Cyangugu]* – *Ntagerura et al* – *Redacted Transcript of 08/07/2002* – Motion, 8 July 2002.

Prosecutor v. *André Ntagerura, Emmanuel Bagambiki and Samuel Imanishimwe,* Case No. ICTR–99–46, TRA001288/2, *[Cyangugu]* – *Ntagerura et al* – *Redacted Transcript of 11/07/2002,* 11 July 2002.

Prosecutor v. *André Ntagerura, Emmanuel Bagambiki and Samuel Imanishimwe,* Case No. ICTR–99–46, TRA001293/2, *[Cyangugu]* – *Ntagerura et al* – *Redacted Transcript of 22/07/2002,* 22 July 2002.

Prosecutor v. *André Ntagerura, Emmanuel Bagambiki and Samuel Imanishimwe*, Case No. ICTR–99–46, TRA001601/2, *[Cyangugu]* – *Ntagerura et al* – *Redacted Transcript of 28/03/2002*, 28 March 2002.

Prosecutor v. *André Ntagerura, Emmanuel Bagambiki and Samuel Imanishimwe*, Case No. ICTR–99–46, TRA001610/2, *[Cyangugu]* – *Ntagerura et al* – *Redacted Transcript of 21/03/2002*, 21 March 2002.

Prosecutor v. *André Ntagerura, Emmanuel Bagambiki and Samuel Imanishimwe*, Case No. ICTR–99–46, TRA001615/1, *[Cyangugu]* – *Ntagerura et al* – *Redacted Transcript of 25/03/2002*, 25 March 2002.

Prosecutor v. *André Ntagerura, Emmanuel Bagambiki and Samuel Imanishimwe*, Case No. ICTR–99–46, TRA001616/1, *[Cyangugu]* – *Ntagerura et al* – *Redacted Transcript of 26/03/2002*, 26 March 2002.

Prosecutor v. *André Ntagerura, Emmanuel Bagambiki and Samuel Imanishimwe*, Case No. ICTR–99–46, TRA001618/02, *[Cyangugu]* – *Ntagerura et al* – *Redacted Transcript of 02/10/2002*, 2 October 2002.

Prosecutor v. *André Ntagerura, Emmanuel Bagambiki and Samuel Imanishimwe*, Case No. ICTR–99–46, TRA001619/2, *[Cyangugu]* – *Ntagerura et al* – *Redacted Transcript of 03/10/2002*, 3 October 2002.

Prosecutor v. *André Ntagerura, Emmanuel Bagambiki and Samuel Imanishimwe*, Case No. ICTR–99–46, TRA001621/2, *[Cyangugu]* – *Ntagerura et al* – *Redacted Transcript of 08/10/2002*, 8 October 2002.

Prosecutor v. *André Ntagerura, Emmanuel Bagambiki and Samuel Imanishimwe*, Case No. ICTR–99–46, TRA001774/1, *[Cyangugu]* – *Ntagerura et al* – *Redacted Transcript of 24/09/2001*, 24 September 2001.

Prosecutor v. *André Ntagerura, Emmanuel Bagambiki and Samuel Imanishimwe*, Case No. ICTR–99–46, TRA001782/1, *[Cyangugu]* – *Ntagerura et al* – *Redacted Transcript of 16/10/2002*, 16 October 2002.

Prosecutor v. *André Ntagerura, Emmanuel Bagambiki and Samuel Imanishimwe*, Case No. ICTR–99–46, TRA001795/1, *[Cyangugu]* – *Ntagerura et al* – *Redacted Transcript of 22/10/2002*, 22 October 2002.

Prosecutor v. *André Ntagerura, Emmanuel Bagambiki and Samuel Imanishimwe*, Case No. ICTR–99–46, TRA001796/1, *[Cyangugu]* – *Ntagerura et al* – *Redacted Transcript of 23/10/2002*, 23 October 2002.

Prosecutor v. *André Ntagerura, Emmanuel Bagambiki and Samuel Imanishimwe*, Case No. ICTR–99–46, TRA001799/1 *[Cyangugu]* – *Ntagerura et al* – *Redacted Transcript of 30/10/2002*, 30 October 2002.

Prosecutor v. *André Ntagerura, Emmanuel Bagambiki and Samuel Imanishimwe*, Case No. ICTR–99–46, TRA001800/1, *[Cyangugu]* – *Ntagerura et al* – *Redacted Transcript of 04/11/2002*, 4 November 2002.

Prosecutor v. *André Ntagerura, Emmanuel Bagambiki and Samuel Imanishimwe*, Case No. ICTR–99–46, TRA001851/2, *[Cyangugu]* – *Ntagerura et al* – *Redacted Transcript of 20/01/2003*, 20 January 2003.

Prosecutor v. *André Ntagerura, Emmanuel Bagambiki and Samuel Imanishimwe,* Case No. ICTR–99–46, TRA001907, *[Cyangugu]* – *Ntagerura et al* – *Redacted Transcript of 21/01/2003,* 21 January 2003.

Prosecutor v. *André Ntagerura, Emmanuel Bagambiki and Samuel Imanishimwe,* Case No. ICTR–99–46, TRA001909/1, *[Cyangugu]* – *Ntagerura et al* – *Redacted Transcript of 24/02/2003,* 24 February 2003.

Prosecutor v. *André Ntagerura, Emmanuel Bagambiki and Samuel Imanishimwe,* Case No. ICTR–99–46, TRA001912/1, *[Cyangugu]* – *Ntagerura et al* – *Redacted Transcript of 11/03/2003,* 11 March 2003.

Prosecutor v. *André Ntagerura, Emmanuel Bagambiki and Samuel Imanishimwe,* Case No. ICTR–99–46, TRA001915/1, *[Cyangugu]* – *Ntagerura et al* – *Redacted Transcript of 24/03/2003,* 24 March 2003.

Prosecutor v. *André Ntagerura, Emmanuel Bagambiki and Samuel Imanishimwe,* Case No. ICTR–99–46, TRA001916/1, *[Cyangugu]* – *Ntagerura et al* – *Redacted Transcript of 25/03/2003,* 25 March 2003.

Prosecutor v. *André Ntagerura, Emmanuel Bagambiki and Samuel Imanishimwe,* Case No. ICTR–99–46, TRA001918/1, *[Cyangugu]* – *Ntagerura et al* – *Redacted Transcript of 27/03/2003,* 27 March 2003.

Prosecutor v. *André Ntagerura, Emmanuel Bagambiki and Samuel Imanishimwe,* Case No. ICTR–99–46, TRA001919/1, *[Cyangugu]* – *Ntagerura et al* – *Redacted Transcript of 31/03/2003,* 31 March 2003.

Prosecutor v. *André Ntagerura, Emmanuel Bagambiki and Samuel Imanishimwe,* Case No. ICTR–99–46, TRA001920/1, *[Cyangugu]* – *Ntagerura et al* – *Redacted Transcript of 01/04/2003,* 1 April 2003.

Prosecutor v. *André Ntagerura, Emmanuel Bagambiki and Samuel Imanishimwe,* Case No. ICTR–99–46, TRA001921/1, *[Cyangugu]* – *Ntagerura et al* – *Redacted Transcript of 02/04/2003,* 2 April 2003.

Prosecutor v. *André Ntagerura, Emmanuel Bagambiki and Samuel Imanishimwe,* Case No. ICTR–99–46, TRA001998/1, *[Cyangugu]* – *Ntagerura et al* – *Redacted Transcript of 05/02/2003,* 5 February 2003.

Prosecutor v. *André Ntagerura, Emmanuel Bagambiki and Samuel Imanishimwe,* Case No. ICTR–99–46, TRA002000/1, *[Cyangugu]* – *Ntagerura et al* – *Redacted Transcript of 11/02/2003,* 11 February 2003.

Prosecutor v. *André Ntagerura, Emmanuel Bagambiki and Samuel Imanishimwe,* Case No. ICTR–99–46, TRA002001/1, *[Cyangugu]* – *Ntagerura et al* – *Redacted Transcript of 13/02/2003,* 13 February 2003.

Prosecutor v. *André Ntagerura, Emmanuel Bagambiki and Samuel Imanishimwe,* Case No. ICTR–99–46, TRA002002/2, *[Cyangugu]* – *Ntagerura et al* – *Redacted Transcript of 17/02/2003,* 17 February 2003.

Prosecutor v. *André Ntagerura, Emmanuel Bagambiki and Samuel Imanishimwe,* Case No. ICTR–99–46, TRA002003/1, *[Cyangugu]* – *Ntagerura et al* – *Redacted Transcript of 18/02/2003,* 18 February 2003.

Prosecutor v. André Ntagerura, Emmanuel Bagambiki and Samuel Imanishimwe, Case No. ICTR–99–46, TRA002053/1, *[Cyangugu]* – *Ntagerura et al* – *Redacted Transcript of* 11/08/2003, 11 August 2003.

Prosecutor v. André Ntagerura, Emmanuel Bagambiki and Samuel Imanishimwe, Case No. ICTR–99–46, TRA002063/1, *[Cyangugu]* – *Ntagerura et al* – *Redacted Transcript of* 13/08/2003, 13 August 2003.

Prosecutor v. André Ntagerura, Emmanuel Bagambiki and Samuel Imanishimwe, Case No. ICTR–99–46, TRA002066/1, *[Cyangugu]* – *Ntagerura et al* – *Redacted Transcript of* 12/08/2003, 12 August 2003.

Prosecutor v. André Ntagerura, Emmanuel Bagambiki and Samuel Imanishimwe, Case No. ICTR–99–46, TRA002960, *[Cyangugu]* – *Ntagerura et al* – *Redacted Transcript of* 06/02/2006 – *Appeals Hearing*, 6 February 2006.

Prosecutor v. André Ntagerura, Emmanuel Bagambiki and Samuel Imanishimwe, Case No. ICTR–99–46, TRA002962, *[Cyangugu]* – *Ntagerura et al* – *Redacted Transcript of* 07/02/2006 – *Appeals Hearing*, 7 February 2006

Prosecutor v. André Ntagerura, Emmanuel Bagambiki and Samuel Imanishimwe, Case No. ICTR–99–46, TRA002964, *[Cyangugu]* – *Ntagerura et al* – *Redacted Transcript of* 08/02/2006 –*Appeals Judgement*, 8 February 2006.

Prosecutor v. André Ntagerura, Emmanuel Bagambiki and Samuel Imanishimwe, Case No. ICTR–99–46, TRA003809/1, *[Cyangugu]* – *Ntagerura et al* – *Redacted Transcript of* 07/07/2006 – *Appeals Judgement*, 7 July 2006.

Gatete (Case No.: ICTR–00–61)

Prosecutor v. Jean Baptiste Gatete, Case No. ICTR–00–61, CONTRA018137, *Gatete* – *Redacted Transcript* 04/11/2009, 4 November 2009.

Prosecutor v. Jean Baptiste Gatete, Case No. ICTR–00–61, CONTRA018674, *Gatete, Redacted Transcript of* 02/03/2010, 2 March 2010.

Prosecutor v. Jean Baptiste Gatete, Case No. ICTR–00–61, CONTRA018748, *Gatete, Redacted Transcript of* 11/3/2010, 11 March 2010.

Prosecutor v. Jean Baptiste Gatete, Case No. ICTR–00–61, ICTR–00–61–0022, *Gatete* – *Prosecutor's Response to the Defense Preliminary Motion Challenging Defects in the Form of the Indictment Pursuant to Rule 72*, 9 May 2003.

Prosecutor v. Jean Baptiste Gatete, Case No. ICTR–00–61, ICTR–00–61–0025, *Gatete* – *Defence Preliminary Motions, Under Rule 72 of the Rules of Procedure and Evidence*, 12 April 2003.

Prosecutor v. Jean Baptiste Gatete, Case No. ICTR–00–61, ICTR–00–61–0029, *Gatete, Decision on Defence Preliminary Motion*, 29 March 2004.

Prosecutor v. Jean Baptiste Gatete, Case No. ICTR–00–61, ICTR–00–61–0036/1, *Gatete* – *Amended indictment, ICTR–00–61*, 10 May 2005.

Prosecutor v. Jean Baptiste Gatete, Case No. ICTR–00–61, ICTR–00–61–0043/1, *Gatete* – *Decision on Defence Motion for Protection of Witnesses*, 10 April 2007.

Prosecutor v. *Jean Baptiste Gatete*, Case No. ICTR–00–61, ICTR–00–61–0046, *Gatete – Request by Ibuka and Avega for Leave to Appear and Make Submissions as Amicus (Pursuant to Rule 74 of the Tribunal's Rules of Procedure and Evidence) in Support of the Prosecutor's Rule11 Bis Request for the Referral of the Case of Gatete …*, 9 January 2008.

Prosecutor v. *Jean Baptiste Gatete*, Case No. ICTR–00–61, ICTR–00–61–0047/ 1, *Gatete – Prosecutor's Response to the "Request by Ibuka & Avega for Leave to Appear and Make Submissions as Amicus (Pursuant to Rule 74 of the Tribunal's Rules of Procedure and Evidence) in Support of the Prosecutor's Rule 11 Bis Request for Referral …*, 8 February 2008.

Prosecutor v. *Jean Baptiste Gatete*, Case No. ICTR–00–61, ICTR–00–61– 0048/2, *Gatete – Defence Reply to the Motion Entitled: Prosecutor's Request for the Referral of the Case of Jean-Baptiste Gatete to Rwanda Pursuant to Rule 11 Bis of the Tribunal's Rules of Procedure and Evidence*, 26 February 2008.

Prosecutor v. *Jean Baptiste Gatete*, Case No. ICTR–00–61, ICTR–00–61–0059/ 1, *Gatete – Decision on Amicus Curiae Requests (Ibuka, Avega and Icdaa) Rule 74 of the Rules of Procedure and Evidence*, 30 June 2008.

Prosecutor v. *Jean Baptiste Gatete*, Case No. ICTR–00–61, ICTR–00–61–0066, *Gatete – Amicus Curiae Brief on Behalf of the Republic of Rwanda*, 23 September 2008.

Prosecutor v. *Jean Baptiste Gatete*, Case No. ICTR–00–61, ICTR–00–61–0068/ 1, *Gatete – Decision on Prosecutor's Request for Referral to the Republic of Rwanda*, 17 November 2008.

Prosecutor v. *Jean Baptiste Gatete*, Case No. ICTR–00–61, ICTR–00–61–0069, *Gatete – Defence Preliminary Motion Alleging Defects in the Form of the Amended Indictment*, 22 May 2009.

Prosecutor v. *Jean Baptiste Gatete*, Case No. ICTR–00–61, ICTR–00–61–0070, *Gatete – Prosecutor's Response to the Defence Preliminary Motion Alleging Defects in the Form of the Amended Indictment*, 27 May 2009.

Prosecutor v. *Jean Baptiste Gatete*, Case No. ICTR–00–61, ICTR–00–61–0073, *Gatete – Decision on Defence Motion Concerning Defects in the Amended Indictment*, 3 July 2009.

Prosecutor v. *Jean Baptiste Gatete*, Case No. ICTR–00–61, ICTR–00–61–0074/1, *Gatete – the Prosecutor's Submission Complying with the Decision on Defence Motion Concerning Defects in the Amended Indictment Dated 3 July 2009*, 7 July 2009.

Prosecutor v. *Jean Baptiste Gatete*, Case No. ICTR–00–61, ICTR–00–61–0086/ 1, *Gatete – Decision on Prosecution's Motion for Judicial Notice of Facts of Common Knowledge*, 21 August 2009.

Prosecutor v. *Jean Baptiste Gatete*, Case No. ICTR–00–61, ICTR–00–61–0088, *Gatete – Defence Motion Raising Defects in the Prosecution Pre-Trial Brief of 19 August 2009*, 3 September 2009.

Prosecutor v. *Jean Baptiste Gatete*, Case No. ICTR–00–61, ICTR–00–61–0088, *Gatete – Defence Motion Raising Defects in the Prosecution Pre-Trial Brief of 19 August 2009*, 30 September 2009.

Prosecutor v. *Jean Baptiste Gatete*, Case No. ICTR–00–61, ICTR–00–61–0091, *Gatete – Prosecutor's Response to 'Defence Motion Raising Defects in the Prosecution Pre-Trial Brief of 19 August 2009'*, 8 September 2009.

Prosecutor v. *Jean Baptiste Gatete*, Case No. ICTR–00–61, ICTR–00–61–010, *Gatete, Motion on Admissibility of Allegations outside the Temporal Jurisdiction of the Tribunal*, 15 October 2009.

Prosecutor v. *Jean Baptiste Gatete*, Case No. ICTR–00–61, ICTR–00–61–0100, *Gatete, Decision on Defence Motion Raising Defects in the Prosecution Pre-Trial Brief of 19 August 2009*, 2 October 2009.

Prosecutor v. *Jean Baptiste Gatete*, Case No. ICTR–00–61, ICTR–00–61–0104/ 1, *Gatete – Decision on Defence Motions for Disclosure Pursuant to Rule 66 (A) (II) and Commencement of Trial*, 13 October 2009.

Prosecutor v. *Jean Baptiste Gatete*, Case No. ICTR–00–61, ICTR–00–61–0115, *Gatete – Prosecutor's Reply to 'Defence Motion on Prosecution Disclosure and Commencement of the Trial' and Motion for Reconsideration of Decision of 13 October 2009*, 16 October 2009.

Prosecutor v. *Jean Baptiste Gatete*, Case No. ICTR–00–61, ICTR–00–61– 0116, *Gatete – Decision on Prosecutor's Motion to Vary List of Witnesses Pursuant to Rule 73BIS(E) of the Rules of Procedure and Evidence*, 19 October 2009.

Prosecutor v. *Jean Baptiste Gatete*, Case No. ICTR–00–61, ICTR–00–61–0128, *Gatete – Motion for Exclusion of Evidence*, 30 October 2009.

Prosecutor v. *Jean Baptiste Gatete*, Case No. ICTR–00–61, ICTR–00–61–0131, *Gatete – Motion for Disclosure of Rwandan Judicial Records Pursuant to Rule 66 (A) (ii) of the Rules of Procedure and Evidence*, 2 November 2009.

Prosecutor v. *Jean Baptiste Gatete*, Case No. ICTR–00–61, ICTR–00–61–0133, *Gatete – Decision on Defence Motion on Admissibility of Allegations outside the Temporal Jurisdiction of the Tribunal*, 3 November 2009.

Prosecutor v. *Jean Baptiste Gatete*, Case No. ICTR–00–61, ICTR–00–61–0166/ 1, *Gatete – the Pre-Defence Brief of Jean-Baptiste Gatete*, 29 January 2010.

Prosecutor v. *Jean Baptiste Gatete*, Case No. ICTR–00–61, ICTR–00–61–0188, *Gatete, Decision on Defence Motion for Exclusion of Evidence and Delineation of the Defence Case*, 26 March 2010.

Prosecutor v. *Jean Baptiste Gatete*, Case No. ICTR–00–61, ICTR–00–61–0240/ 1, *Gatete – Judgement and Sentence*, 31 March 2011.

Prosecutor v. *Jean Baptiste Gatete*, Case No. ICTR–00–61, TRA001643/1, *Gatete – Redacted Transcript of 20/10/2009*, 20 October 2009.

Prosecutor v. *Jean Baptiste Gatete*, Case No. ICTR–00–61, TRA005145/1, *Gatete – Redacted Transcript of 10/3/2010*, 10 March 2010.

Prosecutor v. *Jean Baptiste Gatete*, Case No. ICTR–00–61, TRA005147/1, *Gatete – Redacted Transcript of 09/03/2010*, 9 March 2010.

Prosecutor v. *Jean Baptiste Gatete*, Case No. ICTR–00–61, TRA005152/1, *Gatete – Redacted Transcript of 08/03/2010*, 8 March 2010.

Prosecutor v. *Jean Baptiste Gatete*, Case No. ICTR–00–61, TRA005153/1, *Gatete – Redacted Transcript of 16/03/2010*, 16 March 2010.

Prosecutor v. *Jean Baptiste Gatete*, Case No. ICTR–00–61, TRA005157/1, *Gatete – Redacted Transcript of 22/3/2010*, 22 March 2010.

Prosecutor v. *Jean Baptiste Gatete*, Case No. ICTR–00–61, TRA005158/1, *Gatete – Redacted Transcript of 17/03/2010*, 17 March 2010.

Prosecutor v. *Jean Baptiste Gatete*, Case No. ICTR–00–61, TRA005458, *Gatete – Redacted Transcript of 22/10/2009*, 22 October 2009.

Prosecutor v. *Jean Baptiste Gatete*, Case No. ICTR–00–61, TRA005459, *Gatete – Redacted Transcript of 05/11/2009*, 5 November 2009.

Prosecutor v. *Jean Baptiste Gatete*, Case No. ICTR–00–61, TRA005461, *Gatete – Redacted Transcript of 13/11/2009*, 13 November 2009.

Prosecutor v. *Jean Baptiste Gatete*, Case No. ICTR–00–61, TRA005490/2, *Gatete – Redacted Transcript of 21/10/2009*, 21 October 2009.

Prosecutor v. *Jean Baptiste Gatete*, Case No. ICTR–00–61, TRA005491/2, *Gatete – Redacted Transcript of 03/11/2009*, 3 November 2009.

Prosecutor v. *Jean Baptiste Gatete*, Case No. ICTR–00–61, TRA005506/2, Gatete, *Redacted Transcript of 02/11/2009*, 2 November 2009.

Prosecutor v. *Jean Baptiste Gatete*, Case No. ICTR–00–61, TRA005507/2, *Gatete – Redacted Transcript of 10/11/2009*, 10 November 2009.

Prosecutor v. *Jean Baptiste Gatete*, Case No. ICTR–00–61, TRA005537/2, *Gatete – Redacted Transcript of 12/11/2009*, 12 November 2009.

Prosecutor v. *Jean Baptiste Gatete*, Case No. ICTR–00–61, TRA005592, *Gatete – Redacted Transcript of 08/11/2010*, 8 November 2010.

Other ICTR Documents

ICTR Legacy Symposium – 20 Years of Challenging Impunity, Arusha, Tanzania, 6–7 November 2014.

ICTR, 'Testifying before the International Criminal Tribunal for Rwanda', 06FB002 (Arusha: 2005).

ICTR Office of the Prosecution – Annex B: Statistics from the ICTR's Rape and Sexual Violence Cases (January 2014).

OTP ICTR, 'Prosecution of Sexual Violence: Best Practices Manual for the Investigation and Prosecution of Sexual Violence Crimes in Post-conflict Regions: Lessons Learned from the Office of the Prosecutor for the International Criminal Tribunal for Rwanda', (2014), at www.unmict.org, (last accessed 1 August 2017).

OTP ICTR, 'Prosecution of Sexual Violence', Appendix B, At: https://unictr .irmct.org/sites/unictr.org/files/publications/ICTR-Prosecution-of-Sexual-Violence.pdf, last accessed 30 October 2019.

Prosecutor v. Clément Kayishema and Obed Ruzindana, Case No. ICTR–95–01, ICTR–95–01–1108/1, *Judgement and Sentence*, 21 May 1999.

Prosecutor v. George Ruggiu, Case No. ICTR-97–32-I Judgement and Sentence, 1 June 2000.

Prosecutor v. Grégoire Ndahimana, Case No. ICTR-01–68, *Trial Judgement*, 30 December 2001, at: unictr.unmict.org (last accessed 15 July 2017).

Prosecutor v. Alfred Musema, Case No. ICTR-96–13, *Judgement and Sentence*, 27 January 2000, at: http://unictr.unmict.org (last accessed 15 July 2017).

Prosecutor v. Augustin Bizimungu, Augustin Ndindiliyimana, François-Xavier Nzuwonemeye and Innocent Sagahutu, Case No. ICTR-00–56, ICTR-00–56-1123/1, *Judgement and Sentence*, 17 May 2011.

Prosecutor v. Casimir Bizimungu, Jérôme Bicamumpaka, Justin Mugenzi and Prosper Mugiraneza, Case No. ICTR–99–50, ICTR–99–50–2143/1, *Judgement and Sentence*, 30 September 2011.

Prosecutor v. Édouard Karemera and Matthieu Ngirumpatse, Case No. ICTR–98–44, ICTR–98–44–4803/1, *Judgement and Sentence*, 2 February 2012.

Prosecutor v. Édouard Karemera, Matthieu Ngirumpatse and Joseph Nzirorera (Government 1), Case No. ICTR-98–44, ICTR-98–44-2076/1, *[Government 1] – Karemera et al – Decision on Prosecution Motion for Judicial Notice*, 9 November 2005.

Prosecutor v. Édouard Karemera, Matthieu Ngirumpatse and Joseph Nzirorera (Government 1), Case No. ICTR-98–44, ICTR-98–44-2411/1, *[Government 1] – Karemera et al – Decision on Prosecutor's Interlocutory Appeal of Decision on Judicial Notice*, 16 June 2006.

Prosecutor v. Emmanuel Rukundo, Case No. ICTR–01–70, ICTR–01–70–0393, *Judgement and Sentence*, 27 February 2009.

Prosecutor v. Emmanuel Rukundo, Case No. ICTR–01–70, ICTR–01–70–0400/1, *Appeals Judgement*, 20 October 2010.

Prosecutor v. Ferdinand Nahimana, Jean Bosco Barayagwiza and Hassan Ngeze, Case No. ICTR–99–52, ICTR–99–52–1323/1, *Judgement and Sentence*, 3 December 2003.

Prosecutor v. François Karera, Case No. ICTR–01–74, ICTR–01–74–0141/1, *Judgement and Sentence*, 7 December 2007.

Prosecutor v. Ildéphonse Nizeyimana, Case No. ICTR–00–55, ICTR–00–55 C–0536/1, *Judgement and Sentence*, 19 June 2012.

Prosecutor v. Jean Uwikindi, Case No. ICTR–01–75, ICTR–01–75–AR11bis, *Uwikindi – Decision on Uwikindi's Appeal Against the Referral of His Case to Rwanda and Related Motions*, 16 December 2011.

Prosecutor v. *Juvénal Kajelijeli*, Case No. ICTR–98–44, ICTR–98–44A–0320/1, *Judgment and Sentence*, 1 December 2003.

Prosecutor v. *Laurent Semanza*, Case No. ICTR–97–20, ICTR–97–20–0779/1, *Judgement and Sentence*, 15 May 2003.

Prosecutor v. *Pauline Nyiramasuhuko, Joseph Ndayambaje, Sylvain Nsabimana, Arsène Shalom Ntahobali, and Alphonse Nteziryayo (Butare)*, Case No. ICTR-98–42, ICTR-98-42-A15bis, *Decision in the Matter of Proceedings under Rule 15bis(D)* – *Dissenting Opinion of Judge Hunt*, 24 September 2003.

Prosecutor v. *Pauline Nyiramasuhuko, Joseph Ndayambaje, Sylvain Nsabimana, Arsène Shalom Ntahobali, and Alphonse Nteziryayo (Butare)*, Case No. ICTR-98–42, *Judgement and Sentence*, 24 June 2011, at: unictr.unmict.org (last accessed 15 July 2017).

Prosecutor v. *Siméon Nchamihigo*, Case No. ICTR–01–63, ICTR–01–63–0080/1, *Judgement and Sentence*, 12 November 2008.

Prosecutor v. *Théoneste Bagosora, Gratien Kabiligi, Anatole Nsengiyumva and Aloys Ntabakuze (Military 1)*, Appeal Judgement, 14 December 2011.

Prosecutor v. *Yussuf Munyakazi*, Case No. ICTR–97–36, ICTR–97–36A–0142/1, *Munyakazi* – *Judgement and Sentence*, 5 July 2010.

UN ARCHIVAL DOCUMENTS[2]

United Nations General Assembly

A/47/277–S/24111, *An Agenda for Peace: Preventative Diplomacy, Peacemaking and Peace-Keeping: Report of the Secretary-General Pursuant to the Statement Adopted by the Summit Meeting of the Security Council on 21 January 1992*, 17 June 1992.

A/48/935, *Development and International Economic Cooperation: An Agenda for Development: Report of the Secretary-General*, 6 May 1994.

A/48/PV.93, 48th Session, 93rd Meeting, 14 April 1994.

A/49/516, *Strengthening of the Coordination of Humanitarian and Disaster Relief Assistance of the United Nations, Including Special Economic Assistance: Special Economic Assistance to individual Countries or Regions: Emergency Assistance for the Socio-Economic Rehabilitation of Rwanda*, 14 October 1994.

A/49/PV.21, 49th Session, 21st Meeting, 6 October 1994.

A/50/60 – S/1995/1, *Supplement to an Agenda for Peace: Position Paper of the Secretary-General on the Occasion of the Fiftieth Anniversary of the United Nations*, 25 January 1995.

A/51/7/Add.8, *Financing of the International Criminal Tribunal for the Prosecution of Persons Responsible for Genocide and Other Serious Violations*

---

[2] These records are grouped according to which organ of the UN produced the records.

of International Humanitarian Law Committed in the Territory of Rwanda and Rwandan Citizens Responsible for Genocide and Other Such Violations Committed in the Territory of Neighbouring States between 1 January and 31 December 1994: Ninth Report of the Advisory Committee on Administrative and Budgetary Questions, 29 May 1997.

A/51/789, *Financing of the International Criminal Tribunal for the Prosecution of Persons Responsible for Genocide and Other Serious Violations of International Humanitarian Law Committed in the Territory of Rwanda and Rwandan Citizens Responsible for Genocide and Other Such Violations Committed in the Territory of Neighbouring States between 1 January and 31 December 1994: Report of the Secretary-General on the Activities of the Office of Internal Oversight Services,* 6 February 1997.

A/51/PV.78, *51st Session: 78th Plenary Meeting,* 10 December 1996.

A/52/582–S/1997/868, *Report of the International Criminal Tribunal for the Prosecution of Persons Responsible for Genocide and Other Serious Violations of International Humanitarian Law Committed in the Territory of Rwanda and Rwandan Citizens Responsible for Genocide and Other Such Violations Committed in the Territory of Neighbouring States between 1 January and 31 December 1994,* 13 November 1997.

A/52/784, *Financing of the International Criminal Tribunal for the Prosecution of Persons Responsible for Genocide and Other Serious Violations of International Humanitarian Law Committed in the Territory of Rwanda and Rwandan Citizens Responsible for Genocide and Other Such Violations Committed in the Territory of Neighbouring States between 1 January and 31 December 1994: Report of the Secretary-General on the Activities of the Office of Internal Oversight Services,* 6 February 1998.

A/52/871, *The Causes of Conflict and the Promotion of Durable Peace and Sustainable Development in Africa: Report of the Secretary-General,* 13 April 1998.

A/53/367, *Human Rights Field Operation in Rwanda: Report of the United Nations High Commissioner for Human Rights on the Human Rights Field Operation in Rwanda,* 11 September 1998.

A/53/429, *Report of the International Criminal Tribunal for the Prosecution of Persons Responsible for Genocide and Other Serious Violations of International Humanitarian Law Committed in the Territory of Rwanda and Rwandan Citizens Responsible for Genocide and Other Such Violations Committed in the Territory of Neighbouring States between 1 January and 31 December 1994,* 23 September 1998.

A/53/659, *Report of the Advisory Committee on Administrative and Budgetary Questions,* 11 November 1998.

A/53/PV.47, *53rd Session: 47th Plenary Meeting,* 28 October 1998.

A/54/315-S/1999/943, *Report of the International Criminal Tribunal for the Prosecution of Persons Responsible for Genocide and Other Serious Violations* of *International Humanitarian Law Committed in the Territory of Rwanda and Rwandan Citizens Responsible for Genocide and Other Such Violations Committed in the Territory of Neighbouring States between 1 January and 31 December 1994*, 7 September 1999.

A/54/634, *Financing the International Criminal Tribunal for the Prosecution of Persons Responsible for Genocide and Other Serious Violations of International Humanitarian Law Committed in the Territory of Rwanda and Rwandan Citizens Responsible for Genocide and Other Such Violations Committed in the Territory of Neighbouring States between 1 January and 31 December 1994: Report of the Expert Group to Conduct a Review of the Effective Operation and Functioning of the International Tribunal for the Former Yugoslavia and the International Criminal Tribunal for Rwanda*, 22 November 1999.

A/54/PV.48, *54th Session: 48th Plenary Meeting*, 8 November 1999.

A/55/269, *Situation of Human Rights in Rwanda: Report of the Special Representative of the Commission on Human Rights on the Situation of Human Rights in Rwanda*, 4 August 2000.

A/55/435 – S/2000/927, *Report of the International Criminal Tribunal for the Prosecution of Persons Responsible for Genocide and Other Serious Violations of International Humanitarian Law Committed in the Territory of Rwanda and Rwandan Citizens Responsible for Genocide and Other Such Violations Committed in the Territory of Neighbouring States between 1 January and 31 December 1994*, 2 October 2000.

A/55/512, *Financing the International Criminal Tribunal for the Prosecution of Persons Responsible for Genocide and Other Serious Violations of International Humanitarian Law Committed in the Territory of Rwanda and Rwandan Citizens Responsible for Genocide and Other Such Violations Committed in the Territory of Neighbouring States between 1 January and 31 December 1994: Report by the Secretary-General*, 23 October 2000.

A/55/759, *Financing the International Criminal Tribunal for the Prosecution of Persons Responsible for Genocide and Other Serious Violations of International Humanitarian Law Committed in the Territory of Rwanda and Rwandan Citizens Responsible for Genocide and Other Such Violations Committed in the Territory of Neighbouring States between 1 January and 31 December 1994: Report of the Office of Internal Oversight Services on the Investigation into Possible Fee-Splitting Arrangements between Defence Counsel and Indigent Detainees at the International Criminal Tribunal for Rwanda and the International Tribunal for the Former Yugoslavia*, 1 February 2001.

A/56/836, *Report of the Secretary-General on the Activities of the Office of Internal Oversight Services: Financing of the International Tribunal for the Prosecution of Persons Responsible for Serious Violations of International Humanitarian Law Committed in the Territory of the Former Yugoslavia since 1991: Financing of the International Criminal Tribunal for the Prosecution of Persons Responsible for Genocide and Other Serious Violations of International Humanitarian Law*

Committed in the Territory of Rwanda and Rwandan Citizens Responsible for Genocide and Other Such Violations Committed in the Territory of Neighbouring States between 1 January and 31 December 1994: Follow-up investigation into possible fee–splitting arrangements between defence counsel and indigent detainees at the International Tribunal for Rwanda and the International Tribunal for the former Yugoslavia, 26 February 2002.

A/56/853, Financing of the International Tribunal for the Prosecution of Persons Responsible for Serious Violations of International Humanitarian Law Committed in the Territory of the former Yugoslavia since 1991: Financing of the International Criminal Tribunal for the Prosecution of Persons Responsible for Genocide and Other Serious Violations of International Humanitarian Law Committed in the Territory of Rwanda and Rwandan Citizens Responsible for Genocide and Other Such Violations Committed in the Territory of Neighbouring States between 1 January and 31 December 1994: Comprehensive Report on the Results of the Implementation of the Recommendations of the Expert Group to Conduct a Review of the Effective Operation and Functioning of the International Tribunal for the former Yugoslavia and the International Criminal Tribunal for Rwanda, 4 March 2002.

A/57/PV.36, 57th Session: 36th Plenary Meeting, 28 October 2002.

A/58/140–S/2003/707, Report of the International Criminal Tribunal for the Prosecution of Persons Responsible for Genocide and Other Serious Violations of International Humanitarian Law Committed in the Territory of Rwanda and Rwandan Citizens Responsible for Genocide and Other Such Violations Committed in the Territory of Neighbouring States between 1 January and 31 December 1994, 11 July 2003.

A/59/183–S/2004/601, Report of the International Criminal Tribunal for the Prosecution of Persons Responsible for Genocide and Other Serious Violations of International Humanitarian Law Committed in the Territory of Rwanda and Rwandan Citizens Responsible for Genocide and Other Such Violations Committed in the Territory of Neighbouring States between 1 January and 31 December 1994, 27 July 2004.

A/60/229–S/2005/534, Report of the International Criminal Tribunal for the Prosecution of Persons Responsible for Genocide and Other Serious Violations of International Humanitarian Law Committed in the Territory of Rwanda and Rwandan Citizens Responsible for Genocide and Other Such Violations Committed in the Territory of Neighbouring States between 1 January and 31 December 1994, 15 August 2005.

A/69/734, Financing of the International Residual Mechanism for Criminal Tribunals: Construction of A New Facility for the International Residual Mechanism for Criminal Tribunals, Arusha Branch, 19 January 2015.

A/C.3/52/SR.34, Third Committee: Summary Record of the 34th Meeting, 17 February 1998.

A/C.5/48/SR.57, *Fifth Committee: Summary Record of the 57th Meeting: Financing of the United Nations Observer Mission Rwanda*, A/C.5/48/SR.57, 29 March 1994.

A/C.5/51/SR.39 *Fifth Committee: 51st Session: Summary Record of the 39th Meeting*, 11 December 1996.

A/C.5/52/SR.68, *Fifth Committee: Summary Record of the First Part of the 68th Meeting*, 8 July 1998.

A/C.5/57/L.35, *Financing of the International Criminal Tribunal for the Prosecution of Persons Responsible for Genocide and Other Serious Violations of International Humanitarian Law Committed in the Territory of Rwanda and Rwandan Citizens Responsible for Genocide and Other Such Violations Committed in the Territory of Neighbouring States between 1 January and 31 December 1994*, 4 December 2002.

A/RES/53/213, *Resolution 53/213*, 10 February 1999.

A/RES/60/225, *Resolution 60/225*, 22 March 2006.

United Nations Economic and Social Council

E/1994/SR.8, *Provisional Summary Record of the 8th Meeting*, 14 June 1994.

E/CN.4/1995/7, *Question of the Violation of Human Rights and Fundamental Freedoms in any Part of the World, with Particular Reference to Colonial and Other Dependent Countries and Territories: Report on the Situation of Human Rights in Rwanda Submitted by Mr. R. Degni-Ségui, Special Rapporteur of the Commission on Human Rights, Under Paragraph 20 of Commission Resolution E/CN.4/S–3/1 of 25 May 1994*, 28 June 1994.

E/CN.4/1998/54/Add.1, *Further Promotion and Encouragement of Human Rights and Fundamental Freedoms, Including the Question of the Programme and Methods of Work of the Commission Alternative Approaches and Ways and Means within the United Nations System for Improving the Effective Enjoyment of Human Rights and Fundamental Freedoms Report of the Special Rapporteur on Violence against Women, Its Causes and Consequences, Ms. Radhika Coomaraswamy Addendum Report of the Mission to Rwanda on the Issues of Violence against Women in Situations of Armed Conflict*, 4 February 1998.

United Nations Security Council

S/1994/1115, *Letter Dated 28 September 1994 from the Permanent Representative of Rwanda to the United Nations Addressed to the President of the Security Council: Statement Dated 28 September 1994 on the Question of Refugees and Security in Rwanda*', S/1994/1115, 29 September 1994.

S/1994/1125, *Preliminary Report of the independent Commission of Experts Established in Accordance with Security Council Resolution 935 (1994)*, 4 October 1994.

S/1994/1157/Add.1, *Situation of Human Rights in Rwanda: Third Report on the Situation of Human Rights in Rwanda Submitted by Mr. René Degni-Ségui, Special Rapporteur of the Commission on Human Rights, Under Paragraph 20 of Resolution S–3/1 of 25 May 1994*, 14 November 1994.

S/1994/640, *Report of the Secretary-General on the Situation in Rwanda*, 31 May 1994.

S/1995/134, *Report of the Secretary-General Pursuant to Paragraph 5 of Security Council Resolution 955 (1994)*, 13 February 1995.

S/1999/1257, *Report of the Independent Inquiry into the Actions of the United Nations during the Rwandan Genocide*, 16 December 1999.

S/2000/11989, *Letter from President Pillay to the President of the United Nations Security Council*, 15 December 2000.

S/2002/1375, *Letter dated 16 December 2002 from the Secretary-General addressed to the President of the Security Council*, 19 December 2002.

S/2003/946, *Letter dated 3 October 2003 from the Secretary-General Addressed to the President of the Security Council: Completion Strategy of the International Criminal Tribunal for Rwanda*, 6 October 2003.

S/2004/616, *the Rule of Law and Transitional Justice in Conflict and Post-Conflict Societies: Report of the Secretary-General*, 23 August 2004.

S/2009/258, *Report of the Secretary-General on the Administrative and Budgetary Aspects of the Options for Possible Locations for the Archives of the International Tribunal for the Former Yugoslavia and the International Criminal Tribunal for Rwanda and the Seat of the Residual Mechanism(s) for the Tribunals*, 21 May 2009.

S/2010/574, *Letter Dated 12 November 2009 from the President of the International Criminal Tribunal for Rwanda Addressed to the President of the Security Council: Report on the Completion Strategy of the International Criminal Tribunal for Rwanda (as of 1 November 2010)*, 5 November 2010.

S/2013/310, *Letter Dated 23 May 2013 from the President of the International Criminal Tribunal for Rwanda Addressed to the President of the Security Council: Report on the Completion Strategy of the International Criminal Tribunal for Rwanda (as at 10 May 2013)*, 23 May 2013.

S/2015/884, *Letter Dated 17 November 2015 from the President of the International Criminal Tribunal for Rwanda Addressed to the President of the Security Council: Report on the Completion of the Mandate of the International Criminal Tribunal for Rwanda as at 15 November 2015*, 17 November 2015.

S/PV.3371, *3371st Meeting*, 30 April 1994.

S/PV.3377, *3377th Meeting*, 16 May 1994.

S/PV.3388, *3388th Meeting*, 08 June 1994.

S/PV.3400, *3400th Meeting*, 1 July 1994.

S/PV.3453, *3453rd Meeting*, 8 November 1994.
S/PV.4229, *4229th Meeting*, 21 November 2000.
S/PV.4429, *4429th Meeting*, 27 November 2001.
S/PV.4999, *4999th Meeting*, 29 June 2004.
S/PV.5453, *5453rd Meeting*, 7 June 2006.
S/PV.5697, *5697th Meeting*, 18 June 2007.
S/PV.6041, *6041st Meeting*, 12 December 2008.
S/PV.6228, *6228th Meeting*, 3 December 2009.
S/PV.6678, *6678th Meeting*, 7 December 2011.
S/PV.7155, *7155th Meeting*, 16 April 2014.
S/PV.7192, *7192nd Meeting*, 5 June 2014.
S/PV.7574, *7574th Meeting*, 9 December 2015.
S/RES/955, *Resolution 955*, 8 November 1994.
S/RES/1503, *Resolution 1503*, 28 August 2003.
S/RES/1966, *Resolution 1966*, 22 December 2010.

Other United Nations Documents

CERD/C/SR.1212, *International Convention on the Elimination of all Forms of Racial Discrimination, Summary of Record of the 1212th Meeting*, 26 March 1997.
IT-9S-SI18-PT *Prosecutor v. Radovan Karadzic, Decision of the Application of Rule 73 BIS*, 8 October 2009.

INTERNET MATERIALS

African Rights and Redress. *Survivors and Post–genocide Justice in Rwanda: Their Experiences, Perspectives and Hopes*. (November 2008). At: www .redress.org/downloads/publications/Rwanda%20Survivors%2031%20O ct%2008.pdf (last accessed 16 January 2017).
Hegel, Georg. *Philosophy of Right* Quoted on: www.marxists.org/archive/marx/ works/1853/02/18.htm (last accessed 25 May 2017).
ICC, 'Rules of Procedure and Evidence', At: www.icc-cpi.int/resource-library/ Documents/RulesProcedureEvidenceEng.pdf#page=32, last accessed: 31 October 2019.
ICTR (Press Release), 'Trial of Yussuf Munyakazi Starts'. (22 April 2000) At: http://unictr.unmict.org/en/news/trial-yussuf-munyakazi-starts (last accessed 3 October 2016).
ICTR Statute. At: http://unictr.unmict.org/en/documents/statute-and-cre ation (last accessed 24 May 2017).
Immigration and Refugee Board of Canada. 'Rwanda: Whether People Who Give Testimony at the Trials and Hearings of Those Accused of Genocide and Crimes against Humanity Are Being Harassed,

Intimidated and Threatened'. At: www.refworld.org/docid/3ae6ac5950 .html (last accessed 1 February 2015).

Judge Harhoff Letter. At: www.bt.dk/sites/default/files-dk/node-files/511/6/65 11917-letter-english.pdf (last accessed 1 June 2017).

Labbé, Chine, Fumbuka Ng'wanakilala, and Thomas Escritt. 'Rwanda Court's Forgotten Men Pose Challenge to International Justice', At: www.reuters.com/article/us-un-justice-insight-idUSKCN0HN0N K20140928, last accessed: 19 February 2019.

Mégret, Frederic. 'International Criminal Justice as a Juridical Field'. *Champ Pénal/Penal Field* 13 (2016). At: http://journals.openedition.org/champpe nal/9284 (last accessed 19 December 2017).

Moore, Jina. 'This Is the Story a UN Court Didn't Want Three Rape Survivors to Tell'. *Buzzfeed.* At: www.buzzfeed.com/jinamoore/this-is-the-story-a-un-court-didnt-want-three-rape-survivors?utm_term=.efwZxxYY8#.jaw dwwrrm (last accessed 16 January 2017).

MICT, 'Archives', At: www.irmct.org/en/archives, last accessed: 18 October 2019.

'Children of Conflict', At: www.irmct.org/specials/1000words/index.html, last accessed: 18 October 2019.

'Construction of the Arusha Facility', At: www.irmct.org/specials/arusha-f acility/index.html, last accessed: 1 September 2019.

'International Criminal Tribunal for Rwanda (ICTR) Special Bibliography', At: www.un-ilibrary.org/international-law-and-justice/bi bliography-on-ictr-icty-and-irmct-2018_59527281-en-fr, last accessed: 31 October 2019.

Judicial Records Archive Database (JRAD), At: https://jrad.unmict.org/, last accessed: 24 October 2019.

'Mechanism for International Criminal Tribunals Opens Its New Premises of the Arusha Branch', At: www.irmct.org/en/news/mechanism-inter national-criminal-tribunals-opens-its-new-premises-arusha-branch, last accessed: 1 September 2019.

'Opening of the New Premises of the Mechanism for International Criminal 'Worth a Thousand Words', At: www.irmct.org/specials/1000words/index .html, last accessed: 18 October 2019.

Tribunals Arusha, United Republic of Tanzania, 25 November 2016, '"Together We Built" by Mr. John Hocking', At: www.irmct.org/site s/default/files/statements-and-speeches/161125-registrar-speech-open ing-ceremony-of-arusha-premises-en.pdf, last accessed: 30 October 2019.

'Remarks of Judge Theodor Meron President of the Mechanism for International Criminal Tribunals Opening Ceremony of the New Premises of the Arusha Branch, 25 November 2016, At: www.irmct .org/sites/default/files/statements-and-speeches/161125-president-speech-opening-ceremony-arusha-premises-en.pdf, last accessed: 1 September 2019, 3.

'The ICTR in Brief', At: http://unictr.irmct.org/en/tribunal, last accessed: 19 February 2019

Palmer, Nicola and Phil Clark. 'Testifying to Genocide: Victim and Witness Protection in Rwanda', *Redress* (2012). At: http://protectionline.org/files/2012/11/121029ProtectionReport.pdf (last accessed 17 July 2017).

Power, Samantha. 'Bystanders to Genocide: Why the United States Let the Rwandan Tragedy Happen', The Atlantic Online, September 2001. At: www1.essex.ac.uk/ARMEDCON/story_id/BystandersToGenocideRawanda.pdf, last accessed: 21 September 2019.

Sellers, Patricia. 'The Prosecution of Sexual Violence in Conflict: The Importance of Human Rights as Means of Interpretation'. At: www.ohchr.org/Documents/Issues/Women/WRGS/Paper_Prosecution_of_Sexual_Violence.pdf (last accessed 1 June 2017).

Stewart, James. 'NYU JILP Symposium: New Thoughts about Barayagwiza: Reactions to Policing International Prosecutors'. *Opinion Juris* (5 April 2014). At: http://opiniojuris.org/2013/04/05/nyu-jilp-symposium-new-thoughts-about-barayagwiza-reactions-to-policing-international-prosecutors/ (last accessed 4 May 2017).

UN, 'Documents: Online Archive', At: www.un.org/en/documents/index.html, last accessed: 30 August 2019.

UN General Assembly, Article II 'Convention for the Prevention and Punishment of the Crime of Genocide' At: https://treaties.un.org/doc/publication/unts/volume%2078/volume-78-i-1021-english.pdf, last accessed: 24 October 2019.

UNICTR Archives Website. At: www.unmict.org/en/about/archives-International-criminal-tribunals (last accessed 25 May 2016).

UNSC, 'Statute of the International Criminal Tribunal for Rwanda', At: http://legal.un.org/avl/pdf/ha/ictr_EF.pdf, last accessed: 25 October 2019.

Nvivo. www.qsrinternational.com/nvivo/what-is-nvivo, last accessed: 20 December 2017.

Vladimir Miladinović Website. http://vladimirmiladinovic.blogspot.com/, last accessed: 22 August 2020.

Voices of the Rwanda Tribunal www.tribunalvoices.org/.

PUBLISHED SOURCES

Achebe, Chinua. 1977. An Image of Africa. *Massachusetts Review* 18(4): 782–94.

Adami, Tom. 2007. 'Who Will Be Left to Tell the Tale?' Recordkeeping and International Criminal Jurisprudence. *Archival Science* 7: 213–21.

Agamben, Giorgio. 1998. *Homo Sacer: Sovereign Power and Bare Life*. Stanford: Stanford University Press.

and Martha Hunt. 2005. Genocidal Archives: The African Context. *Journal of the Society of Archivists* 26(1): 105–121.

Akhavan, Payam. 1996. Justice and Reconciliation in the Great Lakes Region of Africa: The Contribution of the International Criminal Tribunal for Rwanda. *Duke Journal of Comparative and International Law* 7: 325–49.

2012. *Reducing Genocide to Law: Definition, Meaning, and the Ultimate Crime*. Cambridge: Cambridge University Press.

Alusala, Nelson. 2004. The Arming of Rwanda and the Genocide. *African Security Studies* 13(2): 137–40.

Anghie, Antony. 2005. *Imperialism, Sovereignty and the Making of International Law*. Cambridge: Cambridge University Press.

Arbour, Louise. 1999. The Status of the International Criminal Tribunals for the Former Yugoslavia and Rwanda: Goals and Results. *Hofstra Law and Policy Symposium* 3: 37–46.

Arendt, Hannah. 2006. *Eichmann in Jerusalem: A Report on the Banality of Evil*. London: Penguin.

Arondekar, Anjali. 2005. Without a Trace: Sexuality and the Colonial Archive. *Journal of the History of Sexuality* 14(1/2): 20–17.

Aukerman, Miriam. 2002. Extraordinary Evil, Ordinary Crime: A Framework for Understanding Transitional Justice. *Harvard Human Rights Journal* 15: 39–96.

Barnett, Michael. 2002. *Eyewitness to a Genocide: The United Nations and Rwanda*. London: Cornell University Press.

and Martha Finnemore. 2005. The Power of Liberal International Organizations. In *Power in Global Governance*, edited by Michael Barnett and Raymond Duvall, 163–71. Cambridge: Cambridge University Press.

Bastian, Jeannette. 2007. Reading Colonial Records through an Archival Lens: The Provenance of Place, Space and Creation. *Archival Science* 6: 267–84.

Bell, Christine. 2009. Transitional Justice, Interdisciplinary and the State of the 'Field' or Non-Field. *The International Journal of Transitional Justice* 3(1): 5–27.

Biju-Duval, Jean-Marie. 2007. 'Hate Media' – Crimes against Humanity and Genocide. In *The Media and the Rwandan Genocide*, edited by Allan Thompson, 343–61. London: Pluto Press.

Bloxham, Donald. 2001 *Genocide on Trial: War Crimes Trials and the Formation of Holocaust and Memory*. Oxford: Oxford University Press.

Boas, Gideon. 2001. Creating Laws of Evidence for International Criminal Law: The ICTY and the Principle of Flexibility. *Criminal Law Forum* 12(1): 41–90.

Bonafé, Beatrice. 2007. Finding a Proper Role for Command Responsibility. *Journal of International Criminal Justice* 5(3): 599–618.

Brown, Kris and Fionnuala Ni Aolain. 2015. Through the Looking Glass: Transitional Justice Futures through the Lens of Nationalism, Feminism and Transformative Change. *International Journal of Transitional Justice* 9 (1): 127–49.

Brown, Richard and Beth Davis-Brown. 1998. The Making of Memory: The Politics of the Archive, Libraries and Museums in the Construction of National Consciousness. *History of Human Sciences* 11(4): 17–32.

Brown, Sara. 2014. Female Perpetrators of the Rwandan Genocide. *International Feminist Journal of Politics* 16(3): 448–69.

Browning, Christopher. 2001. *Ordinary Men: Reserve Police Battalion 101 and the Final Solution in Poland.* London: Penguin Books.

Buruma, Ian. 2009. *Wages of Guilt.* London: Atlantic.

Byrne, Rosemary. 2010. The New Public International Lawyer and the Hidden Art of International Criminal Trial Practice. *Connecticut Journal of International Law* 243(25):243–303.

Campbell, Kirsten. 2011. Victims and Perpetrators of International Crimes: The Problem of the 'Legal Person'. *Journal of International Humanitarian Legal Studies* 2(2): 325–51.

　　2013. The Laws of Memory: The ICTY, Archive, and Transitional Justice. *Social and Legal Studies* 22(2): 247–69.

　　2014. Testimonial Modes: Witnessing, Evidence and Testimony before the International Criminal Tribunal for the Former Yugoslavia. In *The Future of Testimony: Interdisciplinary Perspectives on Witnessing,* edited by Antony Rowland and Jane Jun, 83–113. Florence: Routledge.

Caswell, Michelle. 2014. Defining Human Rights Archives: Introduction to the Special Double Issue on Archives and Human Rights. *Archival Science* 14: 207–13.

Chapman, Audrey and Patrick Ball. 2001. The Truth of Truth Commissions: Comparative Lessons from Haiti, South Africa, and Guatemala. *Human Rights Quarterly* 23(1): 1–43.

Clark, Phil. 2008. The Rules (and Politics) of Engagement: The *Gacaca* Courts and Post-Genocide Justice, Healing, and Reconciliation in Rwanda. In *After Genocide: Transitional Justice, Post-Conflict Reconstruction and Reconciliation in Rwanda and Beyond,* edited by Phil Clarke and Zachary Kaufman, 297–319. London: Hurst Publishers.

　　2010. *The Gacaca Courts, Post-Genocide Justice and Reconciliation in Rwanda: Justice without Lawyers.* Cambridge: Cambridge University Press.

　　2018. *Distant Justice: The Impact of the International Criminal Court on African Politics.* Cambridge: Cambridge University Press.

Clarke, Kamari. 2019. Affective Justice: The Racialized Imaginaries of International Justice. *PoLAR* 42(2): 244–57.

Abel S. Knottnerus and Eefje De Volder eds. 2016. *Africa and the ICC: Perceptions of Justice*. Cambridge: Cambridge University Press.

Combs, Nancy. 2010. *Fact-Finding without Facts: The Uncertain Evidentiary Foundations of International Criminal Law*. Cambridge: Cambridge University Press.

Conley, John and William O'Barr. 2005. *Just Words: Law, Language, and Power*. Chicago: University of Chicago Press: 2nd edition.

Cox, Michael. 2013. Power and the Liberal Order. In *After Liberalism?*, edited by Rebekka Friedman, Kevork Oskanian and Ramon Pacheco Pardo, 103–16. London: Palgrave Macmillan.

Crenshaw, Kimberley. 1991. Mapping the Margins: Intersectionality, Identity Politics, and Violence against Women of Color. *Stanford Law Review* 43 (6): 1241–99.

Cunningham, Clark. 1992. The Lawyer as Translator, Representation as Text: Towards an Ethnography of Legal Discourse. *Cornell Law Review* 77(6): 1298–387.

Daly, Erin. 2008. Truth Scepticism: An Inquiry into the Value of Truth in Times of Transition. *The International Journal of Transitional Justice* 2(1): 23–41.

Danner, Allison and Jenny Martinez. 2005. Guilty Associations: Joint Criminal Enterprise, Command Responsibility, and the Development, and the Development of International Criminal Law. *California Law Review* 93(1): 75–169.

Dauphinee, Elizabeth. 2008. War Crimes and the Ruin of Law. *Millennium – Journal of International Studies* 37(1): 49–67.

Del Ponte, Carla. 2006. Investigation and Prosecution of Large-Scale Crimes at the International Level. *Journal of International Criminal Justice* 4(3): 539–58.

Deleuze, Giles. 1986. *Foucault*, translated by Seán Hand. London: University of Minnesota Press.

1992. What Is Dispositif? In *Michel Foucault: Philosopher*, translated by Timothy Armstrong, 159–69. Hemel Hampstead: Harvester Wheatsheaf.

Dembour, Marie-Bénédicte and Emily Haslam. 2004. Silencing Hearings? Victim-Witnesses at War Crime Trials. *European Journal of International Law* 15(1): 151–78.

Derrida, Jacques. 1995. Archive Fever: A Freudian Impression. *Diacritics* 25 (2): 9–63.

1992. Force of Law: The 'Mystical Foundation of Authority'. In *Deconstruction and the Possibility of Justice*, edited by Drucilla Cornell, Michel Rosenfeld and David Carlson, 3–68. London: Routledge.

Des Forges, Alison. 1999. *Leave None to Tell the Story: Genocide in Rwanda*. New York: Human Rights Watch.

and Timothy Longman. 2004. Legal Response to Genocide in Rwanda. In *My Neighbour, My Enemy: Justice and Community in the Aftermath of Mass Atrocity*, edited by Eric Stover and Harvey M. Weinstein, 49–67. Cambridge: Cambridge University Press.

Dillon, Michael and Julian Reid. 2000. Global Governance, Liberal Peace, and Complex Emergency. *Alternatives* 25(1): 117–43.

Dirks, John. 2004. Accountability, History, and Archives: Conflicting Priorities or Synthesized Strands? *Archivia* 57: 29–49.

Dixon, Rosalind. 2002. Rape as a Crime in International Humanitarian Law: Where to from Here? *European Journal of International Law* 13(3): 697–720.

Douglas, Lawrence. 2001. *The Memory of Judgment: Making Law and History in the Trials of the Holocaust*. London: Yale University Press.

Drumbl, Mark. 2000. Punishment, Post-Genocide: From Guilt to Shame to Civis in Rwanda. *New York University Law Review* 75(5): 1222–326.

2005. *Atrocity, Punishment, and International Law*. Cambridge: Cambridge University Press, 2007.

Pluralising International Criminal Justice: from Nuremberg to The Hague: The Future of International Criminal Justice by Philippe Sands. *Michigan Law Review* 103(6): 1295–328.

Edkins, Jenny. 2003. *Trauma and the Memory of Politics*. Cambridge: Cambridge University Press.

Eltringham, Nigel. 2006. 'Invaders Who have Stolen the Country': The Hamitic Hypothesis, Race and the Rwandan Genocide. *Social Identities* 12(4): 425–46.

2008. 'A War Crimes Community?': The Legacy of the International Criminal Tribunal for Rwanda Beyond Jurisprudence. *New England Journal of International Law and Compliance* 14(2): 309–18.

2009. 'We Are Not a Truth Commission': Fragmented Narratives and the Historical Record at the International Criminal Tribunal for Rwanda. *Journal of Genocide Research* 11(1): 55–79.

2013. Illuminating the Broader Context: Anthropological and Historical Knowledge at the International Criminal Tribunal for Rwanda. *Journal of the Royal Anthropological Institute* 19(2): 338–55.

2014. 'When We Walk Out, What Was It All About?': Views on New Beginnings from within the International Criminal Tribunal for Rwanda. *Development and Change* 45(3): 543–64.

2019. *Genocide Never Sleeps: Living Law at the International Criminal Tribunal for Rwanda*. Cambridge: Cambridge University Press, 2019.

Enloe, Cynthia. 1989. *Bananas, Beaches, and Bases: Making Feminist Sense of International Politics*. London: Pandora.

Erickson, Bonnie, Allan Lind, Bruce Johnson, and William O'Barr. 1978. Speech Style and Impression Formation in a Court Setting: The Effects of 'Powerful' and 'Powerless' Speech. *Journal of Experimental Social Psychology* 14(3): 266–79.

Evans, Richard. 2000. *In Defence of History*. London: Granta Books.

Farge, Arlette. 2013. *The Allure of the Archive*, translated by Thomas Scott-Railton. London: Yale University Press, 2013.

Felman, Shoshana. 2002. *The Juridical Unconscious: Trials and Traumas in the Twentieth Century*. London: Harvard University Press.

　　2014. Fire in the Archive: The Alignment of Witnesses. In *The Future of Testimony: Interdisciplinary Perspectives on Witnessing*, edited by Antony Rowland and Jane Jun, 48–68. Florence: Routledge.

Fergal, Gaynor. 2012. Uneasy Partners – Evidence, Truth and History in International Trials. *Journal of International Criminal Justice* 10(5): 1257–75.

Fink, Joseph. 2005. Deontological Retributivism and the Legal Practice of International Jurisprudence: The Case of the International Criminal Tribunal for Rwanda. *Journal of African Law* 49(2): 101–31.

Foster, Robert, Rick Hosking, and Amanda Nettlebeck. 2001. Introduction. In *Fatal Collisions: The South Australian Frontier and the Violence of Memory*, edited by Robert Foster, Rick Hosking and Amanda Nettlebeck, 1–13. Kent Town: Wakefield Press.

Foucault, Michel. 1972. *The Archaeology of Knowledge and the Discourse on Language*, translated by Alan Sheridan. New York: Pantheon Books.

　　1977. *Discipline and Punish: The Birth of the Prison*, translated by Alan Sheridan. New York: Vintage.

　　1980. The Confession of the Flesh: An Interview with Michel Foucault. In *Power/Knowledge: Selected Interviews and Other Writings 1972–1977*, edited by Colin Gordon, 194–228. New York: Pantheon Books.

　　1984. Nietzsche, Genealogy, History. In *The Foucault Reader*, edited by Paul Rainbow, 76–101. London: Random House.

Franke, Katherine. 2006. Gendered Subjects of Transitional Justice. *Journal of Gender and Law* 15(3): 813–28.

Fujii, Lee. 2009. *Killing Neighbours: Webs of Violence in Rwanda*. London: Cornell University Press.

Gallimore, Tim. 2007. The Legacy of the International Criminal Tribunal for Rwanda (ICTR) and Its Contributions to Reconciliation in Rwanda. *New England Journal of International and Comparative Law* 14(2): 239–66.

Garbett, Claire. 2013. The Truth and the Trial: Victim Participation, Restorative Justice, and the International Criminal Court. *Contemporary Justice Review* 16(2): 193–213.

Gentry, Caron E. and Laura Sjoberg. 2007. *Mothers, Monsters, Whores: Women's Violence in Global Politics*. Chicago: Zed Books.

Goldstone, Richard. 1995. Justice as a Tool for Peace-making: Truth Commissions and International Criminal Tribunals. *Journal of International Law and Politics* 28: 485–504.

2000. *For Humanity: Reflections of a War Crimes Investigator*. London: Yale University Press.

2001. The Role of the United Nations in the Prosecution of International War Criminals. *Washington University Journal of Law & Policy* 5: 119–29.

2009. Interview: Obstacles in International Justice: The Establishment and Efficacy of International Courts. *Harvard International Review* 30(4):80–81.

Goose, Stephan and Frank Smyth. 1994. Arming Genocide in Rwanda, the High Cost of Small Arms Transfers. *Foreign Affairs* 73(5): 86–96.

Gordon, Colin. 1980. Afterword. In *Power/ Knowledge: Selected Interviews and Other Writings 1972–1977*, edited by Colin Gordon, 229–61. New York: Pantheon Books.

Gow, James. 2006. The ICTY, War Crimes Enforcement and Dayton: The Ghost in the Machine. *Ethnopolitics* 5(1): 49–65.

Gready, Paul. 2005. Reconceptualising Transitional Justice: Embedded and Distanced Justice. *Conflict, Security and Development* 5(1): 3–21.

Greetham, David. 1999. 'Who's In, Who's Out': The Cultural Poetics of Archival Exclusion. *Studies in the Literary Imagination* 32(1): 1–28.

Grossberg, Michel. 1998. How to Tell Law Stories. *Law and Social Inquiry* 23 (2): 459–70.

Guichaoua, André. 2015. *From War to Genocide: Criminal Politics in Rwanda, 1990-1994*. Madison: University of Wisconsin Press.

Hagan, John and Levi, Ron. 2005. Crimes of War and the Force of Law. *Social Forces* 83(4): 1499–534.

Halbwachs, Maurice. 1992. *On Collective Memory*. Chicago: University of Chicago Press.

Hansen, Lene. 2013. *Security as Practice: Discourse Analysis and the Bosnian War*. London: Routledge.

Harris, Verne. 2002. The Archival Sliver: Power, Memory and Archives in South Africa. *Archival Science* 2(1): 63–86.

2014. Antonyms of Our Remembering. *Archival Science* 14(3–4): 215–29.

Hazan, Pierre. 2010. *Judging War, Judging History: Behind Truth and Reconciliation*. Stanford: Stanford University Press: 2nd edition.

Henry, Nicola. 2010. The Impossibility of Bearing Witness: Wartime Rape and the Promise of Justice. *Violence against Women* 16(10): 1098–119.

Hilberg, Raul. 1961. *The Destruction of the European Jews, VOL I-III*. London: Yale University Press.

Himadeep, Muppidi. 2005. Colonial and Postcolonial Global Governance. In *Power in Global Governance*, edited by Michael Barnett and Raymond Duvall, 273–93. Cambridge and New York: Cambridge University Press.

Hintjens, Helen. 1999. Explaining the 1994 Genocide in Rwanda. *Journal of Modern African Studies* 37(2): 241–86.

Hoyle, Carolyn and Leila Ullrich. 2014. New Court, New Justice? The Evolution of 'Justice for Victims' at Domestic Courts and at the International Criminal Court. *Journal of International Criminal Justice* 12 (4): 681–703.

Human Rights Brief. 2014. Moving Forward: A Reflection on Current Issues Facing International Criminal Justice with Richard Goldstone. *Human Rights Brief* 21(2): 32–35.

Humphrey, Michael. 2003. From Victim to Victimhood: Truth Commissions and Trials as Rituals of Political Transition and Individual Healing. *The Australian Journal of Anthropology* 13(2): 171–87.

    2003. International Intervention, Justice and National Reconciliation: The Role of the ICTY and ICTR in Bosnia and Rwanda. *Journal of Human Rights* 2(4): 495–505.

Huysmans, Jef and Joao Pontes Nogueira. 2016. Ten Years of IPS: Fracturing IR. *International Political Sociology* 10(4): 299–319.

Jabri, Vivienne. 2010. War, Government, Politics: A Critical Response to the Hegemony of the Liberal Peace. In *Palgrave Advances in Peacebuilding*, edited by Oliver Richmond, 41–57. London: Palgrave Macmillan.

    2013. Peacebuilding, the Local and the International: A Colonial or a Postcolonial Rationality? *Peacebuilding* 1(1): 3–16.

    2014. Disarming Norms: Postcolonial Agency and the Constitution of the International. *International Theory* 6(2): 372–83.

    2017. Colonial Rationalities, Postcolonial Subjectivities, and the International. In *Against International Relations Norms*, edited by Charlotte Epstein, 38–56. Basingstoke: Routledge.

Kelsall, Tim. 2006. Politics, Anti-politics, International Justice: Language and Power in the Special Court for Sierra Leone. *Review of International Studies* 32(4): 587–602.

    2009. *Culture under Cross-examination: International Justice and the Special Court for Sierra Leone.* Cambridge: Cambridge University Press.

Kerr, Rachel. 2004. *The International Criminal Tribunal for the Former Yugoslavia: An Exercise in Law, Politics, and Diplomacy.* Oxford: Oxford University Press.

Kersten, Mark. 2012. Truths, Memories and Histories in the Archives of the International Criminal Tribunal for the Former Yugoslavia. In *Genocide Convention: The Legacy of 60 Years*, edited by Hugo Van der Wilt, Jeroen Vervliet, Göran Sluiter, and Johannes Houwink ten Cate. Leiden: Brill, 2012.

    2016. *Justice in Conflict: The Effects of International Criminal Court's Ending Wars and Bringing Peace.* Oxford: Oxford University Press.

Koopman, Colin. 2008. Foucault's Historiographical Expansion: Adding Genealogy to Archaeology. *Journal of the Philosophy of History* 2(3): 338–62.

Kuperman, Alan. 2007. How the Media Missed the Rwanda Genocide. In *The Media and the Rwandan Genocide*, edited by Allan Thompson, 256–60. London: Pluto Press.

LeBor, Adam. 2006. *'Complicity with Evil': The United Nations in the Age of Modern Genocide*. London: Yale University Press.

Lemarchand, René. 2009. The 1994 Rwanda Genocide. In *The Genocide Studies Reader*, edited by Paul Bartrop and Samuel Totten, 483–507. Abingdon: Routledge.

Mac Ginty, Roger. 2010. Hybrid Peace: The Interaction between Top-down and Bottom-up Peace. *Security Dialogue* 41(4): 391–412.

MacKinnon, Catharine. 1993. Crimes of War, Crimes of Peace. *UCLA Women's Law Journal* 4: 59–87.

1996. Law's Stories as Reality and Politics. In *Law's Stories: Narrative, Rhetoric and the Law*, edited by Peter Brooks and Paul Gewirtz, 232–36. Yale: Yale University Press.

2007. The ICTR's Legacy on Sexual Violence. *New England Journal of International and Comparative Law* 14(1): 211–21.

Madsen, Mikael and Yves Dezalay. 2002. 'The Power of the Legal Field: Pierre Bourdieu and the Law'. In *Introduction to Law and Social Theory*, edited by Reza Banakar and Max Travers. 188–204. Oxford: Hart Publishing.

Magnarella, Paul. 2000. *Justice in Africa: Rwanda's Genocide, Its Courts, and the UN Criminal Tribunal*. Aldershot: Ashgate.

Maier, Charles. 2000. 'Doing History, Doing Justice': The Narrative of the Historian and of the Truth Commission. In *Truth v. Justice: The Morality of Truth Commissions*, edited by Robert Rotberg and Dennis Thompson, 262–75. Princeton: Princeton University Press.

el-Malik, Shiera and Isaac Kamola. 2017. Introduction: Politics of African Anticolonial Archive. In *Politics of African Anticolonial Archive*, edited by Shiera el-Malik and Isaac Kamola, 3–4. London: Rowman & Littlefield International.

Mamdani, Mahmood. 2010. Responsibility to Protect or Right to Punish? *Journal of Intervention and Statebuilding* 4(1): 53–67.

2014. *When Victims Become Killers: Colonialism, Nativism, and the Genocide in Rwanda*. Oxford: Princeton University Press.

Marrus, Michael. 1998. The Holocaust at Nuremberg. *Yad Vashem Studies* 26: 1–32.

Martinez, Jenny. 2007. Understanding Mens Rea in Command Responsibility: From Yamashita to Blaškić and Beyond. *Journal of International Criminal Justice* 5(3): 638–64.

McEvoy, Kieran. 2007. Beyond Legalism: Towards a Thicker Understanding of Transitional Justice. *Journal of Law and Society* 34(4): 411–40.

and Kirsten McConnachie. 2013. Victims and Transitional Justice: Voice, Agency and Blame. *Social and Legal Studies* 22(4): 489–513.

McNulty, Mel. 1997. 'France's Role in Rwanda and External Military Intervention: A Double Discrediting. *International Peacekeeping* 4(3): 24–44.

2000. French Arms, War and Genocide in Rwanda. *Crime, Law and Social Change* 33(1–2): 105–129.

Mégret, Frédéric. 2002. The Politics of International Criminal Justice. *European Journal of International Law* 13(5): 1261–84.

2006. From 'Savages' to 'Unlawful Combatants': A Postcolonial Look at International Humanitarian Law's 'Other'. In *International Law and Its Others*, edited by Ann Orford, 265–318. Cambridge: Cambridge University Press.

Meierhenrich, Jens. 2013. The Practice of International Law: A Theoretical Analysis. *Law and Contemporary Problems* 76(3–4): 1–83.

Melvern, Linda. 2006. *Conspiracy to Murder: The Rwandan Genocide*. London: Verso.

2009. *A People Betrayed: The Role of the West in Rwanda's Genocide*. London: Zed Books: 2nd edition.

Meron, Theodor. 2000. The Humanization of Humanitarian Law. *American Journal of International Law* 94(2): 239–78.

Merry, Sally Engle. 2006. New Legal Realism and the Ethnography of Translational Law. *Law and Social Inquiry* 31(4): 975–95.

Michalski, Milena and James Gow. 2007. *War, Image and Legitimacy: Viewing Contemporary Conflict*. London: Routledge.

Mignolo, Walter D. 2007. Introduction. *Cultural Studies* 21(2–3): 62.

Minow, Martha. 1987. Foreword: Justice Engendered. *Harvard Law Review* 101 (10): 10–95.

1990. *Making All the Difference: Inclusion, Exclusion, and American Law*. London: Cornell University Press.

1998. *Between Vengeance and Forgiveness: Facing History after Genocide and Mass Violence*. Boston: Beacon Press.

2000. The Hope for Healing: What Can Truth Commissions Do? In *Truth v. Justice: The Morality of Truth Commissions*, edited by Robert Rotberg and Dennis Thompson, 235–60. Princeton: Princeton University Press.

2008. Making History or Making Peace: When Prosecutions Should Give Way to Truth Commissions and Peace Negotiations. *Journal of Human Rights* 7(2): 174–85.

Michael Ryan, and Austin Sarat, eds. 1995. *Narrative, Violence, and the Law: The Essays of Robert Cover*. Michigan: The University of Michigan.

Moghalu, Kingsley. 2005. *Rwanda's Genocide: The Politics of Global Justice*. Basingstoke: Palgrave Macmillan.

Moon, Claire. 2006. Narrating Political Reconciliation: Truth and Reconciliation in South Africa. *Social Legal Studies* 15(2): 261–62.

Motha, Stewart and Honni van Rijswijk eds. 2016. *Law, Memory and Violence: Uncovering the Counter Archive*. London: Routledge.

Motha, Stewart. 2018. *Archiving Sovereignty: Law, History, Violence*. Chicago: University of Michigan Press.

Mundis, Daryl. 2005. The Judicial Effects of the 'Completion Strategies' on the Ad Hoc International Criminal Tribunals. *The American Journal of International Law* 99(1): 142–58.

Mutua, Makau. 2001. Savages, Victims, and Saviours: The Metaphor of Human Rights. *Harvard International Law* Journal 42(1): 201–45.

Nagy, Rosemary. 2008. Transitional Justice as Global Project: Critical Reflections. *Third World Quarterly* 29(2): 275–89.

Neuffer, Elizabeth. 2001. *The Key to My Neighbour's House: Seeking Justice in Bosnia and Rwanda*. New York: Picador.

Ngoga, Martin. The Institutionalisation of Impunity: A Judicial Perspective of the Rwandan Genocide. In *After Genocide: Transitional Justice, Post-Conflict Reconstruction and Reconciliation in Rwanda and Beyond*, edited by Phil Clark and Zachery Kaufman, 321–33. London: Hurst.

Nora, Pierre. 1989. Between Memory and History: Les Lieux de Mémoire. *Representations*, 2: 7–24.

Nowrojee, Binaifer. 'Your Justice Is Too Slow': Will the International Criminal Tribunal for Rwanda Fail Rape Victims. In *Gendered Peace: Women's Struggle for Post-War Justice and Reconciliation*, edited by, Donna Pankhurst, 107–36. London: Routledge.

    2005. 'Your Justice Is Too Slow': Will the ICTR Fail Rwanda's Rape Victims? *United Nations Research Institute for Social Development*: 1–28.

Nsanzuwera, Francois-Xavier. 2005. The ICTR Contribution to National Reconciliation. *Journal of International Criminal Justice* 3: 944–49.

O'Reilly, Maria. 2012. Muscular Interventionism. *International Feminist Journal of Politics* 14(4): 529–48.

    2013. Gender and Peacebuilding. In *Routledge Handbook of Peacebuilding*, edited by Roger MacGinty, 72–83. London: Routledge.

Orford, Ann, 2006. A Jurisprudence of the Limit. In *International Law and Its Others*, edited by Ann Orford, 1–35. Cambridge: Cambridge University Press.

Osborne, Thomas. 1999. The Ordinariness of the Archive. *History of Human Sciences* 12(2): 51–64.

Osiel, Mark. 2000. *Mass Atrocity, Collective Memory, and the Law*. New Jersey: Transaction Publishers.

Otto, Dianne. 1996. Subalternity and International Law: The Problem of Global Community and the Incommensurability of Difference. *Social and Legal Studies* 5(3): 337–64.

Pahuja, Sundhya. 2005. The Postcoloniality of International Law. *Harvard International Law Journal* 46(2): 459–469.

Palmer, Nicola. 2012. Transfer or Transformation?: A Review of the Rule 11 bis Decisions of the International Criminal Tribunal for Rwanda. *African Journal of International and Comparative Law* 20(1): 1–21.

2015. *Courts in Conflict: Interpreting the Layers of Justice in Post-genocide Rwanda*. Oxford: Oxford University Press.

Paris, Roland. 2010. Saving Liberal Peacebuilding. *Review of International Studies*, 36(2): 337–65.

Partis-Jennings, Hannah. 2017. The (In)Security of Gender in Afghanistan's Peacebuilding Project: Hybridity and Affect. *International Feminist Journal of Politics* 19(4): 411–25.

Pena, Marianna and Gaelle Carayon. 2013. Is the ICC Making the Most of Victim Participation? *Journal of Transitional Justice* 7(3): 518–35.

Pendas, David. 2006. *The Frankfurt Auschwitz Trial, 1963–1965*. Cambridge: Cambridge University Press.

Peskin, Victor. 2005. Courting Rwanda: The Promises and Pitfalls of the ICTR Outreach Programme. *Journal of International Criminal Justice* 3(4): 950–61.

2008. *International Justice in Rwanda and the Balkans: Virtual Trials and the Struggle for State Cooperation*. Cambridge: Cambridge University Press.

Power, Samantha. 2003. *A Problem from Hell: America and the Age of Genocide*. London: Flamingo.

Prunier, Gérard. 1995. *The Rwanda Crisis: History of Genocide*. London: Hurst & Company.

Quijano, Aníbal. 2007. Coloniality and Modernity/Rationality. *Cultural Studies* 21(2–3): 168–78.

Rancière, Jacques. 2013. *The Politics of Aesthetics*. London: Bloomsbury Publishing.

Redwood, Henry. 2020. Archiving (In)Justice: Building Archives and Imagining Community. *Millennium*. https://journals.sagepub.com/doi/abs/10.1177/0305829820935175 (Online First, October 2020).

and Wedderburn, Alister. 2019. A Cat-and-Maus Game: The Politics of Truth and Reconciliation in Post-conflict Comics. *Review of International Studies* 45(4): 588–606.

Reus–Smit, Chris. 2004. The Politics of International Law. In *Politics of International Law*, edited by Reus-Smit, 14–44. Cambridge: Cambridge University Press.

ed. 2004. *The Politics of International Law*. Cambridge: Cambridge University Press.

Reynold, Henry. 2000. *Why Weren't We Told? A Personal Search for the Truth about Our History*. Victoria: Ringwood.

Richmond, Oliver P. 2006. The Problem of Peace: Understanding the 'Liberal Peace'. *Conflict, Security & Development*, 6(3): 291–314.

and Roger Mac Ginty. 2015. Where Now for the Critique of the Liberal Peace? *Cooperation and Conflict* 50(2): 171–89.

Rodman, Kenneth. 2014. Justice as a Dialogue between Law and Politics. *Journal of International Criminal Justice* 12(3): 437–469.

Rousso, Henry. 2002. *The Haunting Past: History, Memory and Justice in Contemporary France*. Pennsylvania: University of Pennsylvania Press.

Ruzindana, Mathias. 2012. The Challenges of Understanding Kinyarwanda: Key Terms Used to Investigate the 1994 Genocide in Rwanda. In *Propaganda, War Crimes Trials and International Law: from Speakers Corner to War Crimes*, edited by Predrag Dojcinovic, 145–70. Abingdon: Routledge.

Sabaratnam, Meera. 2013. Avatars of Eurocentrism in the Critique of the Liberal Peace. *Security Dialogue* 44(3): 259–78.

SáCouto, Susanna, Leila Sadat, and Patricia Sellers. 2020. Collective Criminality and Sexual Violence: Fixing a Failed Approach. *Leiden Journal of International Law*, 33(1): 207–41.

Sander, Barrie. 2018. Unveiling the Historical Function of International Criminal Courts: Between Adjudicative and Sociopolitical Justice. *International Journal of Transitional Justice* 12(2): 334–55.

2018. History on Trial: Historical Narrative Pluralism within and beyond International Criminal Courts. *International & Comparative Law Quarterly* 67(3): 547–76.

Sarat, Austin and Thomas Kearns. 1993. A Journey through Forgetting: Toward a Jurisprudence of Violence. In *The Fate of Law*, edited by Austin Sarat and Thomas Kearns, 209–74. Michigan: The University of Michigan.

1999. Writing History and Registering Memory in Legal Decisions and Legal Practices: An Introduction. In *History, Memory, and the Law*, edited by Austin Sarat and Thomas Kearns, 1–24. Michigan: University of Michigan.

Schwartz, Joan and Terry Cook. 2002. Archives, Records, and Power: The Making of Modern Memory. *Archival Science* 2(1): 1–19.

Shapiro, Michael. 2015. *War Crimes, Atrocity and Justice*. Cambridge: Polity Press.

Sharlach, Lisa. 1999. Gender and Genocide in Rwanda: Women as Agents and Objects. *Journal of Genocide Research* 1(3): 387–99.

Shepherd, Laura and Caitlin Hamilton. 2016. Gender and Peacebuilding. In *Handbook on Gender and War*, edited by Simona Sharoni, Julia Welland,

Linda Steiner, and Jennifer Pedersen, 467–83. Cheltenham: Edward Elgar Publishing.

Simpson, Gerry. 2007. *Law, War and Crime: War Crimes Trials and the Reinvention of International Law*. Cambridge: Polity Press.

Spivak, Gayatri. 1985. The Rani of Sirmur: An Essay in Reading the Archives. *History and Theory* 24(3):247–72.

1994. Can the Subaltern Speak? In *Colonial Discourse and Post-colonial Theory: A Reader*, edited by Patrick Williams and Laura Chrisman, 90–110. New York: Colombia University Press.

Steedman, Carolyn. 2001. Something She Called a Fever: Michelet, Derrida, and Dust. *The American History Review* 106(4): 1159–80.

2011. After the Archive. *Comparative Critical Studies* 8(2-3): 321–40.

Stoler, Ann. 2002. Colonial Archives and the Arts of Governance. *Archival Science* 2(1): 87–109.

2010. *Along the Archival Grain: Epistemic Anxiety and Colonial Common Sense*. Princeton: Princeton University Press.

Stover, Eric. 2005. *The Witnesses*. Philadelphia: University of Pennsylvania Press.

Straus, Scott. 2006. *The Order of Genocide: Race, Power and War in Rwanda*. London, Cornell University Press.

Teitel, Ruti. 1998. The Universal and the Particular in International Criminal Justice. *Columbia Human Rights Law Review* 30(285): 285–303.

Transitional Justice. Oxford: Oxford University Press, 2000.

Tepperman, Jonathan. 2002. Truth and Consequences. *Foreign Affairs* 81(2): 128–45.

Thompson, Alan, ed. 2007. *The Media and the Rwandan Genocide*. London: Pluto Press.

Thompson, Susan and Rosemary Nagy. 2011. Law, Power and Justice: What Legalism Fails to Address in the Functioning of Rwanda's Gacaca Courts. *The International Journal of Transitional Justice* 5(1): 11–30.

Trotter, Andrew. 2012. Witness Intimidation in International Trials: Balancing the Need for Protection against the Rights of the Accused. *The George Washington International Law Review* 44: 521–36.

Trouillot, Michel-Rolph. 1995. *Power and the Production of History*. Boston: Beacon Press.

Turner, Jenia. 2007. Defense Perspectives on Law and Politics in International Criminal Trials. *Virginia Journal of International Law* 48(3): 529–93.

Uvin, Peter and Charles Mironko. 2003. Western and Local Approaches to Justice in Rwanda. *Global Governance* 9: 219–31.

Velody, Irving. 1998. The Archive and the Human Sciences: Notes towards a Theory of the Archive. *History of the Human Sciences* 11(4): 1–16.

Walsh, Martha. 2009. Gendering International Justice: Progress and Pitfalls at International Criminal Tribunals. In *Gendered Peace: Women's Struggle for Post–war Justice and Reconciliation*, edited by Donna Pankhurst, 31–65. Abingdon: Routledge.

Wedderburn, Alister. 2019. Cartooning the Camp: Aesthetic Interruption and the Limits of Political Possibility. *Millennium* 47(2): 169–89.

White, James. 1990. *Justice as Translation: An Essay in Cultural and Legal Criticism*. Chicago: Chicago University Press.

Whyte, Jessica. 2016. Always on Top? The 'Responsibility to Protect' and the Persistence of Colonialism. In *The Postcolonial World*, edited by Jyotsna Singh and David Kim, 308–24. London: Routledge.

Wieviorka, Annette. 2006. *The Era of the Witness*. Cornell University Press: New York.

Wilson, Richard. 2010. *Writing History in International Criminal Trials*. Cambridge: Cambridge University Press.

Wittmann, Rebecca. 2005. *Beyond Justice: The Auschwitz Trial*. Cambridge: Harvard University Press.

Wood, Nancy. 1994. Crimes or Misdemeanours?: Memory on Trial in Contemporary France. *French Cultural Studies* 5: 1–21.

INDEX

CAMBRIDGE STUDIES IN LAW AND SOCIETY